ANCIENT PERSIA

The Achaemenid Persian Empire, at its greatest territorial extent under Darius I (r. 522–486 BCE), held sway over territory stretching from the Indus River Valley to southeastern Europe and from the western edge of the Himalayas to northeast Africa. In this book, Matt Waters gives a detailed historical overview of the Achaemenid period while considering the manifold interpretive problems historians face in constructing and understanding its history. This book offers a Persian perspective even when relying on Greek textual sources and archaeological evidence. Waters situates the story of the Achaemenid Persians in the context of their predecessors in the mid-first millennium BCE and through their successors after the Macedonian conquest, constructing a compelling narrative of how the Empire retained its vitality for more than two hundred years (c. 550–330 BCE) and left a massive imprint on Middle Eastern as well as Greek and European history.

Matt Waters is Professor of Classics and Ancient History at the University of Wisconsin–Eau Claire. He is the author of *A Survey of Neo-Elamite History* (2000), and his work has appeared in numerous journals, including *Iran*, *Revue d'Assyriologie*, and the *Journal of the American Oriental Society*. Waters is the recipient of fellowships from the American Council of Learned Societies, Harvard University's Center for Hellenic Studies, the Loeb Classical Library Foundation, and the University of Wisconsin–Madison's Institute for Research in the Humanities. He was awarded the Jonas C. Greenfield Prize from the American Oriental Society in 2006 for the best published article in ancient Near Eastern studies in a three-year period by a scholar under the age of forty.

ANCIENT PERSIA

*A Concise History of the Achaemenid
Empire, 550–330 BCE*

Matt Waters

University of Wisconsin–Eau Claire

CAMBRIDGE
UNIVERSITY PRESS

CAMBRIDGE
UNIVERSITY PRESS

32 Avenue of the Americas, New York NY 10013-2473, USA

Cambridge University Press is part of the University of Cambridge.

It furthers the University's mission by disseminating knowledge in the pursuit of education, learning, and research at the highest international levels of excellence.

www.cambridge.org
Information on this title: www.cambridge.org/9780521253697

First published 2014

Printed in the United States of America

A catalog record for this publication is available from the British Library.

Library of Congress Cataloging in Publication Data
Waters, Matthew W. (Matthew William)
Ancient Persia : A concise history of the Achaemenid Empire, 550–330 BCE /
Matt Waters, University of Wisconsin–Eau Claire.
    pages   cm
Includes bibliographical references and index.
ISBN 978-1-107-00960-8 (hardback) – ISBN 978-0-521-25369-7 (pbk.)
 1. Achaemenid dynasty, 559–330 B.C.E.   2. Iran – History – To 640.   I. Title.
DS281.W38   2013
935'.05–dc23   2013027356

ISBN 978-1-107-00960-8 Hardback
ISBN 978-0-521-25369-7 Paperback

To Michelle, Alex, and Ellie

Contents

List of Figures

List of Maps

Achaemenid Royal Inscriptions and Classical Sources

Information on the most frequently cited sources is contained in the following overview, by author and citation format. A. Kuhrt, *The Persian Empire: A Corpus of Sources from the Achaemenid Period*, 2007, contains translations of almost all textual material referenced herein; it is an indispensable tool for study of the Achaemenid Persian Empire. On a smaller scale, M. Brosius, *The Persian Empire from Cyrus II to Artaxerxes I*, 2000, has translations of several texts, and the Internet site Livius.org (http://www.livius.org/aa-ac/achaemenians/inscriptions.html) has translations of many of the royal inscriptions and other resources.

ACHAEMENID ROYAL INSCRIPTIONS

Inscriptions cited refer to the Old Persian versions of the text, unless otherwise noted. They are cited by standard abbreviations: king's first initial, superscripted number (if applicable), and location. Lowercase letters differentiate separate inscriptions from the same site. For example, A^{2}Sd §2 stands for Artaxerxes II, Susa, inscription d, paragraph (or section) 2.

Elamite and Akkadian translations are found mainly in specialized literature. The classic treatment of all versions of most trilingual inscriptions is F. H. Weissbach, *Die Keilinschriften der Achämeniden*, 1911. The most accessible English translation of the Old Persian versions of the royal inscriptions is R. G. Kent, *Old Persian: Grammar, Text, Lexicon*, 1953. Also notable is R. Schmitt, *Naqsh-i Rustam and Persepolis*, 2000.

CLASSICAL SOURCES

Accessible text editions with translation for major authors, including most of those listed below, are published in the Loeb Classical Library series. The Perseus Project (http://www.perseus.tufts.edu) has translations available under its Greek and Roman Materials tab. Citations of major works follow convention by book, chapter (or paragraph), and section number. For example, Hdt. 1.125 refers to Herodotus, Book I, chapter/paragraph 125. An additional number indicates section, for example Diodorus 12.4.4–5 refers to Diodorus Siculus, Book 12, chapter 4, sections 4–5. Authors' biographical information in the following is adapted from *The Oxford Classical Dictionary*, ed. S. Hornblower and A. Spawforth, Third Edition Revised, 2003.

Aelian, c. 156/170–230/235 CE, from Italy. The author of a number of works, including *On the Nature of Animals* and *Varia Historia*.

Aeschylus, c. 525?–455 BCE, from Athens. Preeminent Athenian playwright, his play *The Persians* dramatizes Xerxes' failed invasion of Greece.

Arrian, c. 86–160 CE, from Bithynia in northern Anatolia. Author of a number of works, references herein are to his *Anabasis of Alexander*.

Berossus, late fourth to early third centuries BCE, a Babylonian who wrote a history in Greek for Antiochus I, cited by fragment number and letter. An English translation of the main fragments is available in G. Verbrugghe and J. Wickersham, *Berossos and Manetho*, 1996.

Ctesias, late fifth and early fourth centuries BCE, Greek physician from Cnidus in southwestern Anatolia, who served at the court of Artaxerxes II. Author of a number of works, citations herein are to his *Persica* in twenty-three books, only fragments of which remain. Cited by fragment number and letter and, for longer fragments, paragraph (§) number. An English translation, with Greek text, is available in J. Stronk, *Ctesias' Persian History, Part I. Introduction, Text, Translation*, 2010.

Diodorus Siculus (abbreviated DS), first century BCE, of Sicily, author of what is generally titled the *Universal History* (*Bibliotheka*), of which fifteen books survive.

Herodotus (abbreviated Hdt.), mid-to-late fifth century BCE, from Halicarnassus in southwestern Anatolia. Herodotus is the most important Greek source for Achaemenid Persian history.

Justin, dated variously between the second and fourth centuries CE, author of a Latin epitome of Pompeius Trogus' *Philippic Histories*.

Manetho, early third century BCE, an Egyptian priest from Heliopolis who wrote a history of Egypt from its origins to 342 BCE.

Plutarch (abbreviated Plut.), first to early second centuries CE, Greek priest from Chaeronea in central Greece. Author of a number of works, references herein are to his various Lives, cited by individual life and paragraph/chapter number (§).

Quintus Curtius Rufus (often just Quintus Curtius), first century CE, wrote a history of Alexander the Great in ten volumes.

Strabo, c. 64 BCE–20s CE, from Pontus in northern Anatolia, author of the *Geographica* in seventeen books.

Thucydides (abbreviated Thuc.), c. 460–400 BCE of Athens, a general who wrote an incomplete history of the Peloponnesian War into the year 411.

Xenophon (abbreviated Xen.), c. 430–350s BCE of Athens. Author of numerous works, several of which serve as sources for Achaemenid Persian history: the *Hellenika*, a continuation of Thucydides' history into the fourth century; the *Cyropaedia* ("the Education of Cyrus"), a novelistic account of Cyrus the Great's life; and the *Anabasis*, the account of Cyrus the Younger's failed expedition against Artaxerxes II and the homeward march of his Greek mercenary forces, of which Xenophon was one of the commanders. The *Anabasis* is variously titled in English translation as "The Expedition of Cyrus," "The March Up Country," or "The March of the Ten Thousand."

Acknowledgments

Cyrus the Great and his successors ruled much of the known earth for more than 200 years, and the empire they forged represented something new in its scope and in its durative power. This book's aim is to provide a detailed historical overview of the Achaemenid Persian Empire (circa 550–330 BCE), presented in conjunction with the manifold interpretive problems that historians face in understanding it. In doing so, I have endeavored to consider Achaemenid history in its Near Eastern context, supplying, as much as possible, a Persian perspective even when relying mainly on Greek and other non-Persian sources.

Writing this book has often proven an exercise in regrettable exclusion even more than considered inclusion – and some topics are only scratched on the surface. As a book geared toward English-speaking, novice readers, the citations and further readings (Appendix D) are primarily in English. Translations of ancient texts are my own unless cited otherwise. I have given priority to readability of translation but with every attempt to adhere to the original text's sense. My work of course owes much to the numerous scholars cited throughout, but in particular I would highlight the works of Pierre Briant and Amélie Kuhrt. Their literally voluminous publications have revolutionized the field. Briant's *From Cyrus to Alexander: A History of the Persian Empire* (translated from the original 1996 French version by P. Daniels) and Kuhrt's *The Persian Empire: A Corpus of Sources from the Achaemenid Period* represent culminations of their seminal, and notably ongoing, works. Rather than cite them on almost every page, I will acknowledge my deep debt to their work here, as frequent sources of information and inspiration in this writing.

I would like to acknowledge the Office of Research and Sponsored Programs at the University of Wisconsin–Eau Claire for support of this project. Many friends and colleagues deserve thanks for their help during its course. Pat and Jill Pink have been unstinting with friendship and hospitality on numerous trips to Chicago for research, including many enjoyable discussions on what constitutes quality writing. Javier Álvarez-Mon, Rémy Boucharlat, Beth Dusinberre, Grant Frame, Mark Garrison, Mike Kozuh, Dan Potts, Tessa Rickards, Chessie Rochberg, Margaret Root, David Stronach, and Mónica Vélez graciously and generously assisted with mixtures of advice, illustrations, in-progress work, and moral support. Special thanks to Clyde Smith and Jeff Vahlbusch who, reminding me that I was not writing a book for specialists, provided many useful comments on an early draft. Two anonymous Cambridge University Press referees provided insightful commentary and saved me from several mistakes, at the same time reminding me that specialists may indeed use or consult this book. Beatrice Rehl and Asya Graf, along with a number of other Cambridge University Press staff, were helpful and patient in guiding me through the maze of the publication process. My gratitude to all of them is immense.

Finally, and especially on the subject of patience, I acknowledge the support of my family, to whom I dedicate this work. To note that they put up with a lot is an understatement.

Map 1.1 Achaemenid Persian Empire, with Major Routes. After *Cambridge Ancient History*, Vol. 4, Second Edition, 1988, map 1.

KAZAKHSTAN

Aral
Sea

Caspian Sea

Jaxartes

(Syr Darya)

MASSAGETAE

SAKA HAUMAVARGA

CHORASMIA

Oxus (Amu Darya)

SAKA TIGRAKHAUDA

SOGDIANA

Cyropolis FERGHANA

Merv

Balkh

Aï-Khanoum

Pamirs

MARGIANA

BACTRIA

Mt
Damavand

Tehran

HYRCANIA

PARTHIA

ARIA

AFGHANISTAN

Hindu Kush

Himalayas

Peshawar

GANDARA

PUNJAB

DRANGIANA

ARACHOSIA

Zagros Mts

Dahan-i
Ghulaman

Kandahar

KHUZISTAN

Pasargadae

Anshan Persepolis

SEISTAN

Helmand

SATTAGYDIA?

Multan

Indus

PARSA

CARMANIA

INDIA

Persian Gulf

GEDROSIA

SIND

Land over 1000 metres

| 0 | 200 | 400 | 600 | 800 | 1000 km |

| 0 | 100 | 200 | 300 | 400 | 500 | 600 miles |

Figure 1.1 Tomb of Darius I, top register, Naqsh-i Rustam. Courtesy of the Oriental Institute of the University of Chicago.

1 Introduction: Tracking an Empire

If you should wonder how many are the lands that Darius the King held, behold the sculpted figures who bear the throne, then you shall learn, then it shall become known to you that the spear of the Persian man has gone forth far. Then it shall become known to you that the Persian man has given battle far away from Persia.

Tomb of Darius I, Naqsh-i Rustam, (DNa §4, Figure 1.1)

Darius I (reigned 522–486 BCE) ruled the Achaemenid Persian Empire at the height of its territorial extent: from the Indus River to the Danube River and from the western edge of the Himalayas to the Sahara Desert. In its scope and durability, and in its ability to project and maintain its power, the Achaemenid Empire was unprecedented in world history. Its equal was not seen again until the height of the Roman Empire under Augustus and his successors in the first and second centuries CE.

The Achaemenid Empire retained its vitality for over two hundred years (550–330 BCE) and left a massive, if not always readily discernible, imprint on subsequent Near Eastern and European history. To the ancient Greeks, the Persian Empire was an object of fear and fascination: Persia served as the great "Other" from the Classical period onward. The Greeks framed the historical and cultural narratives of the West, and their perspective led to the development of many key East-West stereotypes that persist today.

THE PHYSICAL ENVIRONMENT

Not surprisingly, an empire that encompassed so much territory (not less than 2 million square miles) included every sort of terrain.[1] The central core of the Empire was southwestern Iran – ancient Parsa (Greek *Persis*), the geographic area synonymous with the name "Persia" that was subsequently applied to the entire country. Parsa, more specifically equivalent with modern Fars, is dominated by the southern part of the Zagros Mountains – a chain running northwest to southeast across western Iran – save for the coastal region along the Persian Gulf and the low-lying plains of Khuzistan, wherein is found the ancient city of Susa. Within the Zagros and its foothills, the scenery and vegetation differ markedly, and temperatures fluctuate between bitterly cold winters and scorching summers. Moving eastward beyond the Zagros one encounters the Iranian Plateau and the forbidding salt deserts of central Iran.

Despite this geographical variety, sufficient annual rainfall allowed agriculture without irrigation in much of Persia, as it did in many other parts of the Empire: northern Mesopotamia (modern Iraq), the Caspian Sea region and Turkey in the north and northwest, and Syro-Palestine (the Levant) to the west. Southern Mesopotamia, a critical component of the Empire, is a different story: irrigation had been necessary since (and indeed an impetus toward) urbanization in the fourth millennium. Other parts of the Empire, notably Egypt, also relied on irrigation. In Egypt, however, the Nile flooded and receded in harmony with the growing season. The Euphrates and Tigris in Mesopotamia flooded at the time of the harvest. A great deal more effort and resources were therefore devoted in Mesopotamia to controlling the flooding of these rivers via irrigation. Success in taming these rivers resulted in a rich agricultural-economy.

Ancient Near Eastern civilizations had been connected by trade for centuries. By the time of the Persian Empire an extensive network had been developed, the maintenance of which was a primary responsibility of the ruling authorities. The main routes ran between Fars (Persepolis) and Khuzistan (Susa) with roads branching in several directions: through Babylon and Mesopotamia northward across Anatolia (Turkey) to Sardis, the famous Royal Road described by Herodotus (see (pp. 111–113), and through the Median capital Ecbatana and eastward across northern Iran, the Great Khorasan Road (better-known as the Silk Road). Similar routes linked the Indus River valley, Egypt and Libya, and all the major centers even in far-flung regions of the Empire. In addition to the land routes, a number of well-traveled sea lanes from India to the Iranian coast and Mesopotamia were also used by the Persians. In the modern territory of Fars in southwestern Iran is the Kur River Basin, home to the Persian capitals of Pasargadae, founded by Cyrus the Great, and Persepolis, founded by Darius I. The remains at Persepolis, approximately 45 miles northeast of the modern city of Shiraz, offer the most eloquent and imposing testimony to the Persian King's majesty (see pp. 141–145).

The term "Persian" in "Persian Empire" is generally understood to refer to the ethnicity of the ruling elite. The Empire itself encompassed scores of different ethnic groups, each with its own history and culture. Even a superficial accounting of these various groups offers a glimpse into the size and complexity of the Empire, but we possess limited evidence for how most people lived their daily lives. In northern Iran were the Medes, to whom much of Chapter 2 is devoted, and the north and east were home to several other Iranian groups as well: Parthians, Hyrcanians, and Areians, to name just a few. Many of these groups dwelled in what are now the countries of Kazakhstan, Turkmenistan, Uzbekistan, Afghanistan, Pakistan, and India. The fiercely independent Scythians, another Iranian group, dwelled along the northern and northeastern edges of the Empire, on the Eurasian steppes.

Mesopotamia, Syro-Palestine, the Levant, and Arabia were home to various Semitic peoples: Babylonians, Aramaeans, Jews, Phoenicians, and Arabs to name only those most prominent in the extant source material. The Empire encompassed northeastern Africa as well and included Egyptians, Libyans, Nubians, and Ethiopians. The Anatolian plateau and the Caucasus Mountains also contained a variety of peoples; the kingdom of Lydia based at Sardis, in western Turkey, was the main power in the sixth century before Cyrus. Finally, the Greeks of Ionia (western coastal Turkey) and even those of the European mainland figure prominently in this story as well — not least because their experience at the time of the so-called "Greek Miracle" (the Classical Period, c. 500–323 BCE) was shaped so profoundly by the Persian Empire's impact.

WHY "ACHAEMENID"?

The history of ancient Iran stretches back millennia. Before the advent of Islam in the seventh century CE, it included the histories of not only the Achaemenids but also their predecessors the Elamites and their successors the Seleucids, Parthians, and Sassanians. The Achaemenid Empire takes its name from Achaemenes, the eponymous founder of the dynasty. Specialists continue to debate the relationships and, even to some extent, the ethnic identity – counterintuitive as that may seem – of the early Achaemenid kings.[2] For Achaemenes, Darius I's distant ancestor, there is no evidence earlier than Darius I's testimony. Darius' privileging of his Achaemenid descent is fundamental to understanding Persian royal ideology.

Cyrus the Great does not mention Achaemenes in his genealogy, and most modern scholars have rejected Darius' implication that he and Cyrus shared descent from Achaemenes. Although the term "Achaemenid Empire" may be somewhat of a misnomer for the early Persian Empire, especially that period prior to Darius I, it is entrenched in the modern literature and will be used herein. The label also distinguishes the historical period in question and differentiates it from the succeeding Seleucid, Parthian, and Sassanian periods in ancient Iranian history. As the focus of this book is the Achaemenid period, to avoid excessive repetition, when the label "Persian" is used throughout it will be understood to refer to the Achaemenid period unless otherwise noted.

SOURCES

As is often noted, but bears repeating, ancient historians cannot choose their sources. The issue is not in deciding what sources to use but in assessing the usefulness and veracity of anything available. This does not mean that all sources are created equal, of course. Significant portions of this text are devoted to the problems of historical analysis engendered by the paucity of the sources as well as the tendentiousness of those that are available.

Most of the documentary evidence for the study of Achaemenid Persia – regardless of place or time of origin – was commissioned by the educated elite: members of the ruling class itself, the privileged among the conquered or peripheral regions, or the bureaucratic class of scribes. Economic and administrative documents, coupled with archaeological evidence, often provide vivid pictures of daily life, but these are sporadic and generally localized.[3] A brief overview of the main sources follows, by way of an introduction to the variety of evidence available – as well as the problems associated with their use and interpretation for reconstructing Achaemenid history.

Archaeology

Archaeological research in the core areas of the Achaemenid Empire has been uneven. In recent decades, upheaval in the Middle East has periodically made excavation difficult, if not impossible. Several important cities in the ancient Near East have been continuously inhabited from antiquity into the modern period – for example, Hamadan in Iran (ancient Ecbatana), Erbil in Iraq (ancient Arbela), and Damascus in Syria – and excavation opportunities in these areas have been limited, regardless of any political considerations.

In Iran itself excavations have been focused in the western part of the country. In Fars, the Persian capitals of Pasargadae and Persepolis, the two most prominent Achaemenid sites, have received the most attention. The city of Susa in Khuzistan was important for centuries as an Elamite center; it became one of the Achaemenid capitals, the one most frequently referenced in the Greek sources. Recent excavations in the Mamasani district (Fars), in Georgia (east of the Black Sea in the Caucasus Mountains), and other places have provided additional insights into Achaemenid-period settlement as well as the influence and impact of the Empire on local populations. Some of the major cities in Mesopotamia, whose histories stretch back for two millennia or more before the Persian Empire, remained important through the Achaemenid period: Uruk, Ur, Nippur, Sippar, and most notably Babylon, to name only a few. Excavations have continued intermittently at these sites, by teams from various nations, since the nineteenth century.

Proper excavation is both meticulous and laborious, and publication of results may take many years. Excavation techniques have advanced since the nineteenth century, from what may generously be termed as mining operations for luxury goods, monuments, and inscriptions: the types of finds that would garner attention in museums. Modern excavations employ scientific, systematic approaches that are far more expensive and time-consuming, and involve analysis and consideration of every find *in situ* (i.e., where it was found in the ground, with context). They are replete with technology – computer mapping, ground-penetrating radar – the expense and complexity of which make necessary the formation of teams composed of various specialists. Museums worldwide display the fruits of these excavations, and their storage areas are often bursting with material not yet published or even studied. Researchers in the field often speak, only somewhat tongue-in-cheek, of excavating their own museums to find the as-yet unanalyzed piece of pottery, or the as-yet unread text, that may change perspectives on key problems in the field.

Written Sources

Until the late nineteenth century CE, knowledge of the Achaemenid Empire's history was based almost entirely on Greek and biblical accounts. To the Greeks we are indebted for western notions of history-writing and historiography. The Persian Empire left an indelible impression on the early Greek historians who chronicled the era, and, through them, on their successors in the Roman period and beyond. Herodotus and Xenophon provide much of the narrative core of Achaemenid Persian history, for better or worse (a bit of each applies). As a function of the Greek source bias, our knowledge of the Empire disproportionately emphasizes the western and northwestern parts of it: western Anatolia (especially the coast, i.e., Greek Ionia) and the Aegean world. Eastern Iran and Central Asia were critical components of the Empire, as a number of references in the sources make clear, but particulars about Persian administration of these regions are scarce. Information about these areas is thus more spotty and speculative.

The Empire's sheer, geographical scope is reflected in sources from several languages. The diversity of local traditions – oral and written – provides multiple perspectives, as well as frustrations, for study of the Persian Empire. Many of these traditions and the languages in which they were transmitted are poorly-understood, some are simply lost. The historian of the Persian Empire faces a herculean task to gather and sift this disparate evidence. A list of the main languages in which relevant source material is preserved is telling: Old Persian, Avestan, Elamite, Akkadian (the Babylonian dialect), Aramaic, Hebrew, Egyptian, Greek, Latin, and Phrygian. The nineteenth-century decipherments of Egyptian (hieroglyphic script) and Akkadian, Elamite, and Old Persian (cuneiform scripts) opened new vistas for Persian history that are still being explored today, especially for new perspectives on the Greek material that by necessity has formed the narrative base of much of Persian history.

The chronology of main events in Persian history is for the most part well-settled, but new discoveries frequently supplement, and sometimes change entirely, our understanding. Not surprisingly, specialists who study the Persian Empire are found in multiple disciplines: Ancient History, Archaeology, Classical Studies, Religious Studies, Indo-Iranian Linguistics, Assyriology, and Egyptology, among others.

The ancient Persians themselves wrote almost nothing – at least, nothing that has survived – in the way of narrative history. As with many ancient peoples, records of the past were kept alive through oral tradition. These "records" manifest themselves in the written sources in a number of compelling, but often puzzling, ways. It is easy to underestimate, or even ignore, how oral tradition has shaped the historical record, but where its imprint may be discerned and contextualized it is instructive.

Royal Inscriptions and Other Documentary Evidence

From the civilizations of Elam, Assyria, and Babylonia – the Achaemenid Persians' imperial predecessors – we possess a variety of public and private records. The most common were royal inscriptions and administrative records. Terse chronicles record significant military or building activities of the kings. Not enough of these are extant, however, to enable writing a narrative account. Persian royal inscriptions relay the kings' ideology, the image of their empire and their rule that they wished to project, and it is for these very reasons that they are among the most important sources for understanding the Empire. They are intentionally formulaic, grounded in the kings' right to rule absolutely. This type of text situates the Achaemenid kings within a long continuum of Near Eastern history.

Careful analysis of these inscriptions reveals insights into individual king's personalities and priorities. From Darius I onward, the inscriptions were frequently trilingual, inscribed in three languages, each in a different cuneiform script: Old Persian (an Indo-Iranian language), Elamite (linguistic affiliation uncertain), and Babylonian Akkadian (an eastern Semitic language). The choice of these three languages, and their linguistic variety, testifies to important aspects of royal ideology and tradition. Sometimes an inscription may have been written in other languages (e.g., Aramaic, Egyptian, Greek, or Phrygian), dependent upon location and audience. From Darius I's reign onward, the royal inscriptions also became rather formulaic; nevertheless, slight differences in wording, emphasis, and occasionally content reveal significant details. Further, important cultural messages may be encoded in the trilingual inscriptions, based upon slight differences in the various versions of the same text; for example, the inclusion, exclusion, or modification of a key word or phrase in the different editions of the trilingual inscriptions may be telling.

A variety of administrative documents also exists. The most common are clay documents written in Elamite or Babylonian cuneiform and parchment documents in Aramaic, the latter in evidence from the utmost corners of the Empire: northwest Anatolia, southern Egypt, and Bactria. Type and content vary, from state archival material to records of private businessmen who contracted with the crown and private individuals. These documents typically reveal more about socioeconomic history than political history, yet thoughtful analysis offers insight into the political as well. They at times provide details about members of the extended royal family and other elites who oversaw a complex and centralized bureaucracy.

Particularly valuable for understanding the central bureaucracy is the important trove of Elamite documents found at Persepolis and dating to the late sixth and early fifth centuries. The Persepolis Treasury and Persepolis Fortification tablets (pp. 103–108) are also notable for the iconographic evidence: the wide variety of imagery preserved is still being tapped by art historians to assess the symbolism and culture of the Persian imperial bureaucracy. Similarly, several private and temple archives from Babylonia offer insights into the workings of the Empire in the provinces. Ongoing study of this vast and varied material continues to supplement and sometimes revise our knowledge of Persian history. Up until 2007 it was considered gospel that the Old Persian script had been used for royal inscriptions only. The discovery of an administrative document written in Old Persian – a document whose significance remains elusive – has forced us to reconsider what had been one of the most steadfast "truths" in Achaemenid historiography.[4]

Hebrew Bible

Several books in the Hebrew Bible contain important information about Persian administration and its concerns in the Levant. As with any source, the audience and aim of each must be considered. Many Persian kings are portrayed positively in these works, because they are set during the so-called Second Temple period in Jewish history, the era after the Babylonian Captivity in which Cyrus' conquest of Babylon enabled a return of many Jewish exiles and a restoration of Jerusalem and the temple of Yahweh.

Greek/Classical Sources

Far and away the richest sources – in quantity, if not quality – for Persian history come from Greek and Roman writers. As noted above, the mainland Greeks lived in the shadow of the great Empire. Many other Greeks, in Ionia and the Black Sea region, were its subjects. There was no shortage of commercial and diplomatic exchange between these various Greeks – most of whom, it should be remembered, lived in independent city-states – and other subjects of the Persian Empire in the eastern Mediterranean as well as the Persian authorities themselves. Many Greeks, especially in the fourth century, served as mercenaries in the Persian army. Despite this frequent and varied contact, we cannot rely on Greek writers to present an unbiased view of Persian government, strategy, or culture.

The phenomenon of narrative, *written* history is traced to the Greeks and mainly to Herodotus, the so-called "Father of History," who lived and wrote in the mid-fifth century BCE. Herodotus is by far the most important non-Persian source for this study, the main narrative source for the period preceding Cyrus the Great's rise through the early reign of Xerxes. Herodotus was an Ionian Greek. He hailed from Halicarnassus, a city on the western coast of Turkey (Ionia) that was well-established as a nexus of west-east interaction; it was also subject to the Persian Empire. Well-read and well-traveled, Herodotus was in a position to offer significant insights into the scale and reach of the Empire, and yet as a Greek from the western frontier of the Empire, he was far-removed from the inner workings of the court and imperial bureaucracy. It is difficult, if not impossible, to trace where or from whom Herodotus gained his information. As with any source discussed herein, the modern historian must make informed choices about the reliability of the information presented.

The meaning of the word "history" (Greek *historia*), as Herodotus used it, was "observation" or "learning," especially "learning by inquiry." The task that Herodotus gave himself was not modest: to record the cataclysmic – note that this is from a Greek perspective – confrontation between Greeks and Persians, when the Persians invaded Greece in 480–479 BCE under the command of King Xerxes. This was a watershed moment in Greek and western history, and Greek intellectuals of that period and thereafter could not help but react to it and its impact. The invasion was, incidentally, far less significant for Persian history. But Xerxes' expedition occupies perhaps one-third of Herodotus' work. Much of the rest is devoted to developments that preceded Xerxes' invasion and thus helps to explain how and why the expedition came to be.

Herodotus' younger contemporaries Thucydides, Xenophon, and Ctesias also authored works helpful to the study of the Persians. The Athenian general Thucydides' masterpiece chronicles the Peloponnesian War between Athens and Sparta and their respective allies. Thucydides periodically shows keen awareness of the Persians' influential and important role in the war – in fact, it was Persian financial support that ultimately enabled the Spartan victory in 404 BCE – but his concern is not with Persia but rather with the Greeks themselves. His work is thus not as informative as we would wish for the Persian Empire.

The Athenian Xenophon, who lived at the turn of the fourth century, is known from a number of historical and philosophical works. The *Hellenica*, essentially a sequel to Thucydides' history, provides the backbone of our historical narrative circa 411 to the middle of the fourth century. Xenophon also partook in an expedition of Greek mercenaries led by Cyrus the Younger, who attempted to overthrow his brother, King Artaxerxes II, in 401. That expedition failed, but Xenophon's account of it and the Greek forces' return (entitled *Anabasis*, usually translated as "the March Up Country") is an important source for that turbulent period of Persian history. It likewise contains much of import for the historical geography of the ancient Near East. Xenophon's *Cyropaideia* ("the Education of Cyrus") is a quasi-historical novel and disquisition on leadership that reflects the Greek fascination with the founder of the Empire, Cyrus the Great. It adds little to our understanding of the history of the period but continues to be mined for social and cultural insights about the Persians.

Another Ionian Greek, Ctesias of Cnidus (a city on the southwestern coast of Anatolia), served as a doctor in the Persian court for over a decade early in the reign of Artaxerxes II, which makes him a rough contemporary of Xenophon. Only fragments and summaries of his *Persica* – a monumental work tracing the histories of Assyria, Media, and Persia to this time – have survived. This mostly-lost work was extremely influential in antiquity, but what remains is in many ways disappointing. As a historical text, defined by modern standards, it is lacking in accuracy and overemphasizes the sensational – surely part of the reason for its popularity. Ctesias' reputation, despite his work's influence, was less than positive, and this outlook has also colored how modern scholarship views his extant work. However, used judiciously, his work also offers many potential insights into Persian history, culture, and court life.

Later writers such as Diodorus Siculus (first century BCE) and Plutarch (c. 100 CE) contain information to fill gaps in the narrative history, though their accuracy and reliability must also be qualified. Other Greek writers, whose works survive only in fragments or quotations by other authors, also provide information on the Persians. Names such as Deinon and Ephorus (both fourth-century BCE writers) will occasionally be referenced herein. Likewise, tragedy, such as Aeschylus' play

The Persians; philosophy, oddments from Plato's and Aristotle's works; geography, such as Strabo's work; and scraps from other genres also provide useful information, but with the same caveats as noted above. The so-called Alexander historians, those who traveled with Alexander the Great during his conquest of the Persian Empire in the 330s and 320s BCE, are also noteworthy. Their works have not survived directly but were tapped by later Roman writers such as Quintus Curtius Rufus (first century CE) and Arrian (second century CE).

Writing Achaemenid History: An Excursus on the Use of Greek Sources for Persian History

It is no accident that many Greek writers other than Herodotus were obsessed with the Persian Empire. Because of the Persian Empire's enormous resources and reach, even the Greeks of the mainland had to consider its policies, as represented by the western satraps (governors). Most often, Greek views of the Empire were suspicious or downright hostile, colored by the stereotypical Greek denigration of "the Other" (non-Greeks), which made the Persians the prototypical barbarians. This is more than slightly ironic when one considers that the Achaemenid Persians were the rulers of a world empire, heirs to – and innovators within – Near Eastern political and cultural traditions that dated almost two thousand years before the Greeks developed writing. The Greek word *barbaros* was initially a label for non-Greeks – specifically those who did not speak the Greek language – and who were, because they were not Greek, inferior.[5] If one could imagine a situation where no Greek sources were available, it is interesting to speculate how modern scholarship would interpret the Greeks as displayed at Persepolis or the tomb reliefs, from the Persian perspective alone: rustic barbarians with goofy hats?

An overview of the Persian Empire must rely on generalizations. Thorough, critical examination of each piece of evidence, with contextualization of its inherent problems, would move far beyond the scope of this book. There are many specialist books and articles that continue to grapple with the details of Persian history, some of which are cited in the footnotes and recommended readings. The reader is asked to keep in mind that the interpretations put forward here are no more than an introductory word. Every source that tells us something about Persian history, from all the various categories above, must be scrutinized for its accuracy, or when we lack supporting evidence – which is often the case – for its potential reliability.

An example from Herodotus may prove useful in this regard. He wrote his history, and notably read excerpts of it aloud to live audiences at Athens and elsewhere, in the late 430s and 420s BCE, a bitter and bloody period of Greek history in the initial stages of the Peloponnesian War. Herodotus invoked what in his view was clearly a better time: that time when much (but certainly not all) of the Greek world united against the overwhelming might of Xerxes' invading army, and by so doing the Greek way of life, its values and its institutions, had prevailed against all odds.

As the so-called "Father of History," he holds pride of place in the development of that discipline, but "history" to Herodotus and others held a different meaning than it does for us. Writing two generations after Xerxes' invasion (in 480–479 BCE), Herodotus had access to eye-witnesses of the invasion, but for those periods that came before – the reigns of Cyrus, Cambyses, and Darius – he was reliant mainly on what his sources told him. As a public performer, Herodotus also knew the value of a good story and did not hesitate to tell one. Ultimately, then, the line between historical fact and hyperbole often seems blurred. It is this line that has preoccupied much of modern scholarship on Herodotus. He was not naïve, but he relayed the information given to him, often with a skeptical aside, and left it to his readers to decide. Some of his accounts of Persian customs seem bizarre and yet others echo, some-times only faintly, important themes highlighted in the Persian kings' own royal inscriptions. Regardless of the means of transmission, it is difficult to view this as a coincidence.

Herodotus was a product of his times, the great intellectual milieu of the fifth-century Greek world, and his work is replete with its ele-ments, for example, interest in medicine, the ordering of the natu-ral world, ethnography, and the relationship between human and the divine. His work is not a loose collection of random accounts and obser-vations but contains a clearly-demonstrable pattern in its arrangement. This makes his history as much a literary achievement as a historical one, but it makes the modern historian's task that much more complex.

For example, Herodotus relates that, at a critical moment in Cyrus the Great's expansionist campaigns, it is the defeated Croesus, once king of Lydia and subsequently Cyrus' "wise advisor" (one of Herodotus' favorite literary character-types), who counsels Cyrus to make the fateful move across the river Araxes to engage his enemy. This reminds the reader to consider that it was Croesus' own hubris in crossing the river to engage the Persians that brought about his defeat by Cyrus (see pp. 39–42). Did this actually happen as Herodotus tells it? Did Croesus become, in truth, an advisor of Cyrus who, in this case, gave Cyrus bad advice as a "payback" for his own defeat? Or was this entire episode an embellishment on Herodotus' part, to emphasize a literary motif? Or is the truth somewhere in the middle? It is these sorts of questions that must be considered time and again in examination of our sources for Achaemenid Persian history.

2   Forerunners of the Achaemenids: The First Half of the First Millennium BCE

IRANIANS INTO IRAN

The Persians were one of many groups of Iranians, who were often demarcated by tribes.[1] Based on assessment of archaeological evidence, scholars believe that Iranian migrations into western Iran may have begun as early as 1500 BCE. The kingdom of Elam was dominant during that time in western Iran, and we have little firm information on the Persians until several centuries later. Archaeologists emphasize how difficult it is to equate specific types of evidence (e.g., a particular style of pot) with specific groups of people. We can only generalize about the earliest migrations of Iranians into the land that would ultimately bear their name. Even some of the most basic questions remain contentious among specialists, such as which route or routes the Persians took into and through Iran. For much of twentieth century, it was held that Iranian migration occurred mainly through the Caucasus Mountains, west of the Caspian Sea. More recently, new discoveries in conjunction with reassessment of old evidence have identified an eastern route as more likely.

Research in ancient Bactria – an area that encompassed modern northeastern Iran, northern Afghanistan, and parts of Turkmenistan and Uzbekistan – has uncovered remnants of an advanced, Bronze Age society that flourished in the centuries around 2000 BCE. Various sites in this area provide evidence of irrigation farming and monumental architecture, markers traditionally associated with early urbanization. As a whole, this area is called the Bactria-Margiana Archaeological Complex (BMAC) or the Oxus Civilization, for the Oxus River (the

Amu Darya) that runs through the region. Margiana was the name of Bactria's neighbor in ancient Iran. It is a matter of ongoing debate whether various Indo-Iranian groups were some of the original inhabitants of the BMAC; whether they simply passed through – over decades, if not centuries – on their way to the Indian subcontinent or to Iran; or whether they had nothing to do with any of it.[2] The linguistic and cultural affiliation between the various Indo-Iranian groups is well-established, but specifics regarding their settlement in Iran remain obscure.

The Persians first appear in the written record of the ninth century BCE, from the reign of the Assyrian king Shalmaneser III (reigned 858–824 BCE). Shalmaneser III and his successors frequently raided territories in the central western Zagros Mountains northwest of the modern Mahidasht, home to Persians and various other Iranian groups. By the middle of the eighth century, the Assyrians had created a formal province of Parsua and controlled the area until Assyria's fall in the late seventh century. Tracking the movements of the Iranians in this period seems a hopeless task; we have no sources from them and few references to them. Assyrian royal inscriptions and official correspondence refer to this region only in the context of military raids, receipt of tribute, or other administrative matters relating to the region's government by Assyria.

The connection between the Persians of the central Zagros and the Persians of southwestern Iran (Fars), the later core of the Achaemenid Empire, is unclear. If migrations continued, in the mid-first millennium from northeast to southwest along the Zagros chain, it is not evident in the available sources, nor have clear traces of such migration been found archaeologically. Some archaeologists consider pottery from the Achaemenid period (found at the major sites of Susa, Pasargadae, and Persepolis) to be stylistically linked to earlier pottery, dating as early as circa 800 BCE, from the Zagros. To date, no compelling explanation has been advanced to explain this linkage, beyond the reasonable – yet unsubstantiated – assumption that at least some migrating Persian groups brought the style with them when they migrated to Fars during the course of the seventh century. But this hypothesis has not found widespread acceptance.

We thus have Persians attested separately in the central Zagros and in Fars, with the former attested somewhat earlier. It is difficult to imagine a large-scale migration through the Zagros Mountains over the course of the seventh and sixth centuries, but it cannot be ruled out. If there was such a movement by Persians who once lived under the Assyrian aegis in the Zagros, this migration may have been one source of the transmission of cultural conventions between Assyria and Persia, such as elements of imperial ideology. An alternative is that two separate groups of Persians migrated into the central Zagros and into Fars, respectively, during roughly the same period in the first half of the first millennium BCE.

ELAM

Elamites were, as far as we can tell, the earliest inhabitants of southwestern Iran. The geographic term Elam comes from Hebrew *'êlām*, and Akkadian *Elamtu*, to describe the land that the Elamites themselves called *Haltamti*. Elamite civilization may be traced to the fourth millennium BCE, roughly contemporary with the earliest Sumerians in Mesopotamia, modern Iraq. The acculturation of Elamites and Iranians, especially the Persians and Elamites of Fars, is a major factor in the rise of the Achaemenid Empire, but it is a phenomenon that is not obvious in the available sources. One needs to dig beneath the surface, both literally and figuratively, to discern it. The lack of appreciation of Elamite influence on the Persians stems in the main from the relative paucity of Elamite material and the difficulties associated with its study. This lack has only begun to be rectified in the last generation of modern scholarship. Figure 2.1 is one such example, a procession portrayed at a long-standing Elamite shrine that scholars have compared to similar processions portrayed at Persepolis.

It is the Elamites who dominate the landscape of the historical period in southwestern Iran, until the Medes and Persians established themselves in the mid-first millennium. Khuzistan and Fars appear to have been the main areas of Elamite settlement. That statement must be qualified, because excavation in eastern Iran has been relatively limited.

Figure 2.1 Elamite rock relief from Kul-e Farah, Izeh, Iran. Courtesy of D. T. Potts.

The Elamite language has been deciphered, but its vocabulary and grammatical elements are less well understood than other languages written in cuneiform scripts, such as the Akkadian used by Elam's neighbors in Assyria and Babylonia. The corpus of surviving Elamite texts is not nearly as large, and for many periods we lack bilingual texts, which are so critical in cracking a language's code. Further, the Elamite language has no clear linguistic relatives to aid translation.[3] Elamite has therefore not been subjected to the same intensity of analysis as Akkadian or Sumerian.

Through the second millennium, the center of Elamite civilization appears to have been in Fars, specifically the city of Anshan, approximately 30 miles west of the future Persian capital Persepolis. Yet the city of Susa, in Khuzistan, is the most visible city, thanks to over a century's worth of archaeological work there that began in the late 1800s CE. Susa was on the eastern edge of the Babylonian flood plain, and as a consequence its history was intertwined with its Mesopotamian neighbors from its beginnings. Its importance persisted into the Persian period, when it became one of the Persian capitals.

Around 1000 BCE, Anshan was abandoned. In the roughly 150 years previous, the Elamite kings, who had styled themselves in their royal titles "King of Anshan and Susa," were at the height of their territorial power and ambition. They even ruled Babylonia for a time in the mid-twelfth century. The written record falls silent shortly thereafter until the eighth century. A large part of the problem in studying Elamite history in Fars during the so-called Neo-Elamite period (c. 1000–550 BCE) is that large-scale settlement there cannot be traced again until the Achamenid period, four centuries later. The most likely reason for the gap in the archaeological record is that semisedentary pastoralism became the dominant way of life during this period. In addition, only a small part of Anshan has been explored. Our assessment of this and many other areas may change dramatically as archaeological excavation proceeds.

It is ironic that the period circa 750–650 BCE is the most well-known of Neo-Elamite history, because the vast majority of documentary evidence for Elamite political history is of Assyrian origin, Elam's rival and nemesis. Assyrian kings left extensive narratives of their military achievements (the royal annals), many of which detail campaigns against Elam. Specialists are still working through these and related materials, many of which were found in the nineteenth-century excavations, and there is much work to be done. The record is much thinner from Elam itself: a smattering of royal inscriptions (most from Susa) that are poorly understood and lack the detail and flourish of the Assyrian annals. We are thus reliant upon the perspective of Elam's enemy for assessment of Elam's history. Beneath the political and economic rivalries (e.g., for control of the important trade routes through the Zagros Mountains), however, was a rich network of cultural ties – including close links between the Assyrian and Elamite royal families of the seventh century. It must be recalled that the histories of Elam and Mesopotamia (Assyria in the north, Babylonia in the south) had been intertwined for centuries; it was not until the rise of the Achaemenid Empire that all these regions were brought under one rule for more than a brief period. Indeed, the history of the seventh and sixth centuries is marked most frequently by Assyria's problems with Elamites and Babylonians, the latter two often working in tandem to thwart Assyrian ambitions. Assyrian sources reveal that the Elamites had great influence, if not direct control, over many of the various Aramaean and Chaldean groups living in southern Mesopotamia.

One of the most powerful Neo-Elamite kings was Shutruk-Nahhunte II, who ruled from 717 to 699 and from whom we have the most Elamite inscriptions. He used the royal titles "King of Anshan and Susa" and

"expander of the realm." Shutruk-Nahhunte's actual political reach, cir-
cumscribed by Assyrian power in the west, may not have approached
that of his forebears in the second millennium, but his royal titles give
insight into his aspirations. Shutruk-Nahhunte's success against Assyria
provided a severe check on the latter's hold of southeastern Babylonia
and the central Zagros in the late eighth century. Shutruk-Nahhunte's
successors through the first half of the seventh century continued to
challenge Assyria. By this time, though, the most consistent fighting
occurred along the Elamite-Babylonian frontier, and the Assyrians generally held the upper hand in the border zones of the central Zagros
Mountains. Yet the necessity of frequent military activity against Elam
in Babylonia and its southern reaches reveals that Assyria, even at the
height of its power under the Sargonid kings (see discussion later in this
chapter), never effectively quieted the region. This assessment is based
on Assyrian sources; the Elamites would have had a different spin on
this running conflict.

Major Assyrian campaigns against Elam occurred with increasing
frequency as the seventh century progressed from every few years to
almost annually. In 653 BCE tensions between Elam and Assyria flared
at the Battle of Til Tuba, along the Ulaya River in Khuzistan. The
Assyrian victory was memorialized in an elaborate palace relief sequence
at Nineveh and in numerous inscriptions.[4] These reliefs are on display
at the British Museum and acquaint the casual viewer – via depictions
of humiliation, torture, and slaughter of enemies – with the cruelty
for which the Assyrians were infamous. It may be countered, however,
that the Assyrians were not much different than their predecessors and
contemporaries in the ancient world. Their public relations were simply
more compelling.

Much of the decade after the Til Tuba campaign was marked by
more forceful and direct Assyrian involvement in Elamite affairs, to
little positive effect. A rapid succession of kings reflected the resulting instability in Elam in the late 650s and early 640s. The political
chaos did not reduce Elamite-Assyrian friction, so in 646 Ashurbanipal
launched another campaign against Elam. This one resulted in the sack
of Susa that, according to the Assyrian accounts, leveled the city. The
devastation, while not atypical, is relayed in dramatic detail: treasuries
were emptied, temples plundered and destroyed, previous kings' graves

exhumed and their corpses dishonored, and countless livestock and people removed to Assyria. It is difficult to assess the accuracy of this type of description. The victor certainly exaggerates, but beyond the hyperbole, we know that that was far from the end of the story for Susa. Scattered evidence reveals that several Elamite kingdoms in Khuzistan and Fars persisted into the sixth century. It is in this milieu that the earliest Persian kings, Cyrus the Great's predecessors, must be located.

ASSYRIA

The Assyrians were a Semitic-speaking people who dwelled in northern Mesopotamia, part of modern Iraq. Their history may be traced for centuries from the late third millennium BCE. The major cities of Nimrud (ancient Calah or Kalhu) and Nineveh were the two main Assyrian centers in the ninth through seventh centuries, and the nineteenth-century excavations at these places proved seminal in founding the modern discipline of Assyriology. Thousands of tablets, most famously from the Library of Ashurbanipal at Nineveh, provide continuing insights into Assyrian history and civilization. The Epic of Gilgamesh, the Epic of Creation (*Enuma elish*), and a variety of other famous myths and legends were uncovered there. In addition, once the cuneiform script was deciphered, a wealth of sources for the history of this period also became accessible: royal inscriptions and annals; correspondence between the king, his officials, and foreign dignitaries; cultic and omen texts detailing aspects of Mesopotamian religion and ritual; and administrative and legal texts revealing – in sometimes mind-numbing but massively useful detail – the bureaucratic workings of empire, temple, and even private commercial interests.

By the time of Tiglath-pileser III (ruled 744–727 BCE), the Assyrians were embarking on a new, imperial phase, one that would make them the largest empire to date and offer a model – ideological and organizational – for the much larger Achaemenid Empire to come later. Assyria reached the height of its power and territorial aspirations in the late eighth and seventh centuries under the Sargonid kings: Sargon II, Sennacherib, Esarhaddon, and Ashurbanipal. The Assyrian Empire controlled or held tributary large areas of south central and southeastern

Turkey (Urartu), northwestern Iran (various Iranian groups), Babylonia, Syro-Palestine (Israel, Judah, Phoenicia, and other small kingdoms), Cyprus, and, briefly, Egypt (Map 2.1).

Many of the Assyrian inscriptions (especially the royal annals) detail the king's military campaigns, and they make manifest the king as the gods' agent who was a moral force, both required and expected to punish enemies and, as a consequence, expand Assyrian territory. How much of this imperial narrative is meant to be taken literally is open to question. It is easy in our day to attribute too much cynicism to Assyrian or Achaemenid Persian claims of divine sanction for military activity and the horrific punishments meted out to defeated enemies. As far as we can tell, though, the Assyrians and other peoples of the ancient Near East took these depictions with utmost seriousness.

BABYLONIA

Babylonia is the geographic term for southern Mesopotamia. The Babylonians, like the Assyrians in the north, were a Semitic-speaking people, who used a slightly different dialect of Akkadian than the Assyrians, though by the eighth century BCE the Aramaic language was becoming the lingua franca of the ancient Near East. The Babylonians constituted various Chaldean and Aramaean tribes, some living in the old urban centers and others in the rural areas, all differing in their level of political organization. Throughout this region's long history it was no small task to keep it under one rule.

The Babylonians placed great store in being the cultural heirs of the Sumerians: the originators of civilization centered in the ancient cities of Ur, Uruk, and Nippur. Babylon itself was younger than these cities but had risen to prominence in the second millennium and retained its august position through the Achaemenid period. Sources for the study of Neo-Babylonian history are similar to those for the Neo-Assyrian Empire. Babylonian royal inscriptions focus on the building and cultic activities of the kings more than on their military deeds. Temple and private archives are in such abundance, however, that the minutiae of some temple households may be tracked at an amazingly detailed level. Records kept in these sanctuaries, from Babylon itself and other major

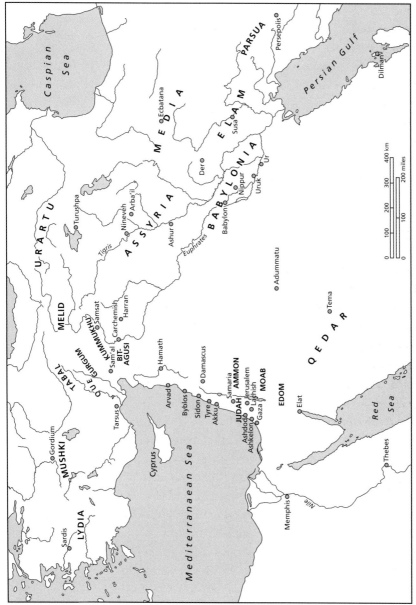

Map 2.1 Assyria and its neighbors. *After Cambridge Ancient History*, Vol. 3, Part 2, Second Edition, 1992, map 3.

27

cities, show a level of continuity in the administration and functioning of these organizations even into the Achaemenid period and beyond.

The Neo-Babylonian Empire's relations with Syro-Palestine and Egypt may be sketched with some confidence, but the situation on its eastern front remains opaque. What of the Medes, who, with the Babylonians, brought about the downfall of Assyria? What of the Elamites, frequent close partners with Babylonia against Assyria at its height? For that matter, what of the Persians themselves during this period, only a generation or two before Cyrus the Great? Answers to these questions remain frustratingly elusive. From Assyria's overthrow (610s BCE) until the reign of the Neo-Babylonian king Nabonidus (556–539 BCE), there is minimal evidence for the political situation in western Iran. The first half of the sixth century remains almost blank.

A Babylonian priest of Marduk, whose name in Greek was Berossos, wrote a history of Babylonia in Greek during the reign of the Seleucid king Antiochus I, within a generation of the Achaemenid Empire's overthrow by Alexander the Great of Macedon in the late 330s. Berossos (Fragment 8b) recorded a tradition that the Babylonian king Nebuchadnezzar married a Median princess, Amytis, the daughter of Astyages. This marriage would have occurred in the late 610s, as Babylonian and Median pressure on Assyria intensified. Presumably, however, Berossos meant Cyaxeres not Astyages, because Cyaxeres was king of the Medes at that time. Astyages was the last Median king, defeated by Cyrus. The word "presumably" is used, because Berossos' confusion makes the tradition suspect, and some scholars reject it as fiction. A lone reference, written three centuries after the fact, does not often inspire confidence, but the study of ancient history is filled with similar examples. What if Berossos' account is true, or contains an element of truth? This might explain the lack of references in the Babylonian tradition to any Babylonian-Median strife, because, in light of a marriage alliance that had done its job, there may have been none. On the other hand, a lack of evidence for conflict does not mean that conflict did not exist. This story reminds us that we have much to learn; discoveries from one site or even of one text may radically change our understanding.

Another piece of Greek evidence also gives pause. The Athenian Xenophon, writing in the early fourth century (roughly one hundred years before Berossos), chronicled his adventures with a Greek mercenary army aiding Cyrus the Younger's revolt against his brother Artaxerxes II. Xenophon makes a passing reference (*Anabasis* 2.4.12) to a "Median Wall," a line of fortifications purportedly built by Nebuchadnezzar that stretched between Sippar and Babylon. Xenophon provides no information about its purpose, but the label itself has been taken to imply a Median threat. Some of Nabonidus' inscriptions about the Medes, whom he labeled with the pejorative Akkadian term *umman-manda* (translated as "horde" or the like), suggest a potential threat in the 550s. But, as Nabonidus' inscriptions further relate, that potential threat was neutralized by Cyrus and the Persians' defeat of the Medes.

ANATOLIAN KINGDOMS

Phrygia

After the fall of the Hittite kingdom in the twelfth century BCE, little is known of Anatolian history until well into the first millennium. The most important kingdoms for our purposes were Phrygia (north central and northwestern Anatolia), Urartu (east and southeastern Anatolia), and Lydia (central western Anatolia). The first of these two kingdoms are mentioned with some frequency in Assyrian sources of the eighth and seventh centuries. Phrygia is sometimes confused with Lydia in modern literature, but they were distinct kingdoms. Little is known of Phrygia's origins in the "dark age" after the Hittite kingdom's collapse, but by the eighth century Phrygia, from its main center Gordion, had encompassed the old Hittite capital of Hattusha (modern Boghazkoy). The Assyrians called this kingdom Mushki, of which a vague echo is preserved in the Greek myth King Midas of the Golden Touch.

Urartu

The kingdom of Urartu was a rival of the Assyrians from the eighth century until the end of the Assyrian Empire. Urartian royal inscriptions are similar to those from Babylonia and Elam, that is, they focus on the king's building activities and his piety to the gods. We rely mainly on Assyrian accounts for reconstruction of much of Urartu's political history, what little there is known of it. Migrating Cimmerians and Scythians in the early seventh century wreaked havoc in Urartu, as Assyrian sources attest these groups did in many areas throughout the ancient Near East. A broken reference in a Babylonian source suggests that Urartu persisted as an independent entity until the time of Cyrus, when it was incorporated into the Persian Empire.

Lydia

The kingdom of Lydia is known to us mainly through the Greek historian Herodotus' account in Book I of his history. Herodotus starts with Lydia because of its rule of the Ionian Greeks, both Lydia and Ionia later subsumed by the rising Persian Empire. Herodotus' history of Lydia, like that of the Medes, contains much of interest to the historian, but it must be considered more legendary than factual. That does not mean, however, that it is entirely fabricated. There is some external corroboration for the Lydian royal house. According to Herodotus, a Lydian courtier by the name of Gyges deposed the king Candaules, married Candaules' wife, and founded a new dynasty. Herodotus' Gyges has been identified with a king of Lydia, *Gugu*, in one of the Assyrian king Ashurbanipal's inscriptions.[5] Gugu's messenger was dispatched to Nineveh to seek assistance against the continuing Cimmerian incursions of the mid-seventh century. Ashurbanipal's inscription emphasizes the wonder that accompanied Gugu's messenger: the distance from which he came (Sardis, in western Anatolia) and the fact that no one at the Assyrian court could understand a word he said. By the time of the Achaemenid Empire, the world had grown smaller; Lydia and other Anatolian territories were administered by Persian satraps, and Sardis was the western edge of the so-called Royal Road. Ashurbanipal's wonder at Gugu's message underlines the great distances and diversity between various regions that were later unified under Achaemenid power.

Classical sources indicate that Lydian power was at least in part based on gold panned from the Pactolus River that ran through Lydia. Many of the Greek city-states of western Anatolia (Ionia) were brought under Lydian rule, and Lydian kings' donations to Greek sanctuaries – especially those of the last king, Croesus, to Delphi – also were the stuff of legend. Croesus sponsored not only Delphi but several other sanctuaries as well, including the famous Temple of Artemis at Ephesus. That temple was destroyed in a fire in the late fourth century but rebuilt; the new Temple of Artemis was designated one of the Seven Wonders of the World. Archaeological finds at Ephesus and elsewhere in Ionia confirm the intensive mingling of Greek and Lydian styles that remained typical throughout the Achaemenid period.[6]

Expanding Lydian influence brought Lydia into conflict with the Medes, a struggle that culminated in a standoff at the so-called Battle of the Solar Eclipse in the year 585. Here is another instance where it is difficult to separate fact from fiction in Greek accounts of this period. Herodotus set the stage for this conflict with his tale of Scythian guests at the Median court of Cyaxeres. The Scythians ran afoul of their benefactor, and, stung by Cyaxeres' insults, they slaughtered and served as dinner (unbeknownst to Cyaxeres) a Median boy, after which they fled to Alyattes, Gyges' great-grandson, in Lydia.[7] Alyattes' refusal to hand over the fugitives led to war. The culminating battle took its name from the solar eclipse that occurred during it, an event so momentous – and one considered of such ill omen – that the combatants ceased the war and negotiated a peace. According to Herodotus, though the names and geography appear confused, the kings of Cilicia and Babylonia (the former perhaps subject to the latter) served as witnesses and the treaty was sealed by a dynastic marriage: Alyattes' daughter Aryenis was married to Cyaxeres' son Astyages.

THE MEDES

No documentary evidence from the Medes themselves has been found. Few confidently identified Median sites have been excavated, and many questions remain about those that have been. Simply identifying a "homeland" of the Medes is a difficult task. The modern city of Hamadan, ancient Ecbatana, served as a capital, which we know from later traditions about Cyrus the Great's victory over Astyages. Median settlements are mentioned in Assyrian sources, starting from the ninth century, throughout the central and northern Zagros Mountains, especially along the Great Khorasan Road towards modern Tehran.

We are thus beholden to Herodotus' account of the rise and organization of the Median Empire, although he was not unique in his consideration of the Medes' importance. Despite the problems with Herodotus' portrayal, until recently it had been generally accepted – at least in outline – as an accurate rendition of the Medes' rise to power. It has thus served as the basis for the picture of the Median Empire that is so prominent in modern scholarship. This is despite its clearly literary elements, and despite the fact that it is hopelessly conflated chronologically. In other words, Herodotus' account of the Medes must be considered more legend than history. Nevertheless, read carefully, Herodotus has things to teach us about the Medes. If for no other reason than a lesson in historiography, a sketch of Herodotus' telescoped tale (1.96–106) is useful.

A Mede named Deioces had designs on taking power, and he took advantage of the general lawlessness of the land. His reputation for justice brought more and more Medes to him to settle their disputes. As his influence grew, Deioces then stepped back; he refused to neglect his own affairs for the benefit of others. When lawlessness soon increased, the Medes decided to make Deioces their king. Once he had accepted the job, Deioces insisted on a bodyguard of spear-bearers and a fortified capital: Ecbatana, constructed with multiple walls, two of which purportedly had battlements plated in silver and gold (1.98). Deioces consolidated his position and then removed himself from sight, thereby making himself exceptional and emphasizing the august status of the king. He further secured his position by implementing certain behavioral protocols, for those few who did gain audience, and by establishing a network of spies and informers. This description matches in theme and outline accounts of the rise of tyrants in Greek city-states, though taken to another, grander level. With regard to the king's exceptionality and the behavioral protocols, historians have noted the parallels with the later Achaemenid court, or rather, the Greeks' stereotypical image of it. Many scholars thus take for granted the literary quality of Herodotus' account of Deioces' rise.

To resume the story, Deioces' successor Phraortes subjugated the Persians and battled the Assyrians. Herodotus then notes a Scythian invasion, which put on hold (for twenty-eight years) the reign of Cyaxeres, who was Phraortes' successor. Despite numerous ingenious attempts, modern scholars have not been able to reconcile large-scale Scythian invasions anywhere in the Near East in the late seventh century BCE. Assyrian evidence testifies to the Scythians' and Cimmerians' threat roughly a generation earlier, during the reign of Esarhaddon. But there is no Assyrian or Babylonian evidence for a "Scythian interlude" during Cyaxeres' rule of the Medes. If this interlude is not simply a literary device, which is the most likely explanation, it seems that Herodotus or his sources conflated the history and chronology of this part of the narrative.

It is important at this point to extend the discussion of the early Medes beyond Herodotus and the Greek tradition. In the last decade, an increasing number of scholars have come to assert that even the outline of Herodotus' account of the Medes, not just the particulars, is inaccurate. With an increase in the accessibility of Assyrian information on the Medes, reconsiderations of this important people and their place in ancient Near Eastern history are currently underway. Assyrian royal inscriptions and correspondence of the eighth and seventh centuries, until circa 650, provide a wealth of detail about the Medes and their interactions with Assyria. Some patterns have emerged.[8] First, the Medes mentioned dwelled in fortified settlements, each headed by a city-lord (the Akkadian term *bēl alī*). Assyrian incursions into Median territory were undertaken to control important commercial routes and to capture horses, for which the Assyrian appetite – to ride, not to eat – was insatiable. There is a striking consistency in Assyrian texts in descriptions of Medes as horsemen, and on sculptures of Sargon's palace at Dur-Sharrukin (modern Khorsabad in Iraq) the Medes are all portrayed with horses. By the end of the eighth century, many areas, especially along the Great Khorasan Road, that the Assyrians identified as "Median" were incorporated into the Assyrian Empire. The Median city-lords of these now Assyrian-held territories were bound to the Assyrian king by loyalty oaths. Evidence for the Medes becomes sparse during Ashurbanipal's reign (669–c. 630 BCE). It is precisely in that period in which we would expect to find a fledgling Median Empire, if such an empire existed. But Assyrian sources for the three decades before Assyria's collapse in the 610s are thin in detail, which makes historical assessment problematic.

The Assyrian evidence is not easily reconciled with the Greek tradition. Through the mid-seventh century, there is no indication of a centralized, Median authority, that is, a sole king, one who could be equated, for example, with Herodotus' Deioces. Modern scholars have attempted to identify some Medes named in Assyrian sources with those of early Median kings mentioned in the Greek tradition. Median local rulers Dayukku (late eighth century) and Kashtaritu (early seventh century) have been equated with Herodotus' Deioces and Phraortes, respectively, but beyond the linguistic gymnastics involved the historical context of each does not offer a good fit. Even if Dayukku and Kashtaritu left an imprint on subsequent Median tradition through oral traditions long since lost, there is no way to forge the two perspectives, Assyrian and Herodotean, into agreement.

What remains in the dark is the critical period circa 650–550 BCE, when the Medes were at the height of their power. It remains unclear how we are to move from Assyrian descriptions of the Medes as seemingly independent city-lords to the Medes as a unified force that Cyaxeres (Umakishtar in the Babylonian sources) was able to unleash against Assyria with such devastating effect in the 610s. Recent approaches have postulated that the Medes were the leaders of a large coalition of mostly Iranian peoples from across northern Iran, a coalition unified by a forceful personality such as Cyaxeres and only for the purpose of defeating Assyria. This coalition, in conjunction with the Babylonians, was successful at that task, but afterwards the coalition splintered. If this reconstruction is accurate, it remains to be reconciled with accounts of the Medes as a major power through the first half of the sixth century, an impression given not only by Greek sources but one alluded to in Babylonian and biblical traditions (such as Jeremiah 25:25–26 and 51:27–28) as well.

3 Persia Rising: A New Empire

CYRUS I IN AN ELAMITE-PERSIAN MILIEU

The Assyrian Empire was at its height during the reign of Ashurbanipal (669–c. 630 BCE). Sources from Assyria on Elam and the early Persians, especially after the Assyrian sack of Susa in 646, are scarce. Scattered Elamite evidence attests to a number of kings that may be dated to this late period (c. 650–550 BCE). But beyond their names, little is known of these individuals: their chronologies, the scope of their rules, and their relationships with one another are all uncertain. Among those kingdoms was the earliest Persian kingdom ruled by Cyrus the Great's forefathers, whom Cyrus lists in the famous Cyrus Cylinder, one of the most important extant pieces of evidence for Cyrus' reign (see discussion later in this chapter). In modern scholarship it has generally been assumed that Cyrus the Great's grandfather (*Kurash* in Akkadian), whom Cyrus named "King of Anshan" in the Cyrus Cylinder, is the same as the Cyrus, King of Persia (*Parsumash* in Akkadian), who sometime in the late 640s sent a delegation to Ashurbanipal.

Cyrus, the King of Parsumash, heard about my victory. He became aware of the might that I wielded with the aid of Ashur, Bel, and Nabu, the great gods my lords, with which I leveled the whole of Elam like a flood. He sent Arukku, his eldest son, with his tribute to Nineveh, the city of my lordship, to pay homage to me. He implored my lordship.[1]

Such descriptions are typical of the aftermath of Assyrian conquests, both in the fate of the antagonist and the ways in which the neighboring rulers rushed to pay their respects and to curry Assyrian favor.

The particulars of the matter, of course, would have been more complicated, even if Ashurbanipal's rhetoric was true at its core. In the version quoted above, Cyrus' son, Arukku, was sent as a hostage to the Assyrian court. This was a common practice, a means of ensuring good relations between the Assyrians and their subjects or distant neighbors. The success of such practices was mixed, however. Roughly a decade before the Cyrus of Parsumash episode, Elamite princes that had been given refuge at the Assyrian court were returned and enthroned in Elam with Assyrian help. But these Elamite princes then turned on their erstwhile benefactors and rebelled, which necessitated further Assyrian military action.

Beyond the political ramifications, this type of exchange – royal children and their entourages living at the Assyrian court – undoubtedly played a role in the transmission of cultural knowledge. In this instance, we know nothing further of Arukku. But what if, after a long stretch at the Assyrian court, he returned home? What sorts of knowledge would he have brought with him? What sorts of commercial or cultural ties might this episode have forged between Assyria and early Persia? Persia was clearly indebted to Elam, Babylonia, and Assyria for modes of imperial organization and ideological expression. How such knowledge was transmitted is rarely easy to specify, and to attribute too much influence to one individual would distort the reality. But an Arukku who spent several years at the Assyrian court – quite likely with elite hostages (whom the Assyrians would have considered "guests") from other areas – would have been exposed to a variety of other peoples and influences, at the highest levels of Assyrian society.

Another piece of critical evidence for the earliest Persian kings is the inscribed seal impression of one "Cyrus, the Anshanite, son of Teispes" (Figure 3.1). This seal impression recurs with some frequency on the Persepolis Fortification Tablets from the reign of Darius I. We do not know the identity of the person who used the seal, but it was clearly a prestige item, perhaps an heirloom. The image portrays a rider running through an enemy, who holds a broken bow – a widespread symbol of defeat and humiliation in the ancient Near East. The rider is presumed to be the Cyrus of the inscription, who is identified with the grandfather of Cyrus the Great, the founder of the Empire. There is ongoing debate about the date of this seal's manufacture, and whether or not the

Figure 3.1 Collated line drawing of PFS 93* from the Persepolis Fortification Archive. Courtesy Persepolis Seal Project.

Cyrus of its inscription may be identified with the Cyrus of Parsumash who paid obeisance to Ashurbanipal. The link is attractive, but it is not a settled issue.[2]

THE FALL OF ASSYRIA AND ITS AFTERMATH

After Ashurbanipal's death, the Assyrian Empire was ruled briefly by his son Ashur-etil-ilani (c. 630–627 BCE) and then the latter's brother, Sin-sharru-ishkun (627–612 BCE). The Babylonians under Nabopolassar began already in the 620s to throw off the Assyrian yoke. An essential source for this period is the so-called Babylonian Chronicle series that records each year's notable political, military, and religious activities. There are several different chronicle texts, each with a different chronological range. Those of main concern here are closely related and often treated as one document. They provide a consistent record from the mid-eighth century through Cyrus' conquest of Babylon in 539 BCE, but there are many gaps. The copies of the chronicles that we possess date to later periods (the Achaemenid period, sometimes later) and may have undergone revisions that we cannot track.

What is most surprising in these accounts is the prominent place given to the Medes in Assyria's downfall. Nabopolassar and the Babylonians had been fighting Assyria for ten years, when the Medes appear in the chronicle: they were involved in an attack on Arrapha (modern Kirkuk, roughly 60 miles east of Ashur) in 615 BCE. In 614, the attacks against Assyrian cities continued, and the Median king Umakishtar (Cyaxeres in the Greek tradition) made a pact of alliance with Nabopolassar, the terms of which the chronicle does not divulge. The great Assyrian capital city of Nineveh was sacked in 612, and in 609 the last Assyrian king, Ashur-uballit II, and the remnants of his army were destroyed near Harran in northwestern Mesopotamia. Thus ended Assyria. The Elamites, whom one might expect to have been involved in their bitter enemy's overthrow, do not appear in any sources relating the downfall of Assyria. The Persians make no appearance either, though references to them in Assyrian and Babylonian inscriptions or chronicles are scarce before Cyrus.

CYRUS' CONQUEST OF THE MEDES

Cyrus' impact on the course of history was broad, if often underrated, and the Near Eastern accounts of his conquests are supplemented by the biblical and, especially, the Greek traditions. Not until the reign of the Babylonian king Nabonidus (reigned 556–539 BCE) do we gain significant insight into the Persians as a rising power. In one of his inscriptions, Nabonidus relayed a dream-omen that occurred to him at the beginning of his reign. The Medes posed a threat to Nabonidus' reconstruction efforts of the Ehulhul temple, dedicated to the moon god at Harran, which had been destroyed during the last stage of the overthrow of Assyria. In the dream dialogue, the god Marduk commands Nabonidus to get to work. Nabonidus expresses concern about the Medes, but his concern is unwarranted. The term *umman-manda* used to describe the Medes has negative connotations in Akkadian literary tradition.[3]

(Marduk replies to Nabonidus) "The *umman-manda* of whom you speak, he, his land, and the kings who go at his side, are no longer a threat." When the third year came, the gods roused Cyrus, king of Anshan, his young servant, against the *umman-manda*. With his small army he dispersed the vast *umman-manda*. Cyrus seized Ishtumegu (Astyages), the king of the *umman-manda*, and took him captive to his land.

This is the first reference to Cyrus the Great, initially as king of the city and region of Anshan in ancient Parsa, modern Fars in southwestern Iran. It appears to date Cyrus' conquest of the Medes to Nabonidus' third year, 553 BCE. One of the Babylonian chronicles dates Cyrus' victory to 550. That account relates Astyages' attack on Cyrus, the defection of Astyages' army to Cyrus, Cyrus' subsequent victory and the sack of Ecbatana (Astyages' royal city), and the removal of plunder from Ecbatana to Anshan.

These two testimonies tell the same story but with some significant variation, which historians attempt to reconcile. The difference in date is one. Since the chronicle series is considered more accurate than royal inscriptions, 550 is the date generally followed. For much of twentieth century scholarship, the reference to "his young servant" in the Nabonidus text was taken to mean that Cyrus was Asytages' servant. This interpretation bolstered the Classical tradition that portrayed the Persians as subject to the Medes. The relationship between the two peoples remains unclear, but to understand the phrase "his young servant" as a reference to Cyrus being a subordinate of Astyages is not a given. The phrase appears to refer to the god Marduk, who chose Cyrus as the instrument to implement his divine will – a common motif in ancient Near Eastern texts for centuries. In positive answer to Nabonidus' concern, Marduk assured Nabonidus that he would send his (i.e., Marduk's) young servant, Cyrus, to destroy the Medes. The phrasing "the kings who go at his (the Median king's) side" is also noteworthy. Although these kings are not specified in Nabonidus' inscription, the Greek writer Ctesias' later account identifies the kings of the Hyrcanians, Parthians, Scythians, and Bactrians as beholden to the Median king (Fragment 8d §46). If these peoples were indeed subject to the Medes, that could have been the basis for a significant Median power in the sixth century.

CYRUS' CONQUEST OF LYDIA AND IONIA

In many modern works, Cyrus' campaign against Lydia is precisely dated to the year 547 BCE, based on an entry in one of the Babylonian chronicles:

In the month of Nisan (= March/April), Cyrus king of Persia mobilized his army and crossed the Tigris River downstream from Arbela (in Assyria). In the month of Ayaru (April/May) [he marched] to ...[4]

The tablet is damaged exactly where the name of the place against which Cyrus marched was written. The difficulty provides an excellent example how the reading of one cuneiform sign, in one text, may impact historical analysis and reconstruction. Depending on whether one reads the crack running through the tablet as hiding one part of a cuneiform sign, or as just a crack in the tablet, makes a difference in what country name is read there: Lydia or Urartu. For much of twentieth-century scholarship, the reading "Lydia" was favored, and that interpretation has had remarkable staying power. Many Achaemenid historians now accept the reading of Urartu (so followed here), and thus for the year 547 assign Cyrus' campaign against that region in southeastern Anatolia, not against Lydia.

Even scholars who accept the reading Urartu in that line of the chronicle still date the Lydian conquest in the 540s, though no longer precisely to 547/546. This interpretation is dependent primarily on evidence from the Classical tradition and, mainly, the sequential order of Cyrus' conquests as given in Herodotus, who is thus our main source for Cyrus' Lydian campaign. Herodotus' detailed account of the Lydian royal house contains all sorts of object lessons relevant to the study of Greek literature, less so for Lydia's history. A classic story in Herodotus (1.53–54) illustrates this. During his preparations to confront Cyrus, Croesus sought the advice of the Oracle of Delphi. The oracle predicted that if Croesus made war against the Persians, he would destroy a mighty empire. Croesus took the oracle to mean that he would be victorious. He was wrong, though he did destroy a mighty empire: his own.

Cyrus met Croesus' army in Cappadocia (central Anatolia). Cyrus' forces were augmented by his conquest of the Medes – which included contingents from northern and eastern Iran – as well as those areas through which Cyrus had marched to confront Croesus. Despite the Persian advantage in numbers, the fighting was inconclusive. With winter fast approaching, Croesus withdrew and disbanded his army, with every intention to resume hostilities in the spring. Cyrus made a surprising, and daring, maneuver: he did not disband his own army but instead pursued Croesus to the Lydian capital, Sardis. Cyrus took Croesus at unawares – as Herodotus puts it, "Cyrus came as his own messenger to Croesus" (1.79) – and defeated him in a pitched battle outside the city. Outnumbered and outmaneuvered, Croesus then took refuge in Sardis, sent desperate pleas to his allies, and was besieged. Just a couple weeks later, some Persians scaled a part of the fortifications that the Lydians had deemed inaccessible, and it was by that route that Sardis was taken.

With the fall of Sardis and capture of Croesus, the Lydian kingdom also then fell. Cyrus was merely getting started, and the historian must again confront questions of chronology and sequence. If the Lydian campaign is dated to the mid-540s BCE, that leaves several years before the firmly dated conquest of Babylon in 539 – a conquest that we may assume was more than a year in the making, despite implications of Cyrus' own testimony. The nascent Persian Empire, still a work in progress, was already a big place. Herodotus indicates (1.153) that, after the fall of Sardis, Cyrus intended to campaign personally against the Babylonians, the Bactrians, the Scythians, and the Egyptians. He delegated the remaining operations in western Asia Minor to subordinates.

In short order, some of the Lydians rebelled. One Pactyes, a Lydian to whom Cyrus had assigned the collection of tribute, instead hired mercenaries and marched on Sardis, where Cyrus' appointee Tabalus (a Persian) had been left in charge. Entrusting local elites such as Pactyes with continued, important roles in the Empire's administration was common later, and this episode suggests the practice began even under Cyrus. In this case, though, the appointment proved to be a mistake. When Cyrus learned of Pactyes' revolt, he dispatched a Median named Mazares: his position reflects the elevated place that some Medes held in Persian administration, even outside the confines of Media itself. Pactyes fled to Cyme, a Greek city on the central western (i.e., Ionian) coast, from where he was passed on to various other Greek cities. The islanders of Chios were induced with a bribe to give him up (Hdt. 1.160).

The Mede Mazares fell ill and died shortly after Pactyes was captured, but not before he began the process of systematically punishing those cities that had helped Pactyes in his revolt. After Mazares died, the Mede Harpagus was sent to finish the job, a job that probably took several months, if not a few years. One by one Greek cities in Ionia were subjugated, some ruthlessly. This rather dark chapter in Greek history is not preserved in much detail, especially when contrasted with the successful resistance of the mainland Greeks against Xerxes' invasion two generations later. This is understandably so, in light of the result during Cyrus' reign: a complete Persian victory. If things had gone otherwise, instead of Marathon, Thermopylae, and Plataea, the western tradition would have perhaps celebrated the battles in west central and southwestern Anatolia, such as Priene, Magnesia, and Phocaea. But these cities were subjugated or destroyed by the Persians, and their territories incorporated into the Empire.

The fate of Croesus varies in ancient traditions. In Herodotus, he became a stock literary character (the wise advisor), a counselor to both Cyrus and his son Cambyses. An earlier tradition implies that Croesus was killed – or removed from the mortal world – during the sack of Sardis. Herodotus portrayed Cyrus intending to do just that, but Apollo's intervention saved Croesus (1.87). The Greek poet Bacchylides (died c. 450 BCE) provided a dramatic rendering of Croesus' intended suicide on a pyre, when the intervention of Zeus and Apollo removed him to the land of the Hyperboreans, a mythical people who dwelled far in the north. Croesus on the pyre occurs in both traditions, but Bacchylides' version implies Croesus' death, couched in divine "removal" to a magical place. Like Herodotus, a later tradition recorded by Justin (perhaps from Ctesias, Fragment 9e) also relates that Croesus was saved by Apollo and that Cyrus granted him territory in a city called Barene near Ecbatana.[5]

CYRUS IN EASTERN IRAN AND CENTRAL ASIA

Herodotus' assessment of Cyrus' strategy after the conquest of Lydia is probably correct. It is easy to envision Cyrus placing higher priority on other areas while leaving mop-up operations in Anatolia to subordinates. Among these other important areas were eastern Iran and Central Asia, the least known but certainly not the least significant areas for the Persians' rise. It is difficult to say much beyond outlining the strategic importance of these areas to the Empire. The evidence is sparse, and the chronology of Cyrus' activities there is impossible to ascertain. Many of the peoples in the extreme northeast were nomadic, but agricultural settlements were widespread. Archaeological surveys have revealed extensive irrigation projects in oases of the Amu Darya (Oxus) River basin. Various individuals and groups from these regions figure prominently in Achaemenid political and military organization subsequently. Bactrian and Scythian forces, especially their cavalry, were renowned throughout Achaemenid history. Cyrus' son, Bardiya, governed the satrapy of Bactria; Darius I's father, Hystaspes, held an important command in Parthia during the crisis of 522 BCE. Other examples abound, but it is impossible to organize them into a narrative. The eastern territories of the Empire figure most prominently in the source material concerning Alexander of Macedon's conquests there in the late 330s and 320s BCE; these territories' political importance during that turbulent time is viewed as characteristic for the entire Achaemenid period.

The regions of Bactria, Hyrcania, Parthia, and Scythia were all incorporated into the Empire at the time of Darius' accession in 522. A later Roman source, Justin (1.7.2), implies that the submission of these northern regions at the time of the Median conquest must have mainly been a formality, as they all subsequently caused Cyrus a great deal of hard campaigning. Further, both Herodotus' and Ctesias' versions set Cyrus' death in the extreme northeast – with the implication being that he campaigned in those regions to the end.

CYRUS' CONQUEST OF BABYLONIA

For Cyrus' conquest of Babylonia we are able to privilege Near Eastern sources once again, but they present their own interpretive issues. Foremost among these sources are the Nabonidus Chronicle (part of the Babylonian Chronicle series noted previously), the famous Cyrus Cylinder, and the so-called Verse Account of Nabonidus. The latter two were commissioned by Cyrus and present his conquest in an idealized manner.

We know from Nabonidus' inscriptions and other Babylonian evidence that Nabonidus himself had been away from Babylon for ten years (c. 553–543 BCE) at the oasis in Teima in northern Arabia. This surprising absence from Babylon, governed in the meantime by Nabonidus' son Bel-shar-usur (or Belshazzar, the Hebrew version of his name from the *Book of Daniel* 5), has been interpreted in a number of ways. Some associate it with Nabonidus' patronage of the moon god, prominent at

Teima. Nabonidus' devotion to him was especially evident in Harran in northwestern Mesopotamia. Because of this, Nabonidus has often been portrayed in a negative light, sometimes even as crazed lunatic. That portrayal was no doubt augmented by the resentment of the priesthoods of other Babylonian deities, if they viewed their sanctuaries as receiving short shrift. It has also been heavily influenced by Cyrus' propaganda and has been tempered only in recent scholarship. An assessment of the advantages gained from Babylonian control of trade routes running through the northern Arabian peninsula has encouraged modern scholars to reevaluate Nabonidus' strategy and the virtues of his efforts there. Nevertheless, his ten-year absence from the city continues to raise numerous questions about his rule and popularity in Babylonia itself. Nabonidus' own inscriptions follow the age-old Mesopotamian pattern of the pious king, one concerned for and active in the building and maintenance of divine sanctuaries. These are some of the very concerns, also formulaic but of utmost importance, expressed by Cyrus in the Cyrus Cylinder.

The preliminaries of the Persian-Babylonian conflict are opaque. It is difficult to understand Nabonidus' extended absence from Babylon if he viewed the Persians as a serious threat during that time. The Babylonians, of course, would have been well-informed of Cyrus' activities: his conquests of the Medes, Urartu, the Lydians, and other regions. It is similarly difficult to link Nabonidus' return to Babylon circa 543 as attributable to concerns about rising Persian power. There is no evidence for such a contention, but it is not hard to imagine a growing sense of unease in Babylonia.

The Nabonidus Chronicle reports that during the summer of 539 the cult statues of gods from various Babylonian cities were taken to Babylon, presumably as a precaution against an imminent Persian attack. Cyrus, on the other hand, implied that Nabonidus' removal of the gods was impious, and Cyrus celebrates his return of those gods to their own cities in his own inscription (Cyrus Cylinder, lines 30–32).[6] As we see even in modern times, it is all about the message. In late September or early October of 539 BCE, a major battle was fought at Opis, north of Babylon, one that resulted in a Persian victory. On October 10 the city of Sippar was captured, and on October 12 Cyrus entered Babylon peacefully and in triumph. Nabonidus was captured. His subsequent fate the chronicle does not reveal; in the Cyrus Cylinder

Figure 3.2 Cyrus Cylinder, Babylon. © The Trustees of the British Museum/Art Resource, NY.

it is noted only that Nabonidus was delivered to Cyrus (line 17). Another Babylonian text – the so-called Dynastic Prophecy, written during the Seleucid period – suggests that Nabonidus was exiled.[7] The Dynastic Prophecy finds echo in Berossus' account (Fragment 10a): the defeated Babylonian king gave himself up before a protracted siege and received territory in Carmania (modern Kerman, in southern Iran), where he eventually died.

Let us consider Cyrus' own version of the Babylonian conquest as given in the Cyrus Cylinder, the longest (by far) inscription that we have that was commissioned by Cyrus himself. The text is inscribed on a clay barrel cylinder (roughly 10 inches long and 4 inches thick), a standard foundation inscription of the type used in Mesopotamia for centuries (Figure 3.2). Foundation inscriptions were dedicated to the gods and deposited as an offering within the foundation or walls of sanctuaries; historians thus conclude that such texts were written for the gods. It is understood, however, that the information contained in these inscriptions, formulaic as it usually was, was also distributed or proclaimed in other ways. The Nabonidus Chronicle (column iii, lines 18–20) refers to a proclamation of Cyrus read to all the people of Babylon. This is perhaps not a word-for-word rendering of what was inscribed on the Cyrus Cylinder, but it is reasonable to assume that the essence was the same: the previous king Nabonidus was unstable and impious; the god Marduk's chosen agent Cyrus was given victory in order to restore peace and harmony, especially the reinstitution of divine offerings and normal workings of his cult; the abandoned sanctuaries would be restored and the gods who dwelled therein returned, with full favors and honors; the displaced peoples would be allowed to return home; and the new king, blessed by the gods, would restore the entire city. The Cyrus Cylinder (line 18) offers a sample of the idealized conqueror entering his new city: "The people of Babylon in their entirety, the whole of Sumer and Akkad, the princes and the governors, all knelt in submission, they kissed his (Cyrus') feet, and their faces brightened."

IMAGES OF CYRUS

One result of Cyrus' conquest of Babylon was the return of Jewish exiles who had been deported to Babylonia, the so-called Babylonian diaspora, after Nebuchadnezzar's sack of Jerusalem in 587–586 BCE. Jewish tradition also suggests that it was Cyrus who was responsible for the rebuilding of the temple of Yahweh in Jerusalem, which had been razed during Nebuchadnezzar's sack. These dramatic changes from the Jewish experience under Babylonian rule explain why Cyrus has such a glowing reputation in Jewish tradition. Indeed, in Second(Deutero)-Isaiah Cyrus is referred to as Yahweh's shepherd (44.28) and his anointed (45.1), the messiah. Isaiah prophesied that Yahweh would take Cyrus by the hand and lead him to victory over all nations; this is reminiscent of Marduk's role in the elevation of Cyrus (Cyrus Cylinder, lines 11–19).

The Book of Ezra (1.2–4 and 6.2–5) contains notice of a proclamation by Cyrus, found during the time of Darius I in the archives of Ecbatana, that authorized the rebuilding of Yahweh's temple in Jerusalem:

In the first year of Cyrus the king, Cyrus the king issued a decree: "Concerning the temple in Jerusalem, let it be rebuilt, the place where sacrifices are offered and burnt offerings are brought ... let the cost be paid from the royal treasury." (excerpted from the Aramaic version of Ezra 6.3–4)[8]

How much of the proclamation is historical is difficult to say; the notation that the expenses will come from the royal treasury is surprising. In any case, there is no traceable action of the rebuilding itself until Darius I's second year. Thus, the proclamation may have been anachronistically attributed to Cyrus' time, because it coincides with the picture presented elsewhere of the Empire's founder. If historical, it is unlikely that this was an isolated incident, that Cyrus made such special provisions only for the Jews of Babylon, though it may seem like it based on the limited evidence.

Cyrus' rise in both the Hebrew and Babylonian traditions is placed in prophetic context: he fulfills both Yahweh's and Marduk's purposes for their chosen people. Such an image, and its consistent application, was not a coincidence; it was carefully tailored by the Persian conquerors to justify their takeover. Cyrus' victory and the dispensations granted to the Jews fit well within a rubric of overarching tolerance, and this has influenced his image even to the present; among specialists, Cyrus' motives are generally understood as more practical than altruistic.[9] The return of gods (the cult statues) to various sanctuaries throughout Greater Mesopotamia was also good policy, one that followed age-old Mesopotamian patterns. Cyrus' return of gods and restoration of sanctuaries simultaneously manifest and entreat divine favor.

CYRUS IN THE GREEK TRADITIONS

Xenophon's *Cyropaedia* ("The Education of Cyrus") is the most admiring of our sources for Cyrus but is also in many ways the least useful for narrative history. The *Cyropaedia* is more romance than history, although it is frequently cited for what it reveals about Persian culture and society as well as about preeminent Persians who figured importantly in the Empire's history. Xenophon's idealized representation of Cyrus' life and reign – Cyrus in effect becomes what in Plato's philosophy would be called the philosopher king – is often impossible to reconcile with the mainstream historical record. Cyrus is the ideal ruler, whom Xenophon uses as a vehicle to explore questions of leadership and government, an ongoing conversation among Greek writers of the Classical period.

Herodotus is our main Greek source, and his version of Cyrus' origins warrants summary here. Notably, Herodotus acknowledges that he knows three other stories about Cyrus (1.95), but he has chosen to relay a version "based on what some Persians say, those who do not wish to glorify the details of Cyrus' life but rather to tell the real story." If

Herodotus considered the version he gave as the least exaggerated of the four, one may wonder how over-the-top the other three were. For such a monumental figure, there were clearly many stories in circulation.

In Herodotus, dreams and portents heralded any significant event. The Median king Astyages had portentous dreams that involved his daughter Mandane urinating so copiously that she flooded not only Ecbatana but also all of Asia. This frightened Astyages, so that when Mandane was of marriageable age he refused to give her to any prominent Mede. Astyages staved off the perceived threat by marrying Mandane to a Persian named Cambyses, "of a noble house and of mild disposition, though he (Astyages) considered him beneath a Mede even of middle rank" (1.107). A subsequent dream alarmed Astyages even more: a vine grew forth from Mandane's private parts and spread over all Asia. There was not much ambiguity there, but Astyages consulted his priests, the dream interpreters, who informed him that any offspring of Mandane would become king and be a threat to him. Astyages summoned the pregnant Mandane home and charged one of his nobles, a man named Harpagus, to destroy the child as soon as it was born. Harpagus in turn gave the job to Mithridates, a humble herdsman, but Mitradates instead exchanged the newborn Cyrus for his own stillborn child, and Mitradates and his wife Spako raised Cyrus as their own son.

This story is another manifestation of an age-old motif of the legendary hero's birth: the child exposed, or of humble origins, who rises to greatness. The story is often called the Sargon Legend, after the birth story of the king Sargon of Akkad (reigned c. 2340–2284 BCE), and associated with many other famous people including the biblical Moses, and Romulus and Remus in the Roman tradition.[10] Cyrus' true identity was revealed when as a boy of ten he was chosen king by the other boys during a game and, in acting the part, he whipped a malcontent who happened to be the son of a Median notable named Artembares. This was a scandal. In questioning the young Cyrus about the incident, Astyages realized he was speaking to his trueborn grandson. The initial omen of Astyages' dream about Mandane, that her offspring would be a king, was presumed fulfilled through Cyrus' playacting the part of king with the other boys. The consequences of this miscalculation have been relayed above: Cyrus ultimately triumphed over Astyages and took his place.

Ctesias also places Cyrus in the Median court, as a ward of Astyages, but not of his bloodline. Instead, Cyrus is given the humblest of origins, named the son of Artadates the bandit and Argoste the goat herder. Scholars have debated the significance of these base origins, because they deviate so much from other versions. Another Artembares, who in Ctesias' version was Astyages' cupholder, served as Cyrus' mentor and foster-father. Through that connection and Cyrus' own aptitude and potential, Cyrus became one of Astyages' foremost lieutenants and advisors. Portents play a large role in Ctesias' story as well, including a flood of urine like in Herodotus, though this time from Cyrus himself as dreamed by his mother.

It is notable that Cyrus is entrenched so firmly in the Median tradition by numerous Greek writers. We have no Median sources per se, but one cannot help but assume that Cyrus' excellent press in Babylonian and Hebrew sources was applied among the Medes as well, which carried over to the Greek tradition. Claims that Cyrus was descended from Astyages would go a long way toward the legitimization of his Median rule.

BACK TO ANSHAN

Given Cyrus' prominence in disparate traditions, it is important to return to Anshan itself, where Cyrus claimed himself and his forebears as kings. Unfortunately, we have little to go on here, because excavations at Anshan have not yet revealed extensive, sixth-century habitation. Mention of Anshan in the extant sources for the seventh and sixth centuries is rare, so it is surprising when the "King of Anshan" (Cyrus) makes such a powerful entrance on the scene. Royal titles are significant markers in understanding what the king represents and what message(s) he wished to convey. With Cyrus we have a very small sampling, and it is necessary to highlight the fact that we have found none of Cyrus' royal inscriptions from Iran itself. The inscriptions from Pasargadae inscribed in Cyrus' name were in fact commissioned by Darius I, in order to bolster Darius' legitimacy (see pp. 148–150).

It is not only in Nabonidus' inscription and the Babylonian chronicle that Cyrus is named "King of Anshan." Cyrus' own inscriptions, from

Figure 3.3 Cyrus Brick Inscription, Temple of Nanna-Suen, Ur. Courtesy of Grant Frame, Associate Curator, Babylonian Section, University of Pennsylvania Museum of Archaeology and Anthropology.

Babylon and from Ur, use the same title. By the time these inscriptions were commissioned, sometime after Cyrus' conquest of Babylon in 539 BCE, Cyrus had already conquered three of the great powers of his day: the Medes, the Lydians, and the Babylonians – and by extension much of the ancient Near East. In the Cyrus Cylinder, line 20, Cyrus arrogates traditional Babylonian titles: "I am Cyrus King of the world, great King, strong King, King of Babylon, King of Sumer and Akkad, King of the four quarters." But earlier in the inscription (line 12) he is referred to as "King of Anshan," as are his four predecessors: Cambyses I, Cyrus I, and Teispes (line 21). On inscribed bricks from a temple in Ur, Figure 3.3, Cyrus again calls himself and his father Cambyses "King of Anshan." The entire inscription reads:

Cyrus, King of the world, King of Anshan, the son of Cambyses,
King of Anshan. The great gods have delivered all the lands into my
hands, and I caused the land to live in peace.

Stamped inscriptions of this sort were commonly used by Mesopotamian rulers. This inscription also uses archaic sign forms, a practice carried over from the Neo-Babylonian period kings. These archaic cuneiform signs evoked a connection to the script used by the earliest kings in the Mesopotamian tradition, from centuries previous, such as Sargon of Akkad. Once again, the new Persian king adopted and adapted older forms to legitimize himself and to locate Persian rule within Mesopotamian norms. But that was not all. The title "King of Anshan" has few antecedents, but most scholars take it as a conscious modification of the traditional Elamite title "King of Anshan and Susa," with emphasis on the former as the seat of Cyrus' family's power. This appears to be Cyrus' initial title, and that of his forebears, another compelling testimony to the Elamite-Persian acculturation that lay at the roots of the Achaemenid Persian Empire's history.

4 From Cyrus to Darius I: Empire in Transition

DEATH OF CYRUS

Cyrus' movements between his conquest of Babylon and his death may only be guessed. The remaining major power not yet conquered was Egypt, which was supposedly one of Cyrus' objectives that drew him away from Lydia (Hdt. 1.153). Perhaps plans were being developed for an invasion of Egypt, plans subsequently implemented by Cambyses, but there is no way of knowing. Babylonian evidence indicates that Cyrus died in August 530 BCE. According to Herodotus, Cyrus reigned for twenty-nine years (1.214) and his final campaign was in the extreme northeast.[1]

Herodotus' account of Cyrus' death focuses on his war with the Massagetae, a Scythian people who lived beyond the Araxes (or Jaxartes, the modern Syr Darya) in modern Kazakhstan. Herodotus here offers another cautionary tale – the limits and consequences of hubris – so one hesitates to take it for literal truth. As he did with Cyrus' birth legend, Herodotus acknowledges multiple versions (1.214) but relates the one he found most plausible. The Massagetae were ruled by a widowed queen, Tomyris, whom Cyrus first attempted to wed and thus gain the territory by diplomacy before conquest.[2] Tomyris rebuffed Cyrus with a warning to stay within his territory: to cease his expansionism or pay the price. Cyrus instead heeded the advice of Croesus, who counseled Cyrus to cross the river and engage Tomyris' forces.

The Persians' initial victory over the Massagetae, led by Tomyris' son Spargapises, was due to a trick. The Persians laid out a great feast and then feigned a retreat, and the Massagetae raided their camp. When the entire Massagetae force became drunk on the wine "abandoned" by the Persians, the Persian forces returned. They killed many of the Massagetae and captured the rest, including Spargapises. Tomyris demanded Spargapises' return with the threat that otherwise, because Cyrus seemed ravenous for blood, she would give him his fill of it. Spargapises committed suicide, and when Cyrus was killed in the subsequent engagement, Tomyris was true to her word: she cast Cyrus' head into a container filled with blood.

Ctesias' story (Fragment 9 §7–8) of Cyrus' death is similar in outline: Cyrus died while campaigning in the far northeast but against a people called the Derbicae. Where these Derbicae dwelled is unclear, but ancient geographers place them in northeastern Iran or Central Asia. Wounded in battle but reinforced by Saka (Scythian) allies, Cyrus lived long enough to defeat the Derbicae and to arrange his succession. Cambyses was appointed king, while Cambyses' brother Tanyoxarkes was granted a vast territory in the northeast – free from tribute – that included Bactria, Chorasmia, Parthia, and Carmania. Herodotus does not assign a formal position to Cambyses' brother, whom Herodotus calls Smerdis.

Cambyses had been groomed for the succession for some time. An entry in the Nabonidus Chronicle noted Cyrus and Cambyses' joint involvement in the Babylonian New Year's festival for 538 BCE, one of the most important events of the Babylonian calendar. Several economic documents from 538 are given the date formula "Cambyses, King of Babylon, and Cyrus, King of lands." This is striking, but it was also short-lived: the joint formula seems to have been used only that one year. Some scholars take it as evidence for co-regency, but the episode remains an enigma.[3] It is unclear why this joint dating formula was used and why it was discontinued. Perhaps the joint dating formula was instituted for continuity during the transitional period of a new conquest, but that remains speculation. Various Classical sources attest to periodic special commands (e.g., Harpagus in Lydia and Asia Minor, Tanyoxarkes in Bactria), but there is no parallel for a Persian co-regency.

KING CAMBYSES

In 530 BCE Cambyses inherited a vast empire, far larger than any previous, and one that had been formulated in just twenty years. Cambyses' royal pursuits are hard to gauge, however, because the record is even thinner for his reign. Cambyses' first order of business would have been arrangements for Cyrus' burial at his tomb in Pasargadae. An incomplete structure found near Persepolis has been identified as an intentional replica of Cyrus' tomb, and it was naturally assumed to have been for Cambyses. But some documentary evidence suggests that Cambyses' tomb lay elsewhere, southeast of Persepolis near modern Niriz, and the evidence pointing there indicates a royally sponsored cult, similar to that associated with Cyrus' tomb.[4]

Cambyses eventually turned his attention westward, where the main power was Egypt. Amasis (reigned 570–526 BCE) had conquered Cyprus and formed an alliance with the Greek ruler Polycrates of Samos, an island off the coast of Ionia. By the 520s Polycrates had become dominant in the Aegean Sea region. This alliance was fractured sometime after Cambyses' accession, and Polycrates offered ships to Cambyses for the Egyptian expedition. Reasons for the switch may only be guessed. Perhaps the intensifying Persian hold on Ionia in conjunction with inducements (or threats?) swayed Polycrates toward Persia. Cambyses' efforts to develop a royal navy, mainly through his Phoenician and Ionian subjects, were no doubt intended for the western front and a planned Egyptian campaign. The territories of the Levant, geographically at the crossroads between Greater Mesopotamia and Egypt, had been a point of contention between rulers of those regions for centuries. Persian control of that region was bound to inflame tensions with Egypt. With an eye on Persian expansionism, Amasis had cultivated good relations with many city-states and sanctuaries in the Aegean world. In 526 Amasis was succeeded by his son Psammetichus III, whose rule was to prove quite short.

CAMBYSES' INVASION OF EGYPT

There is no narrative record of the preparations for the Persian invasion of Egypt in 525 BCE, but they were no doubt extensive. As part of these preparations, Cambyses fostered relations with the king of the Arabs, who controlled the desert route across the Sinai peninsula and could thus enable the successful crossing. The first engagement occurred at the easternmost branch of the Nile delta, the so-called Pelusiac mouth. The Persians put the Egyptians to flight, invaded the Nile Valley, and besieged Psammetichus in his capital, Memphis. There he was protected by fortifications named "the White Wall," which could only be taken with support from a fleet. The city was eventually taken and Psammetichus captured. But he was spared and treated well, as per the pattern of kings previously defeated by the Persians. Herodotus even claims that if Psammetichus had comported himself appropriately he would have been made governor of Egypt (3.15). But Psammetichus subsequently plotted rebellion and was put to death.

Once Egypt was secure, Cambyses intended further military actions both west and south, following the paths of many Egyptian pharaohs. The Libyan oases offered control over strategic western trade routes. Beyond the First Cataract in the south, the kingdom of Kush had always been coveted for its gold. The installation of a Persian garrison at Elephantine – an island in the Nile near modern Aswan – reveals the strategic importance of this area at Egypt's southern boundary.[5] This garrison was one of several similar that were stationed at strategic points throughout the Empire.

Additional Persian expeditions against the oasis of Ammon in the west and against Nubia and Ethiopia in the south ended badly. The particulars may seem far-fetched, but the historicity of these campaigns, including an aborted expedition against the Carthaginians (modern Tunisia), need not be rejected out of hand. The limits of Persian imperialism had not yet been reached. It made sense to secure those borderlands that had been problems for previous Egyptian rulers for centuries. If Herodotus may be believed, the army dispatched to Libya was swallowed in a sandstorm. Cambyses himself led the expedition against Nubia and Ethiopia, but it was abandoned en route: desperate straits culminated in cannibalism among the troops. These misadventures, replete with divine portents and human warnings that Cambyses was going too far, serve as case studies for Herodotus' portrayal of the "mad Cambyses" – more a literary exercise than a historical one. Herodotus records a litany of Cambyses' outrages, overreach, and arrogance – directed not only at Egyptians but also at Persians and even his own family – the paradigmatic example of a stereotypical oriental despot.

Herodotus' "mad Cambyses" shows first of all that the Father of History relied on a negative tradition of Cambyses current in Egypt when Herodotus visited in the mid-fifth century BCE. Herodotus devotes portions of his Book 3 to Cambyses' increasing instability. Cambyses purportedly ordered Amasis' mummy to be disinterred, abused, and finally burned – an insult, to both Persian and Egyptian religions (3.16). Other tombs were opened and cult statues mocked, particularly in the temple of Ptah, an Egyptian creator god whose sacred city was Memphis. The greatest outrage to the Egyptians was the slaying of the Apis bull (3.27–29), a sacred calf that was considered the earthly embodiment of Ptah. The Egyptian king was a central part of the Apis cult, which in turn was directly connected to the office of kingship.

When Cambyses returned to Memphis after the disastrous Ethiopian expedition, he found the Egyptians of Memphis celebrating the birth of a new Apis calf: a new beginning, their god again made manifest. Cambyses snapped. He saw their festival as an expression of joy at his misfortune, and he reacted: stabbing the Apis bull with a knife to the thigh and flogging or slaying many priests. Herodotus subsequently catalogs a cascade of misfortune and misery that brought Cambyses to his own end and shook the entire Empire to its core – the result of Cambyses' impiety. The slaying of the Apis bull makes compelling drama, but it is mostly exaggerated if not fabricated. We have some Egyptian evidence that seems to refute Herodotus' portrayal. Contrary to Herodotus' assertion that the Egyptian priests buried the Apis bull without Cambyses' knowledge, a sarcophagus from a bull buried during Cambyses' reign is engraved with Cambyses' own inscription in traditional Egyptian format:

The Horus Sma-Towy, King of Upper and Lower Egypt, Mesuti-Re, born of Re, Cambyses, may he live forever! He has made this fine monument, a great sarcophagus of granite, for his father Apis-Osiris, dedicated by the King of Upper and Lower Egypt, Mesuti-Re, son of Re, Cambyses, may he be granted long life, prosperity in perpetuity, health and joy, appearing as King of Upper and Lower Egypt eternally.

This inscription states that Cambyses, acting as a typical Egyptian pharaoh, took responsibility for the proper care and burial of the deceased Apis, which is understood to have died during Cambyses' fifth regnal year. If only it were so simple. There are significant problems with our understanding of this sequence: the death and burial of the Apis bull during Cambyses' reign, and the overlap between the birth of a

successor bull and the death of the current Apis. Other inscriptions further complicate matters.[6]

Although the initial inclination is to reject any suggestion that
Cambyses killed the Apis, it cannot be excluded that Cambyses may have
killed a younger calf (the Apis successor) before the death of the one buried in the sarcophagus. The Egyptian evidence reminds us not to take
Herodotus at face value. Some of the changes Cambyses wrought in the
aftermath of the Persian victory must have been unwelcome, perhaps even
unprecedented. For example, a reduction in support for some Egyptian
temples could easily have given rise to negative stories about Cambyses.

The inscription of Udjahorresnet, a naval commander under Amasis
and Psammetichus III who defected to the Persians, also provides some
balance to Herodotus' account. Udjahorresnet's hieroglyphic inscription
is carved on his votive statue from Sais, in the western Delta (Figure 4.1).
The statue holds a small shrine for Osiris, god of the underworld. The
autobiographical inscription chronicles Udjahorresnet's career, with
special emphasis on his service to both Cambyses and Darius I. It is
invaluable as a window on how one of the Egyptian nobility secured a
place for himself in the new order.

Udjahorresnet's inscription provides the only surviving royal titles
for Cambyses beyond Babylonian administrative documents. Cambyses
adopted Egyptian titles (e.g., "King of Upper and Lower Egypt") as
would be expected from a new ruler seeking to place himself in an age-
old tradition. Udjahorresnet himself would have been keen to trumpet
his own titles and achievements – typical in this sort of inscription –
and also to justify his collaboration with the Persians. Udjahorresnet's
inscription, and Cambyses' titles therein, indicate that Cambyses
behaved as did previous kings by restoring order and respecting religious sanctuaries. Udjahorresnet's version is no doubt slanted as well,
but the picture it provides runs directly counter to Herodotus'. It would
not be surprising to discover that the respect Cambyses showed for sanctuaries included those with which Udjahorresnet had been involved,
those in and near Sais, but that is unverifiable. That the Persians presented themselves as pharaohs in the traditional Egpytian manner is not
surprising. Successful integration into Egyptian tradition would make
Persian rule much smoother. As evidenced by subsequent Egyptian
revolts, however, this integration was not always smooth.

Figure 4.1 Statue of Udjahorresnet, Sais, Egypt, housed in the Vatican Museum. Drawing by Tessa Rickards, used by permission.

THE DEATH OF CAMBYSES AND THE CRISIS OF 522 BCE

The length of Cambyses' Egyptian campaign is uncertain, but various sources indicate that Cambyses was returning to Persia in 522 when he died. He had been away for at least three years. Babylonian economic documents reveal that Cambyses died sometime in April and was succeeded by his brother Bardiya. Bardiya ruled for six months, until he was supplanted by Darius. Darius conversely related that Cambyses had killed Bardiya sometime previously and that a look-alike double, whom Darius called Gaumata, rebelled against Cambyses in March of 522. The crisis of 522 was of epic proportions, and the stability of the fledgling Empire was at stake. Various ancient sources relay a story of fratricide; an elaborate cover-up; a body double and impostor on the throne; and a small group of heroes who discover the truth, slay the pretender, and set Persia to rights once again. Despite the fundamental interpretive problems that persist in evaluating the sources, it is clear that the Persian Empire faced a decisive moment. Darius I's eventual, and by no means easy, victory was monumental in its own right and had lasting consequences for the durability of the Empire. The testimonies for this turbulent time are confusing and often contradictory. Separate overviews of the main ones – Darius' Bisitun Inscription and Herodotus' account – are warranted before any attempt at reconciliation.

THE BISITUN INSCRIPTION OF DARIUS I

Mt. Bisitun (or Behistun, English spelling varies) lies about halfway between modern Kermanshah and Hamadan (Ecbatana) on the main east-west road through Media and across northwestern Iran. The Greek name *Bagistanon* probably comes from an Old Persian word *bagastāna*, "place of the gods," which imparts the sacredness of the site. Roughly 200 feet above the road, Darius carved a relief showing himself triumphant over rebel kings, accompanied by two unidentified retainers behind him, and acknowledging the figure in the winged disc that hovers above the scene. This symbol is usually identified with the Zoroastrian god Ahuramazda, whom Darius invokes dozens of times in the accompanying inscription. Flanking and below the relief is the inscription itself chronicling Darius' legitimacy, right to rule, and a narrative of his victories at the beginning of his reign. The inscription is recorded in three languages: Elamite, Akkadian, and Old Persian. The Elamite version is in two copies, the first to the right of the relief and the second to the lower left: reinscribed after the addition of the last rebel king to the relief necessitated the defacement of part of the first version. The Akkadian version is to the left of the relief, and the Old Persian version underneath the relief. Captions in all three languages identify the rebel kings, but not the retainers behind Darius or the winged symbol (see Figures 4.2–4.3). The relief would have been visible from the road, but not the inscription. Copies of the inscription were disseminated throughout the Empire.

Figure 4.2 Darius, Bisitun Relief and Inscriptions, Mt. Bisitun, Iran. Courtesy of the Cameron Archive, Kelsey Museum of Archaeology, University of Michigan.

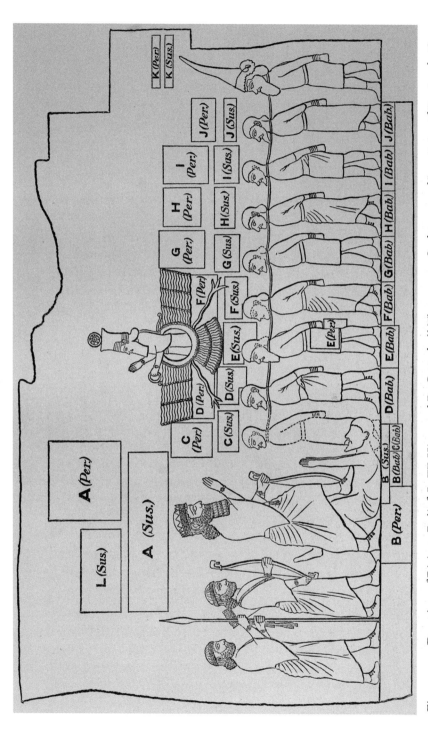

Figure 4.3 Drawing of Bisitun Relief, L. W. King and R. Campbell Thompson, *Sculptures and Inscription of Darius the Great, on the Rock of Behistûn in Persia*, London, 1907, Plate XIII. The capital letters indicate separate inscriptions, and the abbreviations Per., Sus., and Bab. stand for Old Persian, Susian (rather: Elamite, and Babylonian (Akkadian), respectively.

The Bisitun Inscription's significance goes far beyond its place in understanding this critical historical period. It also served as the fundamental document in the foundation of the modern discipline of Assyriology. Bisitun provided the key to the decipherment of the Old Persian, Elamite, and Akkadian cuneiform scripts. The formulaic nature of Achaemenid royal titles allowed patterns in the scripts to be discerned straightaway. The Old Persian script has only a few dozen signs, formally a syllabic system but one not far removed from an alphabet. Old Persian was cracked first thanks to parallels with Avestan and Sanskrit, closely related Indo-Iranian languages. Akkadian and Elamite scripts were more complex, with many more signs. Akkadian was realized to have known linguistic relatives in other Semitic languages such as Aramaic and Hebrew. The Elamite version was eventually translated from the other two versions and based on comparisons with earlier Akkadian-Elamite bilingual texts. In a short overview it is impossible to do justice to the painstaking work, and enormous ingenuity and erudition of the various scholars in the nineteenth century who deciphered these languages.[7] Suffice it to note that the translation of the Bisitun Inscription opened the door to a vast catalog of lost Near Eastern literature, including the Epic of Gilgamesh and many others.

Darius I's trilingual inscription at Bisitun is the only narrative Persian royal inscription extant, and it was the blueprint for subsequent Persian royal ideology. The organization of inscriptions around the relief figures suggests that the Elamite version was inscribed first, then the Akkadian version, and the Old Persian added subsequently. The three inscriptions are meant to be copies of each other, but occasional differences between them – along with the fragmentary Aramaic copy from Elephantine in Egypt – provide much fodder for specialist discussions. The Old Persian (OP) version is considered the primary one, mainly because it is assumed to have been the language of the Persians themselves and because the OP version contains two extra sections, added after the original was complete, that were not added to the other two versions. In the discussion that follows, the parenthetical references to Darius' inscription follow standard scholarly practice: DB (standing for "Darius, Bisitun") followed by the paragraph (§) number, which follows the division into sections of the OP version of the inscription.

Darius' Bisitun Inscription was the official version, and it of course becomes the main source for these events. Darius provides only a brief narration of the circumstances surrounding the first few critical months of 522 (DB §10–14). A summary follows. Darius tersely noted that Cambyses had a full brother named Bardiya, whom Cambyses slew in secret sometime before the Egyptian campaign. Darius described Cambyses' end obliquely, literally "he died his own death" (DB §10). In some modern works, Darius' phrasing is erroneously translated to the effect that Cambyses committed suicide. The wording in all three versions – Elamite, Akkadian, and Old Persian – is straightforward, and suicide is not meant. The ambiguity lies in what the statement "he died his own death" really means, whether Darius was concealing something with such drab wording. No other details are offered.

In March of 522 a man named Bardiya rebelled, and in July he claimed the kingship. This Bardiya was Cambyses' full brother, but Darius claimed otherwise: in the Bisitun Inscription that man who claimed the kingship was Gaumata, an impostor who pretended to be the real Bardiya. The impostor threw the Empire into chaos. The people became disloyal and "the Lie" became great. Darius' antipathy against the Lie – the word is usually capitalized in English translations – reflects a Mazdaean worldview so fundamental to the king's ideology.[8] It is introduced for the first time in the Bisitun Inscription and recurs throughout to describe the reasons for the Empire's descent into chaos under the false kings. Darius as the agent of truth, supported by his god Ahuramazda, is the proper king who overcame the forces of chaos and returned the Empire to its proper order. This is all properly cast in the terms of the victorious king's justification of his right to rule.

According to Darius, the Lie impelled Gaumata to rebel, and this Gaumata represented himself as Bardiya, the son of Cyrus. Subsequent rebels whom Darius defeated were also cast as impelled by the Lie, and most of them claimed descent from prominent figures among their predecessors; for example, two Babylonian rebels claimed to be descended from the famous Nebuchadnezzar II, King of Babylonia in the early sixth century. Darius claimed that the people were terrified of Gaumata, because in order to cover his tracks he slew many who knew the real Bardiya (§13). Nevertheless, Darius, with the help of a few men – at least six of whom are specifically mentioned late in the inscription as his prominent supporters (§68) - was able to kill this Gaumata and his entourage in Media (see Map 4.1, pp. 70–72).

After his vague accounting of the opening gambit, Darius then returned to exact dates in his account, starting with September 29, 522 BCE, for Gaumata's death. How and why Gaumata moved from the place of his initial rebellion in Parsa to a fortress in Media is not explained. In the Bisitun relief, Gaumata is supine, extending his arms imploringly while Darius rests his foot on him in triumph. Darius concluded the section on Gaumata's usurpation with a laundry list of Gaumata's misdeeds and outrages against cult-centers and personal property. This passage is difficult to interpret in its particulars, even if in general it follows the tradition of a new conqueror vilifying the previous regime: one that lacked order. Darius emphasized that he reestablished order by restoring that which had been taken away or destroyed, "in accordance with what had been done previously" (§14). Darius further emphasized that Gaumata had stolen the kingship from Darius' family, which specifically included Cambyses (§10), and that Darius thus restored his family's long established right to rule. His emphasis on descent from Achaemenes forms a central component in Achaemenid royal ideology.

The bulk of the Bisitun Inscription relates the victories of Darius and his lieutenants over the numerous rebel kings who challenged him, primarily in Persia (Parsa) itself, Elam, Babylonia, Media, and other points in northern and eastern Iran. The elimination of Cyrus' sons left an open field for the succession, if there was to be a succession at all – in 522 there was a real threat that the Empire would splinter irrevocably. Armies ranged across the Iranian plateau, the Zagros regions, and Mesopotamia. Darius was relentless, and he recorded his exploits on the model of the Assyrian kings' annals, with a repetitive precision that highlighted his inexorable victory. Each of the rebel armies was defeated, and the rebel kings hunted down and impaled, as in this example with Fravartish (Greek Phraortes):

Darius the King proclaims: I went forth from Babylon and went to Media. When I arrived in Media, at a place named Kunduru, a town in Media, there that Fravartish, who called himself king in Media, came with an army against me to give battle. Then we gave battle. Ahuramazda bore me aid. With the support of Ahuramazda, I completely defeated the army of Fravartish ... Afterward that Fravartish with a few horsemen fled. He went to a place named Raga in Media. Then I sent an army after him. Fravartish was seized and was led to me. I cut off his nose and ears and tongue, and put out one of his eyes. At my gate, bound, he was held. All the people saw him. Later I impaled him at Ecbatana. (condensed from DB §31–32)

The Akkadian version of DB, along with a fragmentary Aramaic copy found in Elephantine in southern Egypt, gives casualty and prisoner figures for many of these battles. We have no independent check on the veracity of these numbers, which run from the hundreds to the thousands and, in two instances – in battles fought in Media (§31) and in Margiana (§38) – perhaps the tens of thousands.[9] Beyond his undeniable military success against imposing odds, Darius' right to rule was sketchy. His blood links to Cyrus' family are stretched, at best, if not entirely fabricated. Darius supplies a Teispes, son of Achaemenes, in his line (DB §2) that links him to Cyrus' ancestor Teispes listed in the Cyrus Cylinder (line 21). Both Darius' father Hystaspes (OP *Vishtaspa*) and grandfather Arsames (OP *Arshama*) were yet living when Darius took the throne. Hystaspes, commanding a military force in Parthia in north central Iran, is specifically mentioned in the Bisitun Inscription (§35) as aiding his son. Herodotus called Hystaspes a governor (Greek *hyparch* – a term loosely applied to ruling officials of varying rank) in Persia itself, but that is different from Darius' account.

HERODOTUS' VERSION OF DARIUS' ACCESSION (3.61–88)

Herodotus called Cambyses' brother Bardiya "Smerdis." Smerdis had initially accompanied Cambyses on the Egyptian expedition. The Ethiopians had sent Cambyses a bow with the message that, when he could draw it, it would be safe to attack them (3.21). Not one of the Persians was able to do so, but Smerdis could bend it, just slightly. Cambyses sent Smerdis home out of jealousy and subsequently had a dream in which he saw Smerdis sitting on the royal throne. Cambyses interpreted this as a threat and dispatched a trusted advisor, Prexaspes, to kill Smerdis in secret (3.30).

Sometime later Cambyses received word of a revolt by Smerdis. By the chronology discussed above (Herodotus himself is not specific), this would be the Spring of 522 BCE. After Cambyses' initial assumption that Prexaspes had betrayed him and that his brother Smerdis yet lived, he soon learned that two Magi brothers had instead rebelled. Herodotus called the first brother Patizeithes and the second brother Smerdis. The second brother had the same name, Smerdis, as Cambyses' brother and, further, they looked exactly alike (3.61). Patizeithes proclaimed that his brother Smerdis was the real Smerdis, installed his brother as king, and sent out heralds demanding allegiance to this false-Smerdis instead of Cambyses, who was at that point en route back to Persia. When Cambyses uncovered the truth of the matter – that it was two Magi brothers revolt- ing against him and that he had killed his brother Smerdis for noth- ing – in rage and despair he sprang into action. The cap of his scabbard fell off as he leaped onto his horse, and he was stabbed in the thigh with his own sword. Gangrene set in the wound, and Cambyses died within a few weeks. The wound was in the exact spot where Cambyses had stabbed the Apis bull, which provided Herodotus another opportunity for a moral lesson (3.64), a fitting end for the "mad Cambyses."

Shortly before his death, Cambyses assembled those noble Persians on campaign with him and gave a tearful confession (3.65) of his mur- der of the real Smerdis and details of the Magian revolt. But he was not believed; the Persian nobles thought Cambyses had made these admis- sions and accusations out of malice. Once Cambyses was dead, Prexaspes denied any involvement; the admission of his murder of a son of Cyrus would not have gone over well. The false-Smerdis thus ruled for seven months, during which he was well-regarded by his subjects (3.67) – because he released them from military service and tribute – and they later regretted his passing. The Magi, seeking to ensure their security, ostensibly won over Prexaspes, who knew their secret. In exchange for his compliance, the Magi promised to make him incredibly wealthy. They asked him to make a public proclamation: to allay any doubts that the Persians were being ruled by anyone other than the son of Cyrus. But Prexaspes instead revealed all during his speech, enjoined the Persians to react against the false rule of the Magi, and then he threw himself from the balcony from which he spoke.

Other Persians had been planning to act. Their leader was named Otanes, whose daughter Phaidymie had been married to Cambyses and then became a wife of the false-Smerdis as well. Herodotus relates a lengthy and entertaining anecdote about Phaidymie's discovery that it was indeed the magus Smerdis who ruled, not Cambyses' brother.

The story allows Herodotus to include some salacious details about the Persian harem and the royal caprice in punishments, both subjects always popular with a Greek audience. Because of the number of royal wives and concubines, Phaidymie had to wait her turn to lay with him. When that time came, Phaidymie was able to confirm that it was the false-Smerdis by the fact that he had no ears, which had been previously removed as punishment by Cyrus.

Otanes shared his suspicions with two other noble Persians, Aspathines and Gobryas. These three each brought one additional person into the group: Intaphernes, Megabyxos, and Hydarnes. The names of these six match, with one exception, those helpers mentioned by Darius in his inscription (DB §68).[10] The group is then joined by Darius, son of Hystaspes. Although the last to join the conspiracy in Herodotus' version, Darius quickly took on the most vocal and forceful role. This Persian "Magnificent Seven" moved quickly, especially when news of Prexaspes' speech and suicide reached them (3.76). Because these seven were among the noblest of Persian families, the palace guards allowed them entry into the inner court. From there they forced their way in and a melee broke out. As Gobryas struggled with the magus he urged Darius to strike, but because it was dark Darius did not wish to hit Gobryas. Gobryas told him to kill both, if necessary, and Darius managed to slay only the imposter.

COMPARISONS

Despite the relative richness of the source material, the circumstances surrounding Cambyses' death and the forces unleashed by it remain opaque. What was the relationship between Cambyses and the real Bardiya? Did Cambyses die first and Bardiya succeed without incident? Or did Bardiya revolt from Cambyses? Were people really expected to believe that Cambyses' murder of Bardiya, if even true, could be kept secret? What was the real relationship between Darius' family and Cyrus' family? Who was the magus Gaumata? Did Cambyses die of natural causes, or does Darius' account hide something more sinister?

Many elements of Herodotus' account are difficult to reconcile with Darius' Bisitun Inscription, so the truth remains elusive. For example, Herodotus' summary statement that the false-Smerdis' rule was well-received is not easily reconciled with Darius' assertions of chaos (DB §13–14), though it would hardly be expected that Darius would paint his predecessor's rule in a favorable light. There are a number of other curious elements here as well beyond the fantastic tale of the impostor's usurpation. Herodotus' seven-month reign for the false-Smerdis may be made to fit into Darius' chronology (counting inclusively) from Gaumata's revolt in March to his death in September of 522 BCE. Darius gave few details about the death of the impostor, only that Darius and a few others slew him at a fort in Media.

As is evident by now, Darius' account invites a great deal of skepticism. Indeed, many modern scholars believe that Darius killed the real Bardiya – even though the circumstances around Bardiya's rule and relationship with Cambyses remain unclear – in his seizure of the throne. Darius as the victor was in a position to write the history but his account, despite its primacy, must be read with a careful eye. Even a casual read suggests important details were either glossed or ignored. Careful study reveals a number of questionable components of Darius' claims to legitimacy, and it throws large parts of his version of his rise into question. Realistically, of course, we should not expect Darius to provide an objective account, at least not by our standards. Darius' foremost goal was to legitimize his succession.

Darius' late and initially secondary involvement in Herodotus' version also raises questions. In another part of his account (3.139), Herodotus relays the story of a Greek from Samos named Syloson, who gave Darius his cloak while both were in Egypt during Cambyses' invasion. After Darius' accession, Syloson received rule of the island of Samos in gratitude. In that anecdote Herodotus labeled Darius a person of no great importance, but the fact that Darius was in Egypt as a member of Cambyses' personal guard indicates otherwise. Herodotus' description "of no great account" has meaning only relative to Darius' later position as king. In fact, Darius was a "spear-bearer" (Greek *doruphoros*) of Cambyses. The same title in Old Persian (*arshitibara*) accompanies the image of Gobryas (another of the Seven, and Darius' father-in-law) engraved on Darius' tomb – clearly a position of high honor. But in any event, reading Herodotus makes it plain that Darius had no a priori claim to the throne.

FISSION OR FUSION?

If one considers the situation in the Empire in the immediate aftermath of Cambyses death, there was no guarantee who would rule. Numerous individuals put themselves forward as kings, and the Empire that Cyrus and Cambyses had assembled was in real danger of splintering. How did Darius secure sufficient support to win the throne? The narrative of his military victories – all, of course, reflecting Ahuramazda's divine favor – constitutes the bulk of the Bisitun Inscription, which in the end is a victory monument. And even though it is all about Darius, the new king acknowledged the names, lineages, and ethnic backgrounds of many of his supporters and enemies. He also specified the locations and dates of various battles. Other members of the Persian "Magnificent Seven" are named as active participants in the battles: Intaphernes against a Babylonian revolt (DB §50); Hydarnes against rebellious Medes (DB §25); and Gobryas against an Elamite revolt (DB §71).

Darius' father Hystaspes and the satraps Vivana and Dadarshi are also explicitly named by Darius. It appears that they held their respective positions before Darius became king, which means that they were appointed by Cyrus or Cambyses. Hystaspes held a military command and may have been a satrap, though Darius does not use that term for him, Old Persian xšaçapāvā. Vivana was the satrap of Arachosia and battled the rebel Vahyazdata there (DB §45). Dadarshi was the satrap of Bactria and battled the rebel Frada in Margiana (DB §38).[11] All three are identified as Persians. Thus, beyond the six coconspirators, Darius had additional supporters who held important positions based in the north (Parthia), east (Arachosia), and northeast (Bactria) – directions from a compass point based in Fars. It is difficult to determine the political and military strength of these individuals, even relative to the forces arrayed against them, because we lack the necessary demographic information[12] Darius relied upon these men to defeat rivals on the Iranian plateau and in eastern Iran, while Darius himself and other commanders addressed threats in the core of the Empire: Parsa (Fars) itself, Elam, Media, and Babylonia. These regions were the mainstays of Cyrus' family's power, and it is probably not a coincidence that they gave Darius so much difficulty.

APPENDIX – DARIUS' WAR FOR THE SUCCESSION

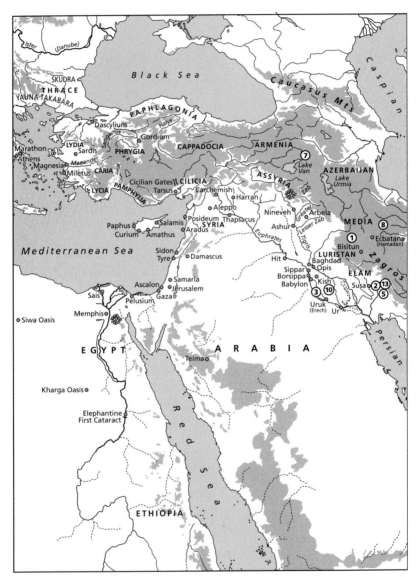

Map 4.1 Main Battles Mentioned in the Bisitun Inscription. After *Cambridge Ancient History*, Vol. 4, Second Edition, 1988, map 1.

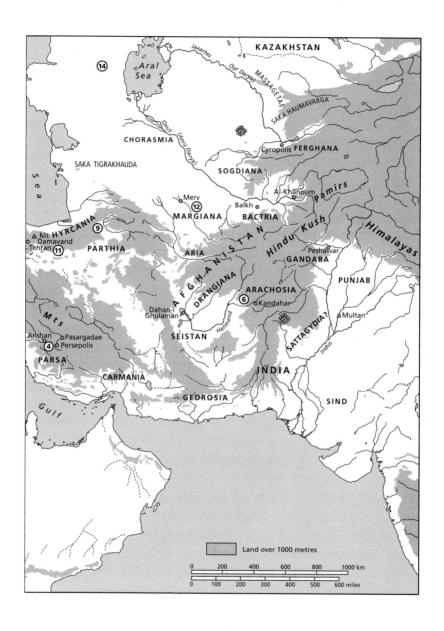

Map 4.1 offers a visual aid for the geographic scope of the resistance encountered by Darius, as he himself relayed in the Bisitun Inscription. Darius provides at some points an impressive specificity (e.g., with regard to most dates) and at others quite the opposite (e.g., the exact circumstances of the slaying of the purported impostor). The locations indicated on the map are only approximated by region and numbered roughly in order of sequence; there is much uncertainty and overlap. In several instances, there were multiple engagements over time. Was military action in a given place continuous or sporadic between given dates?

See Amélie Kuhrt *The Persian Empire: A Corpus of Sources from the Achaemenid Period* (pp. 140–158) for a precise chronology, translation of the Old Persian version, and copious notes and references.

1: Gaumata slain in Media, September 522
2: Against Acina in Elam, October 522
3: Against Nidintu-Bel/Nebuchadnezzar III in Babylonia, October 522 and December 522
4: Against Vahyazdata in Parsa, December 522, May 521, and July 521
5: Against Martiya in Elam, December 522
6: Against Vahyazdata's army in Arachosia, December 522 and February 521
7: Against Armenians, December 522, May 521 (two battles) and June 521 (two battles)
8: Against Medes and Fravartish in Media, December 522, January 521, and May 521
9: Against Fravartish's supporters in Parthia and Hyrcania, March 521 and July 521
10: Against Arakha/Nebuchadnezzar IV in Babylonia, August 521 and November 521
11: Against Cicantakhma in Sagartia (location of this region uncertain), October 521
12: Against Frada in Margiana, December 521
13: Against Athaimaita in Elam, 520
14: Against Skunkha in Scythia (location uncertain), 519

DB §21 also indicates rebellions in Egypt, Assyria, Sattagydia, and Scythia (location of last two uncertain), but no further details about any of those are provided in the Bisitun Inscription.

5 Darius, the Great King

DARIUS TRIUMPHANT – BISITUN REVISITED

Darius' victory in 522–521 BCE was by no means a sure thing. The Bisitun Inscription makes plain the widespread extent and ferocity of the resistance Darius faced. Darius repeated several times (DB §56, §57, §59, and §62) that he accomplished the defeat of the nine rebels in "one and the same year," though his own dating seems to belie this claim: Gaumata was slain in late September 522, and Darius' generals were still subduing the last of the rebels in December 521. A great deal of scholarly ingenuity has been applied to reconciling Darius' statements.[1] Rather than insist on the literal truth – which is not a vain enterprise, because Darius himself makes much of it – one might instead ask why the "one and the same year" was so important to Darius that he made the claim. In the end, it was another way to solidify his legitimacy: by divine favor (of course), by descent (exaggerated), by fitness to rule (standard for any king), and by military might (ultimately, the key element).

As always, one must examine earlier traditions for parallels, of which there are many. The "nine kings in one year" motif occurs several times in the Akkadian king Naram-Sin's inscriptions, more than sixteen centuries earlier. Darius tapped into an ancient convention. Part of the Persian genius lay not only in their successful co-opting of the past but also in their innovations based on it. The Persians had great respect for their Mesopotamian and Elamite forebears, and they borrowed (and modified) both textual and iconographic modes of expression. The Bisitun relief's imagery hearkens back to elements of the stele of Naram-Sin (reigned c. 2213–2176), among many others (Figure 5.1).

Figure 5.1 Stele of Naram-Sin, King of Akkad. Photo Credit: Gianni Dagli Orti/The Art Archive at Art Resource, NY.

Naram-Sin's stele had been plundered from Sippar in the early twelfth century by the Elamite king Shutruk-Nahhunte I, who took it to Susa and added his own inscription in Elamite. The stele was found in Susa by Jacques Jean Marie de Morgan during his excavations at the very end of the nineteenth century. A separate statue plinth also found in Susa bears an inscription of Naram-Sin in which he referred to his victories in nine battles in one year.[2] This antiquarian connection appealed to the Persian kings as much as it did to their predecessors. It is possible that these monuments were on display at Susa in Darius' time and, if so, they would certainly have had an impact on him.

Other themes prominent in the Bisitun Inscription also find precedent. The Babylonian king Nabopolassar (626–605 BCE) emphasized the truth of his assertions in his inscription. Neo-Assyrian kings frequently cast their rebellious opponents as liars.[3] This phenomenon, an emphasis on truth that accompanies the rightful sovereign by virtue of divine favor, was thus not new, but one may credit Darius for taking it to another level as he disparaged his enemies as both rebels and liars. "One man called Gaumata, a magus, he lied and claimed 'I am Bardiya, the son of Cyrus.' He made Persia rebellious" (DB §52). And on it went for each of the challengers Darius had defeated. Most of the other rebels adopted the names of prominent kings who ruled previously in those areas. One Persian rebel, Martiya, claimed to be Ummanunu, after a previous king in Elam; another Persian, Vahyazdata, also claimed to be Bardiya. Two Babylonian rebels each styled himself after the famous Nebuchadnezzar and claimed to be the son of Nabonidus. Two Iranian rebels (one Mede, one Sagartian) claimed to be of the line of the Median ruler Cyaxeres.

To return to the fantastic elements of the story, the impostor-double appears not only in the Bisitun Inscription (Gaumata) and Herodotus (the magus Smerdis) but also in Ctesias (there called Sphendadates; Fragment 13 §11–16) and in later tradition as well. Many scholars find even the outlines of this story improbable: that Cambyses slew his real brother (Bardiya) in secret and that a magus later impersonated Bardiya so successfully that few suspected. And yet there is some precedent for the phenomenon of a royal double. In previous Near Eastern history, disastrous omens threatening the king's person were countered by what was called the substitute-king ritual.[4] A substitute would be chosen (often someone of limited mental capacity) who would literally take the king's place on the throne. The substitute wore the king's clothes and the royal accoutrements, sat on the throne, ate the king's meals, and even slept in the king's bed. The real king, meanwhile, stayed hidden. This way, the disastrous fate that had been preordained for the king would fall upon the substitute instead. Nothing was left to chance: the substitute-king would be killed at the end of his term (in Assyrian times, usually one hundred days), thus ensuring that no harm fell upon the real king – so it was believed. The substitute-king ritual was even performed during Alexander the Great's reign in 323 BCE, in a vain attempt to forestall his death. Some scholars have postulated that such a ritual might lay behind Darius' fantastic tale of the impostor-double. While an ingenious idea, there is no way to tell for certain. In any event, if there was a substitute, it would not have been for Darius. And if Darius did indeed kill a substitute – let us assume the substitute was for Bardiya – the question as to what happened to the real Bardiya remains. Darius' assertion that Cambyses killed his brother, the "official version," invites skepticism.

A later addition to the Old Persian version of the Bisitun Inscription (§71–76) celebrated victories over an Elamite named Athamaita in Elam and against a Saka named Skunkha. The Saka here were the Scythians of the "pointed-cap," who are generally understood to have been Scythians of Central Asia in the extreme northeast of the Empire. Remarkably, Darius chose to have Skunkha the Scythian, but not Athamaita, engraved at the end of the line of the original liar-kings. The original relief included the nine kings defeated by Darius: Gaumata supine and the eight others in a line, with hands behind their backs and a rope around each of their necks. Skunkha's addition necessitated the deface-ment of part of the inscription to the right of the relief, the first Elamite version. The whole Elamite version was then reinscribed to the lower left of the relief, below the Akkadian version and to the left of the Old Persian version.

To note that this was a significant modification is an understate-ment. Something about the victory over Skunkha must have held great significance for Darius. What that may have been is generally not con-sidered in modern scholarship, but here is one possibility. According to Herodotus, Cyrus died while on campaign against the Massagetae (1.201–214), a Scythian group in the extreme northeast of the Empire. Perhaps Darius considered his victory over the Scythians of such impor-tance – he succeeded in the region where the great Cyrus had failed – that he made special provision for its commemoration in the Bisitun relief. Of course, this is speculation, and all appropriate qualifiers must be kept in mind.

CONSOLIDATION AND EXPANSION

In Herodotus' version of the crisis of 522 BCE, it was not a forgone conclusion that Darius would be king. In a famous passage (3.80–83), Herodotus relates a debate about the best form of government. This debate supposedly occurred between three of the conspirators against the magus: Otanes, Megabyzus, and Darius. Otanes argued for democ-racy, Megabyzus for oligarchy (or aristocracy), and Darius for monarchy. Although Herodotus insisted that the debate truly occurred, his read-ers – ancient or modern – have every right to be skeptical. Such a debate is easily imagined in fifth-century Athens, but it is inconceivable in a late sixth-century Persian context. Even if the Persian Empire was then still in a transitional phase from its tribal days, there could not have been much doubt about continuing monarchical rule – especially after a successful thirty-year run under Cyrus and Cambyses. Herodotus' motivation for insisting on the historical truth of the debate remains opaque, but the debate itself must be considered in light of Herodotus' ongoing examination of forms of government – in this case, the strengths and weaknesses of democracy vis-à-vis the alternatives.

Next, according to Herodotus, it was necessary for the Seven conspirators to select which of them would be king. Already we are far-removed from Darius' assertions of legitimacy and lineage in the Bistiun Inscription, but the special place accorded his helpers (listed at DB §68) provides a link. In Herodotus, the initial chief conspirator, Otanes, chooses to step aside – making no claim on the throne – with the understanding that he and his descendants would remain absolutely free, not subject to the king's authority except by their choice and on condition that they adhere to Persian laws. Otanes' avowed detachment was apparently short-lived. In Herodotus, we find Otanes soon in charge of military operations in Asia Minor, especially against the Ionian island of Samos (3.141–149). Otanes the military commander must have followed royal directives. One may thus consider Otanes' prominent place in Herodotus' narrative, and the special privileges due him and his family, to reflect a pro-Otanes source that Herodotus used for this part of his account.

Herodotus then returned to a favorite motif, omens and the supernatural, for the next stage: the actual selection of the king among the remaining six conspirators. They staked this momentous decision on whose horse would neigh first the following morning at a prearranged meeting spot (3.84–87). Modern scholars have discerned echoes of horse oracles associated with royal ritual in ancient Iran, perhaps the ultimate origin of Herodotus' exaggerated and garbled version. Darius' groom Oibares arranged a clever trick – for which Herodotus himself gave two versions, more indication that the story was a popular folktale – whereby the night before Oibares allowed Darius' horse to mate with his favorite mare at the designated spot. The next morning, when Darius' horse reached that spot and caught the scent, the horse leaped forward and neighed. That alone fulfilled the omen, but Herodotus for good measure added a simultaneous flash of lightning and a crash of thunder, a divine omen of approval, to seal the deal.

Darius moved swiftly to consolidate his newly won throne. Darius married the daughters and wives of his predecessors: Atossa and Artystone (daughters of Cyrus), Parmys (daughter of Bardiya/Smerdis), and also Phaidymie (daughter of Otanes). Other recorded marriages included a previous one to a daughter of Gobryas and a later one to Phratagune, Darius' own niece (daughter of his brother Artanes), the last mainly for purposes of preserving Artanes' estate within the extended family. Through his marriages to Cyrus' daughters, Darius joined himself to Cyrus' family, another means by which he strengthened his hold on the throne.

A certain Oroites posed another challenge to Darius. The story is known only from Herodotus (3.120–128). Oroites had been appointed by Cyrus as satrap (or governor) of Lydia. While the false-Smerdis ruled, Oroites remained in Sardis and took no part in the war of succession. It may be assumed that Oroites remained loyal to Cyrus' family or, perhaps more likely, was only biding his time. Oroites murdered one of Darius' messengers (3.126), because the message did not please him. Presumably, Darius was looking for support in his gambit for the throne. The rejection of the message and murder of the messenger was a statement to Darius: an act of defiance and rebellion. Once secure in his power, Darius dispatched another messenger, this one to test the loyalty of the Persians around Oroites. A series of communiques was given to be read in succession by the royal secretary, each with a different order for Oroites' guards. Once he was comfortable that the guards' ultimate loyalty was to the king, the messenger directed the secretary to read the final communique: the order to put Oroites to death. Regardless of the historicity of this specific anecdote, it illustrates how the king's power was upheld by his loyal officials and troops in the provinces. Another holdover from the Cambyses era, a man named Aryandes who governed Egypt, also posed a challenge to Darius (Hdt. 4.166). At some point during the reign of Darius, Aryandes began to mint coins with the intent to make himself the equal of Darius. Aryandes thus went beyond the normal satrapal prerogatives for minting, and Darius considered it an act of rebellion. Aryandes paid the price with his life.

Darius was not content merely to reassemble the Empire that Cyrus and Cambyses had built. Darius pushed the boundaries of the Empire eastward by incorporating the Indus River valley region (modern Pakistan and parts of India). Subsequent royal inscriptions that list the Empire's holdings include Old Persian *Hidush*, a province named for the

Figure 5.2 Darius Statue, Susa. Courtesy of the French Mission at Susa, dir. J. Perrot.

Indus River. Darius also expanded Persian territory in northeast Africa. Herodotus records a Persian expedition across Libya that culminated in Euesperides, identified with modern Benghazi (4.200–204). Some of the inhabitants of Barca, also in Libya, were deported to Bactria, at the extreme opposite end of the Empire. There is little information about the chronology and details of these conquests, but they are both usually dated in the 510s BCE.

A partially preserved statue of Darius, crafted in the Egyptian style but found near a monumental gate in Susa, offers insight into Darius' rule and representation in Egypt (Figure 5.2). It stood about 10 feet tall on a pedestal and survived intact up to the chest. One of the folds of Darius' garment has a short inscription in Elamite, Akkadian, and Old Persian versions. The inscription invokes Ahuramazda, celebrates Darius' victory in Egypt, and contains Persian and Babylonian royal titles. A much longer hieroglyphic inscription on the garment's right folds and base is done in the traditional Egyptian manner. Darius assumes Egyptian titles (e.g., "King of Upper and Lower Egypt) and incorporates Egyptian imagery. The text sets Darius firmly in Egyptian tradition by linking the king with the Egyptian gods Re and Atum of Heliopolis. The central image of the base shows the tying of the Egyptian knot – a centuries-old symbol of Egyptian unification (Upper and Lower Egypt). The subject peoples of the Empire, identified by hieroglyphic captions, are all portrayed in the Egyptian style and actually hold up the pedestal on which the statue of Darius stands. Clearly Darius, like Cambyses, understood the importance of portraying himself as a right and proper Egyptian king in that tradition.

Darius also undertook major construction work in Egypt that included the digging of a canal from the Nile to the Red Sea, an act commemorated by four inscribed stelae. The best preserved is from a place called Kabret, roughly 80 miles north of Suez. It includes a typical Egyptian image: royal figures facing each other, but here with Persian dress and crowns, underneath a winged disk.[5] The text contains a succinct statement taking responsibility for the building of the canal, which had been a major undertaking. Herodotus indicates (2.158) that it had been started by the Egyptian pharaoh Necho roughly a century earlier, but it was brought to completion by Darius.

THE SCYTHIAN-DANUBE EXPEDITION

Darius also campaigned against a group of Scythians in southeastern Europe, in the Danube and Black Sea regions. Herodotus is our main source. This region's proximity to Ionia and Greece, and heavy Greek settlement in the area, meant that the Persian activity there was much closer to home for the Greeks. There were undoubtedly many Greek stories circulating about the expedition several decades later during Herodotus' time. But Herodotus was more interested in Scythian customs and way-of-life. Most historians date the campaign sometime in the later 510s BCE. Details of the military campaign are sparse, and interpretations of its significance vary widely.

The main logistical challenge involved the crossing of the Bosporus – the narrow strait between the northern tip of the Propontis (modern Sea of Marmara) to the Black Sea – by means of a pontoon bridge. Such a feat required massive resources, engineering skill, and will. This crossing was both precedent for and parallel to Xerxes' more famous crossing of the Hellespont preceding his invasion of Greece in 480. Herodotus was not able to locate Darius' crossing precisely, but to his reckoning it was roughly in the middle of the strait; Darius left inscribed stelae to commemorate the occasion (4.87), but these have not been found. Darius also directed his fleet to sail to the Ister (the Danube) via the Black Sea and to build a bridge for his army there. We have no clear statement of Darius' objectives, whether they involved additional conquest or a display of Persian might in a distant land, or both. Herodotus' contention – that Darius sought vengeance for Scythian depredations against the Medes roughly one hundred years previous – seems a stretch. But because in the late 330s BCE Alexander the Great cast himself as taking revenge for Xerxes' invasion roughly 150 years before him, we perhaps should not reject such propagandistic claims out of hand. Herodotus judged the campaign a failure, because Darius ultimately withdrew, but a more sober assessment of his possible objectives, and a consideration of his subsequent moves, tempers that negative judgment.

Herodotus' concludes his account of the Scythian campaign with Darius' ordering one of his generals, Megabazus, to subjugate Thrace, that is, southeastern Europe (4.143). His terse account relates Megabazus moving through Thrace and subjugating all the peoples in the area. Not nearly as entertaining as his ethnographic observations on the Scythian campaign, Herodotus' brief report on Megabazus still offers important details about Persian military ambitions. In the lists of conquered peoples and territories included in some royal inscriptions (see Figure 6.2, p. 97), this area was called in Old Persian *Skudra*.[6] The Persians held this territory, or parts of it, for some time – apparently even after Xerxes' campaign against Greece in 480–479. In his *Life of Alexander* (36.4), Plutarch quotes the fourth-century historian Deinon, who noted that the Persians kept water from the Nile and the Danube in their treasury, manifest symbols of their dominion.

Darius pushed the frontiers of his empire in every direction from Persia: northeast (Skunkha and the "pointed-cap" Scythians), southeast (the Indus River region), southwest (Libya), and northwest (Thrace). The Persian Empire at its territorial height thus comprised territories stretching from the Aral Sea and the western edge of the Himalayas (Central Asia) to the Sahara (Africa), and from the Indus River Valley (Indian subcontinent) to the Danube (southeastern Europe) – the first world empire, indeed. Darius demarcates its boundaries in trilingual inscriptions from Persepolis (DPh) and Ecbatana (DH).

Darius the King proclaims: This is the kingdom that I hold: from the Scythians who are beyond Sogdiana all the way to Kush, from Hidush all the way to Sardis, which Ahuramazda, greatest of the gods, granted me. (DPh §2)

Sogdiana is in the extreme northeast of the Empire, so the inscription refers to the Scythians of Central Asia. Kush refers to Nubia (the Sudan), and Hidush the Indus Valley. The satrapal seat at Sardis controlled the northwestern territories.

DARIUS AND THE AEGEAN PERIPHERY

As noted above, when Darius returned from his Scythian campaign he left Megabazus in charge of subjecting the rest of Thrace, a geographic area encompassing parts of modern Bulgaria, northeastern Greece, and the European portion of Turkey. Persian military activity there gives the impression of long-term, strategic planning. Thrace was a region rich in raw materials, especially timber and precious metals, and also manpower (Hdt. 5.23), of interest not only to the Persians but also to Macedonia and Athens. Details on Megabazus' campaigns are thin, but reading between the lines in Herodotus indicates that the Persians took a systematic approach to establishing forts and supply depots.

At Darius' command Megabazus also subjugated and deported a group of peoples called the Paeonians, who dwelled in the areas north of Macedonia. Herodotus' story (5.14–15) of how Megabazus out-flanked the Paeonians with help from guides from Thrace reveals a common-sense approach: the incorporation of local assistance. Megabazus then sent envoys to Macedonia, where they received earth and water, standard tokens of submission (see pp. 123–125), from the Macedonian king, Amyntas. This made Macedon a vassal kingdom (5.17–18), though Herodotus relays an incredible tale circulating in his day to counter the Macedonian submission to the Persian king's authority. Amyntas supposedly entertained the Persian envoys at a lavish feast, during which the increasingly intoxicated Persians demanded to see, and then sit with, the Macedonian royal women. The Persians could not keep their hands off the women, and the situation escalated. Amyntas' son, Alexander (the subsequent King Alexander I), then persuaded the Persian delegation into believing that these women would be available for sex with them. Instead, however, Alexander and his cohorts dressed themselves as women, went to the drunken and lecherous Persians, and killed them all. Herodotus notes that when other Persians came seeking their countrymen, Alexander bought them off and married his sister Gygaea to the leader of the search party, a certain Bubares. This story shows Herodotus at his entertaining and frustrating best. Scholars give little credence to the story of the Persian party massacre – one always must consider how such tales originate[7] – but a marriage alliance between the Macedonian royal family and a Persian nobleman is credible enough. Such diplomatic marriages were one way in which ties between Persians and their subjects were reinforced.

Darius solidified his hold in Ionia, Thrace, and the Aegean Islands through appointments of Greek natives as city rulers, the so-called tyrants. The Greek term *tyrannos* was used for a ruler who came to power through illegal means, independent of whether that ruler himself was considered a good ruler or bad. Over time the term *tyrannos* came to have generally negative connotations, though, as does its English derivative "tyrant" – its use herein reflects the original Greek connotation. These men included Coës of Mytilene and Histiaeus of Miletus, the latter of whom was also given control of territory in Thrace along the Strymon River. The mainland Greeks come into increasingly sharp focus during the late sixth century as well. For those Greeks who were paying attention, Persian expansion in the northern Aegean must have created some unease – and, in some cases, opportunity. The tyrant of Athens, Hippias (son of the famous Peisistratus), fled to Darius sometime after his exile in

510. Subsequent political infighting in Athens, with one faction receiving Spartan support, led to involvement with the Persian Empire that had major ramifications for subsequent Athenian and Greek history.

In 507, the Athenian faction not supported by the Spartans sent an embassy to Artaphernes, the satrap in Sardis and Darius' brother. Artaphernes' question – "Who are these people?" – is a recurring motif in Herodotus. Herodotus' message here, reflective of his work's main focus on the Greek resistance to Xerxes' invasion in 480, is that the Persians would know soon all about these people, the Greeks. The Persians at this juncture in Herodotus' narrative had no knowledge of the Athenians, and when they (or other mainland Greeks) appeared before the Persians they were curiosities. Artaphernes' response was straightforward. If the Athenians wished the support of the King, they must offer earth and water, an act that manifested submission to the King. Herodotus' account then becomes quite terse, and scholars debate the historical significance of this episode. The Athenians agreed to give earth and water – Herodotus does not expressly say that they did do so, but that is the implication – and then returned home, where they were censured for their behavior (5.73). There may be some revisionist history here, more than fifty years after the Artaphernes affair and more than thirty after Xerxes' invasion. Athens had been a leader in the fight against Xerxes and, during Herodotus' time, was at the height of its power in the Aegean, often at Persian expense. Athens leading the Greek fighting against Persia in the mid-fifth century did not fit well with an Athens submitting to the King even two generations earlier.

For some historians, interpretation of the embassy to Artaphernes in 507 impacts the analysis of all subsequent Athenian action vis-à-vis Persia. If the Athenian embassy offered earth and water as Artaphernes demanded, the Persians would conclude that Athens was subject. The exact expectations on both sides of the arrangement are nowhere described, but it is beyond doubt that in any such exchange the Persians were the dominant party. The Persians appeared to view the offering of earth and water both as a diplomatic agreement and also a solemn oath. Breaking the bond was an insult, and it required the King to respond. Athens broke it.

THE IONIAN REVOLT

Persian expansion in Thrace was accompanied by operations in the Aegean Islands. As we have seen, Persian-supported tyrants ruled in several places, including the island of Samos. A failed campaign against the island of Naxos (in the middle of the Aegean, west in a line from Halicarnassus in Ionia) served as a catalyst for a wider revolt, or series of revolts, between 499 and 494 BCE. Herodotus devotes a great deal of space to the preliminaries of the revolt – more than to the course of the revolt itself. For him it was the main precursor to Xerxes' campaign against the Greek mainland in 480–479.

In Herodotus' portrayal, the revolt ultimately stemmed from the misadventures of one man, Aristagoras, tyrant of Miletus and nephew of Histiaeus. Aristagoras convinced the satrap Artaphernes to sponsor a campaign against Naxos, once approval from the King had been granted. A certain Megabates, Artaphernes' cousin (Hdt. 5.32), was appointed commander of the Persian forces, supported with troops supplied by Aristagoras. A quarrel between Megabates and Aristagoras resulted in the former betraying their plans to the Naxians and thus sabotaging the expedition – a charge so ridiculous that no one takes it seriously. Finding himself on the outs with both Megabates and Artaphernes, Aristagoras decided to revolt. He was supported by a secret message from his uncle Histiaeus in Susa, who was seeking an excuse to return home and hoped that Darius would give him a command. Aristagoras convinced several other Ionian cities to rebel. Seeking powerful allies, Aristogoras then visited the Greek mainland. His attempt to convince Sparta to support him failed, but he was successful in garnering ships and men from Athens and from the city of Eretria on the island of Euboea, just off the eastern coast of Attic peninsula.

Herodotus portrays his fellow Ionians as a hapless group and, by extension, downplays the significance and spread of the revolt. Even in a tradition that framed great events around personal desires or vendettas, Herodotus overemphasizes too much the personal here. Most historians do not give much credence to Aristagoras' singular role in initiating the revolt, identifying the causes rather in economic or other factors, such as the oppressiveness of Persian-supported tyrants. Any one of these is hard (if not impossible) to substantiate with our current evidence. Save for one tantalizing reference in an administrative document from Persepolis – a record of rations given to a certain Datiya traveling on royal business between Sardis and Persepolis in 494 BCE, perhaps in conjunction with the final phases of the revolt – we lack Persian sources that would offer a different perspective.[8] A number of Carian and other non-Greek cities in southwestern Anatolia also revolted, as did the island of Cyprus, a key Persian possession in the eastern Mediterranean (5.108–116). These areas were reconquered relatively quickly, especially Cyprus: its strategic importance made it a greater priority for the Persians.

Regardless of how much responsibility Aristogoras may have had (or not) in starting it, the revolt was not a one-man show. Aristagoras, supposedly fearing Darius's reaction, fled to Thrace where he died. The rebellion did not seem to miss him, because it took the Persians more than five years to quell it. After Aristagoras' death, Histiaeus, Darius' former favorite and Aristogoras' uncle, successfully schemed for his return to Ionia from Susa. Artaphernes in the meantime had discovered that Histiaeus encouraged Aristagoras to revolt, but Histiaeus escaped to the Hellespont before Artaphernes could harm him. In a curious aside, Herodotus notes that Histiaeus had communications with several Persians in Sardis who supported the revolt (6.4). Artaphernes discovered this treason and tricked Histiaeus' supporters into revealing their true stripes, so that they were put to death. Histiaeus himself was captured later, after the fall of Miletus, and impaled – the standard punishment for rebels.

The rebels' success was initially spectacular, though short-lived. Much of the capital of Sardis was burned during a surprise attack, including the sanctuary to the goddess Cybele (5.102). This act rebounded upon the Greeks later, when Xerxes destroyed many Greek temples. Although the Athenians withdrew after this initial success, Herodotus emphasizes their involvement in an anecdote that heightens the tension between Persia and Athens (5.105). When Darius heard the news of the burning of Sardis, his initial reaction was to dismiss the Ionians, because they would soon be brought to heel. But he asked who the Athenians were, just as Artaphernes had done previously. Once informed, Darius, swearing vengeance upon Athens, took his bow and shot an arrow into the sky. He then instructed a servant to repeat to him three times at every meal, "My lord, remember the Athenians" – an anecdote with great entertainment value.

The Ionian rebels took control of the Hellespont, the shipping lane from the Black Sea to the Aegean, and aided the Cypriots in their rebellion. The strategic value of both these places shows what was at stake: control of the northwestern territories of the Empire. In response, the Persians were methodical and ruthless, and they did not discriminate. Each city-state was dealt with individually. In some, the previous tyrants or suitable successors were restored to power; in others democratic governments were left unmolested. The most important factor was a willingness to adhere to Persian authority. By 494 the Persians were focusing their efforts on Miletus itself, the seat of the revolt. A great sea battle at Lade, off the coast of Miletus, resulted in a Persian victory, abetted by the defections of many Ionian ships. Persian efforts to splinter the Ionian alliance had been successful. After the victory, Miletus was besieged and ultimately sacked; its inhabitants were sold into slavery or deported, and its main sanctuary at nearby Didyma was burned.

Mop-up operations continued through the following year (493 BCE) as the Persians reasserted their authority throughout Ionia. They carried through on threats made earlier, before Lade, for those who did not submit. Select girls were sent to the royal court, boys were made into eunuchs. Many cities and sanctuaries were burned – as express punishment for the rebels' assault on Sardis – and Ionia was, as Herodotus put it, enslaved a third time (6.32): the first by the Lydians, the second by Cyrus, and the third now by Darius. The Persian response was not only military. The satrap Artaphernes subsequently undertook an administrative reorganization of all of Ionia (6.42). This included the establishment of boundaries, the fixing of tribute, and the creation of a system in which disputes were subject to arbitration. Herodotus mentions these acts with approval and notes that they minimized the quarreling among the inhabitants of Ionia and established a lasting stability.

DARIUS' SECOND AEGEAN CAMPAIGN
AND THE BATTLE OF MARATHON

After the revolt, Darius dispatched a new military commander to Ionia, his son-in-law Mardonius. Mardonius was the son of Gobryas, one of the

Seven who overthrew the magus impostor, and was married to Darius'
daughter Artozostre. Herodotus relays that Mardonius overthrew all
the tyrants in Ionia and replaced them with democracies (6.43). This
statement has caused much consternation among historians, who find
it difficult to fathom. At minimum, it is an exaggeration, and other
evidence contradicts Herodotus' blanket statement – for example, the
tyrant of Samos, Aeaces, the son of Syloson, continued to rule. For the
Persians on the other hand, the form of local government under their
rule was less important than that government's conscientious delivery
of tribute and adherence to Persian policies. The Persians were nothing
if not pragmatic and mindful of local circumstances in their approach to
governing the provinces. Persian projects on their northwestern frontier
were stymied for seven years by the Ionian Revolt. Once finally quelled,
Mardonius worked to finish what Megabazus had started. Whether the
imperial enterprise of expansion was sufficient impetus in its own right,
or whether the Ionian revolt and its consequences had changed the strategic calculus in that region, is open to debate. Despite Herodotus' dramatic portrayal of Darius obsessed with revenge, Persian ideology did
require a response to those who participated in the revolt.

Herodotus claims that Mardonius' expedition in the northern
Aegean had Athens and Eretria as its main targets, but this is suspect.
Mardonius' campaign should probably be viewed as the reassertion of
Persian power in Thrace and Macedonia. A sequel was being planned: a
direct naval strike across the Aegean that would encompass a multitude
of islands (the Cyclades) and lead through to Eretria and Athens (Map
5.1). According to Herodotus, Darius first sent out heralds demanding
earth and water, as well as messengers to those Ionian cities already
beholden to him ordering that they prepare warships and transports
for the campaign. All the islanders agreed to submit earth and water,
as did many on the Greek mainland, but Herodotus does not name
names (6.48–49). In any event, the Persians met resistance on some of
the islands – suggesting that Herodotus exaggerated or that the tokens
were given in bad faith.

The Persian forces gathered at a traditional mustering spot, the
Aleian plain in Cilicia, east of Tarsus in the northeastern Mediterranean.
Artaphernes, the son of Artaphernes the satrap of Sardis (and thus
Darius' nephew) and Datis, a high-ranking Mede (perhaps the same

as the Datiya mentioned above), commanded the expedition. The fleet sailed to Ionia and, from Samos, directly across the Aegean through the Cyclades Islands (6.94–95). Naxos was successfully taken and plundered, likewise Carystus. On the other hand, the Persians made offerings at Delos – sacred to the Greek gods Apollo and Artemis – and repatriated a statue of Apollo there. We see again the Persian strategy of outright conquest coupled with select support to win over opposition. The campaign continued on to Eretria where, after fierce fighting, two prominent individuals betrayed the city and opened the gates to the Persians. A later source notes that these two were given grants of land, a typical reward for service to the King. The city was plundered, the inhabitants captured and deported, and the temples burned in retaliation for the burning of Sardis at the start of the Ionian revolt. The captives were deported to Susa and resettled near there (Hdt. 6.119).

The next stop was Athens, or, more specifically, the plain of Marathon, some 26 miles northeast of the city. This region was chosen so that the Persian cavalry might be used to maximum advantage. The deposed tyrant of Athens, Hippias, who had fled to Persia previously, accompanied the expedition. He provided inside information to the Persians and, had the expedition been successful, would presumably have been reinstalled as tyrant, beholden to the King. But here the Persians fell short. Herodotus relays at great length the battle and its preliminaries. The Athenians, weak in cavalry but with a strong infantry contingent, waited out the Persians and attacked as they were preparing to depart. A fierce battle ensued, as the Persians extricated their forces from the plain and prepared to sail around the Attic peninsula to attack the city itself on the west side of it. But the Athenians covered the 26 mile march – thus the origins of the modern race, the marathon – just in time and their position prevented another Persian landing. The Persian fleet remained off Phaleron (Athens' harbor at the time) for an unspecified amount of time before it departed.

We have no Persian sources to offer insight on the Battle of Marathon, so Persian goals and perspective must be extrapolated from the Greek accounts. For the Persians it was a minor setback at the end of an otherwise successful campaign. Conversely, it is hard to overstate the importance that this battle had for the Athenian mindset and civic pride, but that is best appreciated elsewhere (see the entries under Appendix

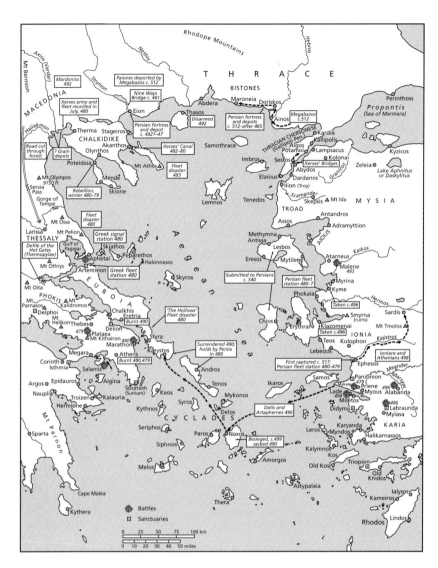

Map 5.1 Persian Campaigns in the Aegean during the Reigns of Darius I and Xerxes. After *Cambridge History of Iran*, Vol. 2, 1985, map 13.

D). Until then Persian forces had been viewed as objects of terror (Hdt. 6.112). By Herodotus' time roughly sixty years later, after the rise in Athenian hegemony in the Greek world thereafter, the Battle of Marathon had become lionized – and canonized – as the first stand against barbarian oppression on the Greek mainland. Despite claims in some modern works, it is unlikely that the Persians were planning – at least with this particular expedition – a wider domination of all Greece. If Athens and the other Greek city-states had folded like cards, there is no doubt the Persians would have welcomed the opportunity to establish mechanisms of lasting control – they already had much experience with this. But the campaign of 490 looks much more like a punitive expedition than an all-out invasion.

6 Mechanics of Empire

KINGS, QUEENS, AND THE ROYAL COURT

The power and importance of the King is a recurring theme throughout the book, and the particular ideology that evolved from and shaped
the King's status will be discussed in a separate section (pp. 147–151).
The King of kings was the sun around whom all else revolved. From
his physical stature to his dress and presentation, all was carefully managed and controlled to highlight his august position. The King's robe
and accoutrements marked him from others, mainly by a special type
of crown, a tiara called in Greek the *kidaris*. Most of our descriptive
evidence comes from Greek sources, though the archaeological record – especially the sculptures from Persepolis – is of course of critical
importance. Quintus Curtius Rufus (3.3.17–19) describes the King's
elaborate attire as including a purple tunic interwoven with white, a
gold-embroidered cloak, and a gold belt from which he often wore a special dagger, called in Greek an *akinakes*. This dagger was one of Elamite-
style, suggesting a carryover from the preceding period; remains of two
scabbards have been found in Central Asia. Garb and accessories would
differ, of course, depending on the occasion and whatever function (ceremonial, military, cultic) in which the King was engaged at that time.
Some elements of the King's wardrobe were not unique to him, such as
the *akinakes* (Figure 6.1), the wearing of which signaled royal favor. The
King and members of the nobility also frequently wore false beards and
are portrayed with such in the iconography, a tradition that was very
old. The King's beard, though, was generally longer and more elaborate
than others.

Figure 6.1 Dagger (*akinakes*) Worn by the King's Weapon-Bearer on the Treasury Relief (and see Figure 7.1), Persepolis. Courtesy of the Oriental Institute of the University of Chicago.

The court apparatus of the King's nobles, advisers, guardians, scribes, and a multitude of others, were all cogs in the imperial machine. They all worked toward the same goal, and all were dependent on each other for success. The King's centrality was all-important – among other ways this is seen in battle, when the safety of the person of the King overrode other considerations – but nevertheless the King was dependent on an elite class of nobles for his power and successful government. But this dependence worked both ways: members of the nobility were absolutely dependent upon royal favor for their positions and prerogatives, and such could be removed. Herodotus tells the story of one of Darius' helpers against the magus, Intaphernes, who overstepped his authority in dispensing punishment to some of Darius' guards when they prevented Intaphernes from seeing the King (3.118–119). Darius viewed this act as a threat to his position, and Intraphernes was put to death, along with several members of his family.

Stunning displays of the disbursement of royal favor are found in descriptions of the royal table, elaborate feasts that involved veritable armies of attendants and entertainers as well as enormous quantities of food and drink. Numerous Greek and Roman sources refer to the phenomena, and Elamite and Babylonian documentation allude to the requisition of foodstuffs and other supplies.[1] Gifts distributed, marks of royal favor, might include grants of land; special clothing, precious metalwork, or jewelry (markers of elite status); an *akinakes*; or any number of other objects, even bequests and favors. In the Intaphernes anecdote just mentioned, Herodotus specifically notes that Intaphernes used his *akinakes* to cut off the ears and noses – compare the similar punishments meted out by Darius as described in the Bisitun Inscription – of the King's guards. That *akinakes* was a sign of high favor; it would of course been taken from Intaphernes immediately upon his arrest: not simply because it was a weapon but also for its symbolic significance, the loss of royal favor and the loss of his position.

The queen held a similarly august position to the King but one that is harder to track. The King could have several wives and concubines, but only one would be primary, the queen herself. She and the queen mother were prominent in a hierarchy that included secondary wives, concubines, and palace staff. The royal women were enormously powerful and influential, but in ways that often defy the stereotypes rampant in Greek sources. Their influence was both social and bureaucratic, as documents from Persepolis testify to their range of landholdings and economic activity. The Persepolis Fortification tablets (see discussion later in this chapter) contain dozens of references to the royal women Irtashduna and Irdabama. These women controlled significant landholdings with large retinues of staff and servants, interacted constantly with high (male) officials on official and private business, and went on long journeys.[2] Irtashduna has been identified with the Artystone of Greek sources, the daughter of Cyrus whom Darius married upon taking the throne. Irdabama appears to have been even more influential, another one of Darius' wives or perhaps even his mother; she has not been confidently identified with any women named in the Greek tradition.

Direct influence of the royal women on royal policy or the like is anecdotal and stems mainly from the Greek tradition, more appropriate to the study of Greek literary tropes than Persian politics. Herodotus provides a good example when he attributes Darius' decision to attack Greece to Queen Atossa's influence (3.134), a scene that Herodotus nicely sets in the king and queen's bedroom. One might compare Hera's machinations to distract Zeus from the Trojan Wars (*Iliad*, Book 14, lines 300f.). Without a doubt the Persian court saw its share of court intrigue and jockeying for influence, but the particulars are difficult to assess.

Greek sources revel in a Persian court overflowing with sexual intrigue and, as a consequence of the projected dominance of the
women and eunuchs, they portray an overarching sense of effeminacy.
According to this perspective, the queens and concubines were seques-
tered, a perspective that (at least for royal women) does not match up
with other evidence such as that for Irtashduna and Irdabama alluded
to earlier in this chapter. Athenaeus, writing around 200 CE but attributing his information to a fourth-century BCE Greek writer named
Heracleides, claims that the Persian kings slept all day in order to be
awake all night to indulge in music and sex with his concubines. To
note that this is exaggerated seems superfluous, but Greek and Roman
audiences loved it. A similar perspective underlies the biblical Book of
Esther, which hinges on finding a new queen, or favorite, a process that
involves King Ahasuerus (Xerxes) vetting his numerous concubines to
discover Esther.[3]

The Greek fascination with opposites and inversion also found ready
application in the eunuchs of the Persian court. Eunuchs seem to play
an outsized role in almost every aspect of court politics and intrigue.
In Xenophon's *Cyropaedia* (7.5.59–65), Cyrus the Great gives a long
disquisition on eunuchs and their virtues for upholding royal security,
an idealized justification of their existence and utility. Ctesias' *Persica*
also highlights eunuchs, especially their influence and prominent roles
at court. Greek fascination with eunuchs and an overestimation (willful
or not) of their influence did much to foster the widespread view of the
Achaemenid Empire as effeminate and lacking vigor. Our sources attest
to numerous instances of eunuchs in lower-level domestic staff positions,
as attendants of princesses or concubines and tutors of royal children.
Castration of young males who were to become eunuchs occurs usually
in contexts of tribute or punishment, and only in exceptional cases did a
eunuch rise to a significant position. One example is Hermotimus, who
was highly honored (as Herodotus phrases it, 8.105) by Xerxes; but
many questions remain about the historicity of this episode as well.

Eunuchs as portrayed in Greek sources more often than not corre-
spond to literary prototypes, extremes exemplifying unwavering loyalty
or base treachery. A certain eunuch Bagapates, prominent in Ctesias'
Persica (Fragment 13 §9, §13, §15–16, §23), typified both. Bagapates
held an influential position under Cyrus and Cambyses, arranged for the

magus to take Cambyses' place, then helped Darius and his coconspirators to kill the magus, and in the end died after sitting beside Darius' tomb for seven years. This is taken to mean that Bagapates served as the tomb's caretaker in an utmost expression of loyalty. In light of dramatic twists and turns of his long career, one cannot help but view him as a literary composite to appeal to a Greek audience. Other examples abound. Not only were eunuchs liminal figures because of their physicality (as castrated males) but frequently because they were placed in the middle (literally and figuratively) of competing interests at the royal court. The excess of eunuchs in the Greek accounts may also be attributed to Greek conflation and confusion of official titles at the Achaemenid court. But there seems to be as many difficulties in the modern historiography on these issues as there are in the original source material. Achaemenid court titles, of course, would not have been Greek but rather Persian — or Assyrian, Babylonian, or Elamite for those labels and court functions inherited from their imperial predecessors. Uncertainty over translation of titles and the functions implied by them has magnified the confusion in identifying actual eunuchs named in the Classical sources.

ADMINISTRATION OF THE EMPIRE

The Persians displayed their ingenuity in their organizational and administrative systems, adopted and adapted from their predecessors. Any study of the Empire's administration starts with the King, whose power was absolute. He was the focal point of a complicated nexus of bureaucracy and personal relationships by which the Empire was ruled. A main difficulty in understanding the administration of the Achaemenid Persian Empire is the assessment of the kings' so-called "*dahyu*-lists." The Old Persian word *dahyu* (plural *dahyāva*) is best understood in context — it may mean either "people" or "country," and is usually translated as the former. The context is not always clear. The royal inscriptions vary in number of *dahyāva* given. Some of these *dahyāva* may have corresponded roughly to provincial territories within the preceding empires, territories that the Persians incorporated via conquest. In scholarly literature they are sometimes called "satrapy-lists" or the like.

DAHYĀVA LISTS

DB §6	DPe §2	DSe §3	DNa §3	XPh §3
Persia	Elam	Media	Media	Media
Elam	Media	Elam	Elam	Elam
Babylonia	Babylonia	Parthia	Parthia	Arachosia
Assyria	Arabia	Areia	Areia	Armenia
Arabia	Assyria	Bactria	Bactria	Drangiana
Egypt	Egypt	Sogdiana	Sogdiana	Parthia
Those of the sea	Armenia	Chorasmia	Chorasmia	Areia
Sardis (Lydia)	Cappadocia	Drangiana	Drangiana	Bactria
Ionia	Sardis	Arachosia	Arachosia	Sogdiana
Media	Ionians of the plain	Sattagydia	Sattgydia	Chorasmia
Armenia	Ionians by the sea	Maka	Gandara	Babylonia
Cappadocia	Lands beyond the sea	Gandara	India	Assyria
Parthia	Sagartia	India	Saka who drink *haoma*	Sattagydia
Drangiana	Parthia	Saka who drink *haoma*	Saka with pointed hats	Sardis
Areia	Drangiana	Saka with pointed hats	Babyonia	Egypt
Chorasmia	Areia	Babylonia	Assyria	Ionians who dwell by the sea
Bactria	Bactria	Assyria	Arabia	Ionians who dwell across the sea
Sogdiana	Sogdiana	Arabia	Egypt	Maka
Gandara	Chorasmia	Egypt	Armenia	Arabia
Scythia	Sattagydia	Armenia	Cappadocia	Gandara
Sattagydia	Arachosia	Cappadocia	Sardis	India
Arachosia	India	Sardis	Ionia	Cappadocia
Maka	Gandara	Ionians of the sea	Saka across the sea	Dahae
	Saka	Skudra beyond the sea	Thrace	Saka who drink *haoma*
	Maka	Thrace	Ionians who wear the *petasos*	Saka with pointed hats
		Ionians beyond the sea	Libya	Thrace
		Caria	Nubia	Akaufaka
			Maka	Libya
			Caria	Caria
				Nubia

Figure 6.2 Lists of *dahyāva* in Royal Inscriptions.

There are several *dahyu*-lists from the inscriptions of Darius and one from Xerxes. Each list includes both peoples and places, the latter not necessarily synonymous with the boundaries of a formal satrapy. In Figure 6.2 they are generally listed as regions.[4] It is not always clear whether a particular term (i.e., the name of a *dahyu*) refers to a group of people or the land in which they live, or both. For example, to most Persians the Greeks – living in hundreds of independent city-states in Ionia and Greece itself – were mostly indistinguishable, and they were labeled generically by the Old Persian word *Yauna*, a rendering of the word "Ionia." There are many ambiguities and peculiarities; for example, it is not entirely clear to whom Darius refers by "those of the sea" (DB §6). Some lists (DPe and XPh) attempt to differentiate these fractious *Yauna*, distinguishing the Ionians who lived in the sea (islanders) from those who lived across the sea, whose location is not specified – north of the Black Sea, in parts of Thrace, in Greece proper? One group of Ionians is even identified by the type of hat the people wore (DNa §3). Scythians (Saka) were also sometimes differentiated by their taste in hats or their use of a particular beverage (*haoma*, associated with Zoroastrian ritual contexts). It becomes clear that classification was not necessarily consistent across these lists.

Some scholars have attempted, by comparing these *dahyu*-lists in Darius' and Xerxes' inscriptions, to track the territorial expansion or contraction of the Empire, but such attempts are often as vain as they are ingenious. Beyond the Bisitun Inscription, it is impossible to date any royal inscriptions with precision. That the descriptions of *dahyāva* seem to vary – based on parameters that we do not fully understand – causes historians no small vexation. Many assume that Xerxes' list (XPh §3) dates after his failed invasion of Greece. If so, it does not appear to have affected the inclusion of various *Yauna* in his list. We should not expect it to. Because these inscriptions are expressions of imperial ideology, one may infer that the lack of specificity (as we seek it) was not necessarily unintentional. In other words, these lists portray the King's idealized perception of his dominion and do not necessarily delineate actual, imperial control, especially on the fringes of the Empire. For example, the territorial extent of the King's dominion over the Scythians (OP *Saka*) is unclear. The King may have received gifts and tribute from these Scythians, but his view and their view on their formal incorporation into the Empire may have been different.

TRIBUTE TO THE KING AND COINS

Herodotus 3.89–95 offers an overview of the Empire's satrapies and their respective tributes, broken down into specific amounts. This passage is an important, if often misunderstood, piece of evidence for the Empire's organization. Whether Herodotus' tallied tribute – a total of 14,560 talents, an absolutely staggering sum of money into the billions of dollars in today's terms, though any such conversions are extremely difficult and notoriously unreliable – has any basis in reality is open to debate. Significant components thereof were more likely to have been paid in kind rather than in coin or precious metal, so some of the numbers must be estimated equivalents.

On what was Herodotus' list based? For a long time, this account formed the core of any discussion of Achaemenid satrapal organization, and it is certainly a starting point for assessing the extent and wealth of the Empire. Nonetheless, scholars are still divided over its interpretation to this day. Some view it as a reasonably coherent overview of the satrapy system but one that is heavily Hellenized and, as a consequence, contains several irregularities. Other scholars assert that it has no historical worth whatsoever and is, rather, entirely a creation of Herodotus based on Greek literary conventions, including those of Greek epic.[5]

Revenues of all sorts poured into the satrapal capitals and from there to the king. The assessment and collection of tribute, or revenues in general, was a complex system that is difficult to categorize succinctly. The organizational elements were attributed to Darius I, but even if he reformed the system there was certainly tribute collected by his predecessors; it was a long standing practice before the Achaemenids. Terminology is not always straightforward, since Herodotus distinguishes some peoples as having given gifts (Greek *dāra*) instead of tribute (Greek *phoros* and variants), such as the Ethiopians. The distinction may have been relative. Beyond this, tribute might also include additional elements such as troop levies and what we would term taxes: payments from royal holdings (granaries, fisheries, mines) either in kind or in coin, for the maintenance of government officials.

There was no one size fits all approach. A people called the Uxians, who lived in the mountains between Khuzistan and Fars, presumably had a special relationship with the King whereby they were given gifts not to harass the Persians, who could not control them. This perspective – which fits the Greek stereotype of the weakness of the Persian king – comes once again from later Greek sources (e.g., Arrian 3.17) and is misleading. A special relationship may have applied here through a gift exchange: to the effect that the Uxians retained their internal autonomy but acknowledged Persian suzerainty. Such an arrangement was hardly unique. A multitude of sources in Elamite, Babylonian, and

Figure 6.3 Persian gold daric. © The Trustees of the British Museum/ Art Resource, NY.

Aramaic reveal the complexity of the system, the extent of Achaemenid reach and effective control.

The application of coinage to the payment of tribute is also a subject of frequent discussion, though, as noted, payment in kind or in weighted precious metals was more common. Coined money had been in use in Lydia and Greece for some time before Darius I, who appears to have been the first to command minting silver or gold royal coinage. We find the most references to Persian coins (and not only of Persian issue) in context of payments to Greek mercenaries in the later fifth and fourth centuries, although that usage was hardly exclusive. The most famous type was the gold daric: it portrayed the King in various poses as an archer, sometimes also with a spear (Figure 6.3), another striking image of the royal ideology. But this type of coin was worth a lot of money and would have been difficult to use in daily exchanges where, if coinage was used, it would have been in silver. Gold darics could be used in commerce, but they may have been primarily prestige items, doled out as a sign of royal favor.

SATRAPS AND PROVINCIAL PERSONNEL

The satraps, the "protectors of the kingdom," were the King's most important officials, typically members of the Persian elite if not the extended royal family. The word "satrap" (Old Persian *xšaçapāvan*) may be considered equivalent to the governor of a province, one level below the King, while the term "satrapy" (from the Greek *satrapeia*, derived from the Old Persian term) refers to a province. Classical sources use different words when referring to the political hierarchy of the Achaemenid Empire, and this engenders confusion; for example, it is uncertain whether the Greek title *hyparchos* (variously translated as "governor," "lieutenant governor," or even "ruler") refers to a Persian satrap or an official who reported to the satrap. Since various Greek authors used the terms so fluidly, it is no wonder that modern scholars have such difficulty with them. But we are not reliant only on Greek evidence. For example, the archive of Arshama (Greek *Arsames*), the satrap of Egypt during the later fifth century, offers extensive information on the day-to-day operations of that important satrapy's administration (see p. 189).

The formal creation of the Achaemenid satrapy system has been attributed to Darius I, but it has become increasingly clear that Cyrus and Cambyses initiated the system through adoption and adaptation of preexisting structures. The resulting administrative units were occasionally modified in light of political circumstances but remained relatively intact throughout the Achaemenid period. It is not possible to demarcate fixed boundaries of satrapies, especially on modern maps, but they frequently coincided with natural ones such as major rivers. Creation of a satrapy usually involved the replacement of the previous king or ruler of a region by a Persian satrap, appointed by the King. Thus the King became an additional level of administration superimposed upon previous kingdoms and territories now incorporated into the Persian Empire. Local officials were often retained but became subordinate to the satrap.

Continuity of satrapal rule through generations of the same family indicates that the appointment became almost dynastic in some areas, whether the satrap was initially a local ruler, as in the case of Mausolus in fourth-century Caria (southwestern Anatolia), or a royal appointee from a Persian elite family, as in the case of Artabazus in Hellespontine Phrygia (in northwestern Anatolia). Artabazus and his descendants provide an unbroken line from 479 BCE well into the fourth century. Artabazus was a cousin to the royal family, thus a part of the extended Achaemenid clan, and this connection underlines the Persian nobility's stake in the Empire. The King depended upon his satraps' loyalty for the Empire's smooth functioning and stability, and the satrap depended upon the King for his position. There were occasions when a satrap spurred destabilization through revolt, especially in the context of a disputed royal succession.

While satraps had a great deal of independence in the day-to-day operation of their provinces, foreign policy was another matter. The satrap was ultimately responsible to the King. It is easy – because we have voluminous evidence of various types – to visualize frequent and ongoing communications between the King's court and the satraps on a variety of matters. Each satrapy had its own administration that was connected with the overarching administrative net through which the King controlled the Empire. Satraps were not only responsible for the security of their provinces but also for the collection and delivery of taxes and tribute as well as for the maintenance of roads and other networks of communication. When the King sought military forces for a major campaign, it was the satrap's responsibility to assemble the requested forces from his area.

Royal secretaries and military personnel, responsible directly to the King, were key components of satrapal administration. These individuals and their retinues helped to govern the satrapy and to maintain consistent and reliable communication with the King. They also served as tangible reminders that the satrap owed his position to the King. Greek sources contain many examples of a satrap's deference to the King in matters of foreign affairs, in response to one or another request by a Greek city-state for assistance or a change in policy. It is easy to interpret such hedging as a satrap's evasion, but the realities of Achaemenid hierarchy and bureaucracy insist otherwise. Herodotus' story of Darius I's handling of the recalcitrant Oroites (see p. 78) provides a paradigmatic example of the King's authority in the provinces: a mechanism of royal control and an illustration of the consequences of insubordination.

The stereotyped view of the detached or cloistered King, prominent in much of twentieth-century scholarship, has become much less compelling. There is ample reason to assert that the King was well-informed of his satraps' activities, and that a satrap in good standing (i.e., one not in open rebellion) consistently deferred to the King on any matters beyond his jurisdiction or prerogative. A fine line may separate satrapal independence from satrapal revolt, but the weight of the evidence indicates satrapal adherence to royal directives. In other words, satraps were aware not only of their responsibilities to the royal administration but also of the sorts of initiatives they could, or were expected to, undertake. Evidence from Greek, Aramaic, and Elamite sources attests to a high degree of imperial organization and control.

The functioning of the Empire demanded reliable communications between center and periphery. Finds such as bullae from Daskyleion (the satrapal capital of Hellespontine Phrygia, in northwestern Anatolia) and Aramaic documents from Bactria attest to bureaucracies, comparable with and connected to the central one, even in the far-flung provinces.[6] Access to provisions and storehouses along the royal roads required authorization, as demonstrated by a number of documents in Aramaic and Elamite, along with Herodotus' more widely-known description of the Royal Road from Sardis to Susa (see discussion later in this chapter). Herodotus' account finds corroboration in an Elamite administrative document from the central administration in Persepolis, a disbursement from the satrap Artaphernes for a group traveling to Persepolis.[7] This mundane communiqué illustrates the control the king and his satraps had over their officials in these far-flung areas.

THE PERSEPOLIS TABLETS: PERSIAN ADMINISTRATION, ECONOMY, AND STRATIFICATION

In the 1930s CE, excavators at Persepolis found two stashes of tablets, one from the so-called Treasury in the southeastern part of the terrace and the other deposited within the fortification wall of the northeastern part of the terrace. Thus the names Persepolis Treasury Tablets (PTT) and Persepolis Fortification Tablets (PFT) indicate the find spots, not the contents, of the tablets. The first group (PTT) is relatively small, 129 useful texts (not including additional fragments), which range in date between 492 and 457 BCE, from the reigns of Darius I to Artaxerxes I. The second group (PFT) is enormous in number but more limited in chronological scope (c. 509–493 BCE, during the reign of Darius I). The number of PFT documents ranges from 4,000 to 30,000 or more, but this depends upon who is counting and with what parameters. Higher counts often include fragments (pieces of broken texts). Studies devoted to the Fortification archive emphasize the variety in the corpus: tablets with Elamite (cuneiform) text; tablets and tags written in Aramaic (ink and incised); and many un-inscribed tablets. Only a portion of the Elamite tablets has been published. There are also a few but important anomalies, including tablets inscribed in Greek, Akkadian, Phrygian, and even Old Persian.

Another important component of the Fortification archive is the diversity of seals applied to the tablets. There are more than 1,100 distinct seals impressed on the published Elamite tablets and many more on the unpublished ones. The seals are an integral part of the administrative process, as the sealings on a tablet may in themselves communicate the agents involved in the transaction as well as the specific locale. The seals portray a range of activity, and their rich iconography is invaluable as an index for Persian visual arts and culture. While the breadth of the archive necessitates its piecemeal study, each piece must be considered part of a cohesive administrative unit. Even though enormous strides have been made in our understanding of the archive, in many respects this venture is still nascent. What follows is only an introduction to the evidence and what it offers for the study of Achaemenid history.

Nearly half of the Fortification texts date to the years 500–499 BCE and almost two-thirds of the Treasury tablets date to the year 466. The administrative region concerns mainly the wider Persepolis region itself, of course, but the corpus contains references to almost all parts of the Empire between Sardis and India, especially those texts that deal with supply distributions for travelers on official business. It should be emphasized that these clay tablets were only one part of the administrative apparatus. The nature of cuneiform texts makes them more durable than parchment, wax boards, and the like, on which a great deal of record keeping was also done. Despite the size of the Fortification archive, once again we are reminded that we have only a piece of the entire puzzle.

The Fortification texts deal mainly with foodstuffs and livestock — their collection, storage, and redistribution. The tablets provide important data on the organization of labor; economy and fiscal management; the demography and cartography of the Empire's core; operations of state institutions at a basic level; religious practices and cultic personnel; travel on state business; and a host of other social and cultural aspects of

Achaemenid Persian history. None of this incredible detail and sophisti-
cation should be too surprising. Such advanced organizational control had
persisted already for several centuries in both Mesopotamian and Elamite
traditions, traceable as far back as 2100 BCE and the Ur III period.

Workers were generally labeled *kurtash*, an Elamite word that escapes
consensus as to its exact translation. It may be misguided to narrow
the term's definition too much. Workers were of varying sorts: those
who worked in the fields and shops controlled by the administration
and those who labored on the massive, ongoing construction projects at
Persepolis. They encompassed varying levels of specialization and socioeconomic status. Usually a given worker's specialty is not indicated,
only the amounts of rations received, which for most workers amounted
to a subsistence wage. Disbursements to workers were usually in-kind,
meaning quantities of foodstuffs, though some Treasury tablets record
payment of silver.

Another interesting feature of the *kurtash* is the range of their eth-
nicities: Arabs, Bactrians, Babylonians, Egyptians, Elamites, Ionians,
Thracians, among several others. Who were these people and why were
they working at Persepolis? How did they get there? These questions
have no easy answers. Some of the royal inscriptions – for example
Darius I's "foundation charter" from Susa (DSf) – associate specific ethnic groups with specific materials or craftsmanship, an inclusive manifestation of the Empire and its diversity. People of varying ethnicity
mentioned in these tablets may have been brought to Persepolis for
similar reasons, whether by virtue of a specific call or by force, required
to work on select projects for the King. Deportations may have been
one means of their presence, such as the Eretrians (see p. 89) labeled
by the central administration with the generic term "Ionian" used for
all Greeks. But as reasonable as such a suggestion seems, it is not obvious that such specific populations of deportees were among the *kurtash*.
That even Persians could be labeled *kurtash* gives pause to any assumption that the word indicates deportees.

The man in charge of the Persepolis administration from 506–497
BCE was named Parnaka (Greek *Pharnaces*), identified by two inscribed
seals in Aramaic on numerous tablets. The first one (labeled in the literature PFS 9* for "Persepolis Fortification Seal number 9," Figure 6.4)
labels him simply as "Parnaka." A second seal (PFS 16*, Figure 6.5),

Figure 6.4 Collated line drawing of PFS 9* from the Persepolis Fortification Archive. Courtesy Persepolis Seal Project.

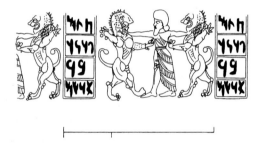

Figure 6.5 Collated line drawing of PFS 16* from the Persepolis Fortification Archive. Courtesy Persepolis Seal Project.

substituted by official order in an Elamite tablet (PF 2067), replaced the first one and bears the label: Parnaka, son of Arsham. Aramaic *Arsham* is Old Persian *Arshama* and Greek *Arsames*. Scholars generally agree that, based on Parnaka's evident high rank and his filiation, he is none other than Darius I's uncle, brother of Darius' father Hystaspes. Further, this same Parnaka is the father of Artabazus, whom Xerxes made satrap of Hellespontine Phrygia.

Parnaka oversaw a vast hierarchy of officials who supervised, in turn, discrete areas of the administrative organization. It is to these various functionaries that Parnaka, or his immediate subordinates (also of high rank), sent orders for disbursements. Instructions thus followed a chain of command, and there was generally a clear allocation of responsibility and accountability. Officials in charge of warehouses – where grain, wine, or other goods for disbursement were stored – were required to keep careful records. Every year accountants prepared inventories that were sent to the central office in Persepolis where the "books" were kept. Parnaka or his lieutenants thus had relatively easy access to information about inventories at any of the warehouses throughout the districts linked to this central administration.

High-ranking officials received commensurately greater allocations than lower-level workers. For example, three texts (PF 654, 665, 669[8]) give a glimpse of Parnaka's own allocations and allow us to reconstruct his daily "payment": two sheep, 90 liters of wine, and 180 liters of flour. The quantities provided are obviously too great to be consumed by one person. Other elites similarly received quantities far too high for any one individual to consume. Such disbursements may have been redistributed to that individual's subordinates, credited for future withdrawals as necessary, or perhaps exchanged for other commodities or silver. Large outlays may also have been applied to special occasions or feasts at the royal table, which was attended by a careful hierarchy and performance, with many layers of significance. It is likely that some of the large disbursements to the elite may have been meant for just such purposes, though the tablets themselves generally only indicate the materials disbursed, not the intended use.

The Persepolis texts offer insights into the stratification of Persian society, but of course the emphasis is on a bureaucratic hierarchy and the people who work within it or for it. Rations (payments) distributed to *kurtash* workers at Persepolis varied in amount by age and gender, though amounts could vary widely based on locale and jobs performed.[9] Pregnant women received special rations, and in some cases those who bore sons then received higher amounts than those who bore daughters. We assume the *kurtash* lived in families, but the circumstances of these families elude us. What happened when the children grew up? Did they remain *kurtash* and start their own families through marriages at the same social level or status?

And the evidence for other members of Persian society, even the lower echelons of citizens, is slimmer yet. All people, regardless of social status, were the king's *bandakā*, the Old Persian word that is sometimes translated as "slaves" but is usually better rendered as "subjects" or "servants." Archaeological evidence offers enormous insight into daily life but at very specific locations.[10] The scope and diversity of the Empire also does not lend itself easily to broad categorizations, though the daily life and tasks of a small farmer may not have differed much in Fars than in central Anatolia. The royal inscriptions refer in general terms to "the strong" and "the weak," but even moving beyond the inscriptions' ideological context such classifications are not very useful in understanding Persian social stratification beyond a very general level. When members of the lower classes appear in the documentary evidence, it is usually in anecdotal contexts; for example, the Roman Aelian writing circa 200 CE tells the story of a Persian man, Siniates, who met Artaxerxes II unexpectedly and scrambled to find a suitable gift for the King. Siniates scooped some water from a nearby river, named after Cyrus, and offered it to the King with a benediction for his long reign and a promise of more suitable gifts once Siniates returned home. Artaxerxes received the gift with full approval, and he rewarded Siniates for this piety with gifts of his own: a Persian robe, a gold cup, and a hefty sum of money (Aelian, *Varia Historia* 1.32). Of course, this anecdote tells us more about the relationship between king and subjects than it does about Siniates' way of life.

THE PERSIAN ARMY

Persian military forces were drawn from all areas of the Empire, members of the elite corps (see Figure 6.6 for an example) as well as conscripts levied for local action or for major campaigns. Thus the label "Persian" is not to be understood as describing the ethnic makeup but rather the troops' allegiance, fighting under Persian officials or commanders. As has been seen, however, the command structure was not thoroughly Persian by any means either, save at the very top of the hierarchy, including most satraps and of course the King himself. The Old Persian word *kāra* may be translated either as "army" or as "people." This reveals the army's ultimate origin – among the Persians themselves, many of whom came to form the corps of the standing army – as it results in occasional confusion in modern translation. When *kāra* appears in a text, it is not always evident to us whether the people as a collective group or the specific subset of the army is meant.

Herodotus gives a full and colorful account of the vast and diverse forces of the imperial levy, the full army and navy of Persians and subject

Figure 6.6 Frieze of Archers, Palace of Darius, Susa. © RMN – Grand Palais/Art Resource, NY.

peoples, when he tallies the vast forces that Xerxes arrayed against Greece in 480 BCE. Herodotus also names many of the commanders, an elaborate depiction of the peoples of the Empire with descriptions of their clothing and equipment (7.61–100). For example, both Persians and Medes were arrayed in felt caps, colored tunics over scale mail, trousers, wickerwork shields, and a variety of weapons. Ethiopians (Nubians) wore leopard or lion skins and carried large bows. Paphlagonians wore woven helmets and carried small shields and spears. That Herodotus' entire portrayal better describes a parade than a battle array has long been understood. But it typifies the diversity of peoples and weaponry that the Persian commanders had to weld into an effective fighting force. Persian forces, both infantry and cavalry, were renowned for their use of the bow: a frequent tactic was the unleashing of storms of arrows from behind a shield wall or for horsemen to harry the enemy with volleys of arrows.

Scholars debate the effectiveness of the Persian forces' armor and tactics especially in the context of Xerxes' invasion of Greece in 480 and Alexander's invasion of the Persian Empire in the late 330s. Herodotus (9.62) describes the final crush of the Persians against the Spartans at the Battle of Plataea in 479:

> On the one hand the Persians were no less than the Greeks in courage
> and strength, but the Persians were without shields and, beyond this,
> were unskilled and not the equal of their opponents in experience.

This passage offers just one example of the persistent problems of source evaluation. When Herodotus says that the Persians were "without shields" (Greek *anoploi*), what does that mean? Were the shields lost in battle? Was this contingent of the Persian army simply not carrying shields? And which group was it, ethnic Persians or some other? Some translate *anoploi* as "without armor," which adds another layer to the problem. The Spartans were the most (by far) professionalized Greek soldiers of their day, so even the elite corps of the Persian army would have had their hands full against them. Beyond the elite, levied troops from the provinces of course did not have the same sort of armor, weaponry, or tactics as did, for example, the Persian Immortals and similar contingents. Numerous other passages in Greek sources provide similar perspectives: heavily armed Greek infantry, fighting in tight phalanx formations, trumped the (as generally described in Greek sources) light armed, less experienced, inferior Persian infantry every time – except when they did not. It is difficult to sift the Greek stereotypes from the realities of individual battles. That the Persians were able to conquer and retain so much territory for so long testifies to their army's effectiveness.

The elite Persian force, numbering 10,000 according to Herodotus (7.83), was called the Immortals. Whenever one of their number died or was wounded or ill, another would take his place so the number of the battalion always remained 10,000. They were the most effective, and feared, Persian infantry force, and clearly comprised elite members of Persian society: men of prominent families or high rank. One thousand of them had gold pomegranates on their spears, some of whom comprised the king's personal bodyguard, and the other 9,000 had silver. Herodotus' incidental detail that the Immortals were conspicuous

for their gold (bracelets or other marks of status and honor), and that
they were accompanied by wagons bearing concubines and many servants, indicates that we are not dealing with the rank and file. Prestige
items are frequently mentioned in conjunction with Persian officers and
nobles, a phenomenon that also fed Greek stereotypes of Persian effeminacy and weakness. But these items were more symbolic than practical
and communicated entirely different messages – honor and status – in
a Persian context.

Greek sources often highlight the prominence and skill of Greek
mercenaries, and from that perspective it was only thanks to better
trained and better equipped Greek professionals that the Empire was
able to field any sort of worthwhile fighting force in the fourth century. This trope contributed heavily to the stereotype of the effeminate,
decaying Persian Empire before its fall to Alexander the Great. And
even though Greek mercenary forces were an increasing phenomenon
in the fourth century, and certainly used by Persian commanders, their
significance often seems overestimated in Greek sources.

COMMUNICATION NETWORKS – THE ROYAL ROAD

Reliable and efficient communications throughout the Empire were
a necessary component for its success (see Map 1.1). The construction, maintenance, and guarding of an extensive network of roads and
bridges required a great deal of engineering expertise, manpower, and
expense. The Persians adopted and adapted their predecessors' systems,
and greatly expanded them, to facilitate communication across vast
distances. Individuals or groups on state business carried sealed documents that allowed access to supplies or provisions en route to their
destination.

The most famous of these roads, though it was only one of many,
was what Herodotus called the Royal Road from Susa in Elam to Sardis
in Lydia (5.52–53). Any "royal" road would have, in fact, run through
Persepolis and points eastward, so Herodotus' terminology reflects a
Greek view, which usually viewed Susa as the main Achaemenid capital. From the west it ran through Cappadocia and Cilicia in Anatolia to
Armenia and then south through Arbela – along the Tigris River – and

on toward Susa. Herodotus notes that there were 111 royal staging posts interspersed on it and mentions several of them specifically (5.52). By his calculations this route ran roughly 1,500 miles and took a journey of ninety days. That was for a traveler in no great haste. Royal dispatches could move with surprising speed, a relay system with fresh horses and messengers at each staging post. Herodotus also describes these royal messengers: "There is nothing mortal that travels faster than these messengers ... for as many days as the whole route there are horses and men stationed, one horse and one man set for each day. Neither snow, nor rain, nor heat, nor night hinders them from accomplishing the course laid before them as quickly as possible. After the first one finishes his route, he delivers the instructed message to the second, the second does likewise to the third; from there in rapid succession down the line the message moves." (8.98)

There were similar routes in all directions from the Empire's core in Fars.[11] Ctesias alludes to other roads running from Mesopotamia and Persia proper to Central Asia. The primary route to Bactria across northern Iran is called in modern works either the (Great) Khorasan Road or, for later periods, by its better known appellation the Silk Road. Administrative documents from Persepolis, Syro-Palestine, and Egypt record disbursements to travelers in all directions. From the Persepolis documentation we gain a sense of the itineraries of a number of the network of roads running between Susa and Persepolis. An Aramaic document tracks travelers journeying from northern Mesopotamia to Damascus and on into Egypt, with several stops along the way listed by name.

Large work crews were involved in the construction and maintenance of these roads. Herodotus' account of Xerxes' invasion of Greece describes roadmakers at work, not infrequently the army on campaign. The main roads, constructed wide enough to allow chariots or wagons to travel on them, served to move military forces quickly, but they were also used by travelers or merchants to transport cargo. Roads also at times had to cross obstacles such as rivers. Some permanent bridges, such as one spanning the Halys River in Anatolia, were guarded by a fort. Pontoon bridges allowed crossing of other rivers, for example, at many spots on the northern Tigris and the Euphrates Rivers and their tributaries. Temporary pontoon bridges afforded the means for Persian armies to cross into Europe: Darius I over the Bosporus on his campaign against the Scythians and Xerxes' bridge over the Hellespont against the Greeks. Of course, rivers and larger waterways were sometimes part of the route. Diodorus Siculus (14.81.4) records a journey on a well-known route at sea along the coast of Cilicia, on land from northwestern Syria to the Euphrates, then down the river to Babylon. Similar sea trading routes connected other parts of the Empire to the core, such as through the Persian Gulf and along the southern coast of Iran to the Indus Valley.

7 Xerxes, the Expander of the Realm

THE DEATH OF DARIUS AND THE ACCESSION OF XERXES

Stung by the defeat of his forces at Marathon, Darius was furious and immediately began to prepare a much larger campaign. At least this is what Herodotus tells us (7.1) – not that the Father of History would have had any chance of knowing Persian strategic concerns in 490 or, for matter, Darius' actual words. Herodotus supplies such details, some perhaps from oral tradition, for dramatic effect. That Darius intended another campaign would be no surprise; the Persians were relentless, after all, but no short-term preparations can be confirmed. Darius died in 486, and his son and successor Xerxes had, on his succession, far larger problems than Greece. Herodotus offers no details about Darius' death but notes that he reigned for thirty-six years, a number confirmed by Babylonian documentation. The latest text to Darius' reign dates from late December 486; the first to Xerxes' reign is from early December of the same year, so there may have been some confusion, even in Babylonia, as to the exact date of the transition. Ctesias indicates that Darius died of illness (Fragment 13 §23).

The succession of Xerxes was not without controversy. Herodotus sets his story (7.2–3) near the end of Darius' reign, when Darius was compelled to choose a successor before he went on campaign, "according to the law of the Persians." There is no other record of such a Persian practice, and Herodotus' reference to it here is a bit odd. Darius had undertaken many campaigns previously, as Herodotus himself related without mention of the succession. It is probably a rhetorical statement that served Herodotus' literary purpose here. Regardless, the issue turned on which son should be successor: his eldest son from his first marriage (before he became king) or his eldest son after he became king. By his earlier marriage to a daughter of Gobryas, Darius had three sons, the eldest of whom was named Artobazanes. Xerxes was the eldest child from Darius' marriage to Atossa, the daughter of Cyrus, after Darius ascended to the throne. Xerxes' descent, and the timing of his birth, became the compelling arguments. Herodotus has these arguments presented to Darius by an exiled Spartan king named Demaratus. Demaratus later accompanied Xerxes on his invasion of Greece and became one of Herodotus' stock characters, the wise adviser. Herodotus adds that the influence of Xerxes' mother, Atossa, would have carried the day in any case, because she had such enormous influence upon Darius. But Atossa's purported influence, as described by Herodotus, represents the popular Greek stereotype of the dominant (and often domineering) position royal women held at the Persian court. Herodotus is unsubstantiated here.

Xerxes himself provides some backdrop for Herodotus' story, as he makes oblique reference to a succession controversy in an inscription from Persepolis (XPf §4). "Xerxes the King proclaims: Darius had other sons as well, but thus was the desire of Ahuramazda: Darius my father made me greatest after himself. When my father Darius died, by the favor of Ahuramazda I became king in my father's place." The rest of the inscription emphasizes Xerxes' continued building works at Persepolis and reinforces the continuity between Darius and Xerxes. No specifics of his mother, birth order, or succession politics are revealed here, nor would we expect them to be. The only salient point is that Darius, and of course Ahuramazda, chose Xerxes; therefore, Xerxes is the rightful king. It is usually presumed to be Xerxes standing behind the enthroned Darius in the so-called Treasury Relief (Figure 7.1) at Persepolis, though the figures are not labeled.[1]

The new King Xerxes was immediately confronted by a revolt in Egypt that had actually begun before Darius' death. By virtue of its geography and its wealth, Egypt had greater strategic significance than any other western region. We know little about the revolt beyond allusions in Classical sources, so it is difficult to gauge its magnitude or Xerxes' response. Herodotus notes that Xerxes crushed the revolt and

Figure 7.1 Treasury Relief, Persepolis. Courtesy of the Oriental Institute of the University of Chicago.

adds the cryptic note that he made Egypt "more enslaved than it was under Darius" (7.7). It is difficult to determine what that means, but the response appears to have been effective. Xerxes installed his full brother, Achaemenes, as satrap there, and the sources indicate no serious trouble on the Egyptian front for roughly two decades.

Xerxes also faced one, and perhaps two, revolts in Babylonia, an area of course even more important than Egypt. A few Babylonian economic documents name two kings who reigned for only a few months: Bel-shimanni and Shamash-eriba. Details elude us here also. The main trouble appears to have been localized in northern Babylonia, including Babylon itself. Dates proposed for the rebellion have ranged from 484 to 479 BCE, and the latter date carries heavy interpretive significance. If a revolt in Babylon could be dated to 479, it would impact analysis of Xerxes' actions against Greece, with wide-ranging ramifications. Most scholars now accept a date of 484, based on a thorough analysis of the relevant evidence.[2]

Both Herodotus and Ctesias relate a story of Xerxes visiting the ziggurat of Babylon, the god Marduk's sanctuary, and either plundering the temple or violating a tomb. Herodotus claims that Xerxes removed a solid gold statue and in the process killed the priest who tried to stop the sacrilege (1.183). Ctesias offers a more convoluted story (Fragment 13b). Xerxes opened a sarcophagus, which bore an inscription indicating that whoever opened it must make sure it was filled with oil. Xerxes was unable to fill it, despite his continued efforts. Of course, this was a bad omen, and Xerxes' failed expedition against Greece and his assassination by his own son (see discussion later in this chapter) were regarded as manifestations of divine displeasure with his impiety.

A lively debate continues as to whether Xerxes truly did any of these things. It remains unclear whether the stories are simply anti-Persian sentiment expressed in Greek sources or whether certain Babylonian rituals were misinterpreted by the Greeks. With regard to Ctesias' story, it has been suggested that it stemmed from confusion with a well-attested ritual that involved the pouring of oil on foundation walls.[3] Modern interpretations often trace these stories to reaction against Persian reprisals for the Babylonian revolt, though Herodotus makes no mention of a revolt in Xerxes' reign.

XERXES' ROYAL INSCRIPTIONS

Xerxes left numerous dedications on buildings and sculptures at several sites, though mainly at Persepolis, second only to Darius in the number extant. The basic formula established by Darius persisted: Ahuramazda is the king's main benefactor, and the king is an Achaemenid. As has been noted, this template – emphasizing divine legitimacy and royal lineage – was one used by Near Eastern kings for centuries. With Xerxes the formula was reinforced. Not only was Xerxes a son of Darius, thus an Achaemenid, but through his mother Atossa he was also descended from Cyrus the Great. All subsequent kings likewise had to be of Achaemenid descent, even if born of secondary wives. There is some irony, then, that all the kings except Darius himself could draw their bloodline to Cyrus as well (see Appendix C).

Attempts to read significance into minor variations in Xerxes' titles – for example, "king of lands" or "king of this earth far and wide" – are generally met with skepticism. Not surprisingly, there is heavy emphasis on his continuation of Darius' legacy: in the ideological sense of his capabilities as an effective ruler and in the tangible sense of his construction work at Persepolis. A trilingual inscription from the *apadana* at Persepolis (XPg) offers an example: "Xerxes the Great King proclaims: By the favor of Ahuramazda, King Darius, who was my father, did much that is good. And by the favor of Ahuramazda, I added to what had been done and I built more. May Ahuramazda, together with the gods, protect me and my kingdom." Another inscription, in Old Persian only (XPl), is almost an exact copy of one from Darius' tomb (DNb), but this one bearing Xerxes' name also enumerates the royal qualities – physical, mental, and emotional – that typified a proper king.

Xerxes' most famous royal inscription is the so-called *daiva*-inscription, in which Xerxes makes forceful but vague reference to punishment meted out against those who did not worship Ahuramazda but instead worshipped *daivā* (the long *a* indicates the plural form) – a word roughly translated as "demons" or false gods.

And among these lands there was a place where *daivā* were worshipped.
By the favor of Ahuramazda I subsequently destroyed the sanctuary of the *daivā*, and I commanded "The *daivā* will no longer be worshipped!"
Where formerly the *daivā* were worshipped, there I worshipped Ahuramazda as appropriate. (XPh §4)[4]

In this inscription Xerxes reasserts Achaemenid royal ideology and elaborates the centrality of Ahuramazda to the King's, and by extension the Empire's, success and well-being. The inscription begins and ends with invocation of Ahuramazda. It begins with the god's creation of the world and of heaven; it ends with a blessing for the one who obeys Ahuramazda's law (understood as manifest in the King) and who worships him appropriately, and it adds a benediction for the god's protection of Xerxes, his house, and his realm.

Xerxes' imprecation against the *daiva*-worshippers has received much attention in modern treatments of XPh. The very existence of the *daivā* stands in antithesis to Ahuramazda, the epitome of righteousness, a contrast that impacts our understanding of Achamenid religious practices. Xerxes' sentiment here parallels that of Darius in the late addition to the Bisitun Inscription (DB §71–76) identifying the failure to worship Ahuramazda as an offense, a marker of rebellion. This is clearly an ideological signpost, but as a motivator of applied strategy it is much more problematic. It is one thing for the king to cast rebels as liars or enemies of the king's god, but it is another to assume that the king actively sought to compel others to the worship of Ahuramazda. As a practical matter we do not see this sentiment beyond formal expressions in the royal inscriptions and, in fact, there is plenty of evidence that contradicts a notion of exclusive worship of Ahuramazda (see pp. 155–156).

Xerxes takes Darius' sentiment one step further but only in this one inscription. In it, Xerxes' claims are strident but not specific: he restored order by defeating offenders. In those places where the *daivā* were worshipped – and, by extension, where Ahuramazda was not worshipped – Xerxes made certain that the proper worship of Ahuramazda was (re?)-instituted. What does that mean? Is Xerxes referring to Babylonia, Greece, Egypt, somewhere else? Perhaps the best answer is all of them and none of them – by that it is meant that Xerxes' expression is an idealized one: a powerful, but generalized, expression of the royal ideology that may not apply to one specific episode or place. We cannot say that Xerxes did not specifically apply these sentiments to one or more of his conquests, but we also cannot find evidence that the compulsory worship of Ahuramazda was instituted anywhere.

Xerxes' *dahyāva*-list (XPh §3, see Figure 6.2, p. 97) is notable as the longest such list on record. Unlike the general east-west arrangement (from the center, Parsa) found in Darius' lists, there is no clear rationale for the order given in XPh. We do not know the exact date of this inscription. If it was commissioned after Xerxes' failed invasion of Greece (480–479 BCE), there is no acknowledgement of any loss of territory. From the ideological perspective, we should not expect to find one. The Greeks by the sea and beyond the sea are listed. There are two new *dahyāva* here as well: the Dahae of Central Asia and the Akaufaka, whose location is unknown. We cannot track the historicity of these conquests, but it is not an accident that Xerxes' list is longer. Regardless of the impact of the Greek campaign, Xerxes had to develop his father's territorial dominion further. The ideology demanded it of the king, "the expander of the realm" – a traditional concept in Near Eastern royal ideology and an actual title used by some Elamite kings. It is notable that Xerxes' *dahyāva*-list is the last extant. Whether it is a matter of not having found one from subsequent kings, or whether the formal presentation of a list was later deemed no longer necessary, is unclear. Some scholars would correlate the latter possibility with a cessation of Persian expansionism after Xerxes – an assessment that matches our (thin) extant record, and makes perfect sense within that record, but one that in the end cannot be currently confirmed.

XERXES AND THE INVASION OF GREECE – SOURCES
AND PROBLEMS

The Persian invasion of Greece in 480–479 BCE is one of the most readily identifiable sequences in both Achaemenid Persian and Greek history. Our image of Achaemenid Persia is usually one of a tyrannical enemy that unleashed an overwhelming onslaught against the freedom-loving Greeks, who, because of their society's values and virtues, were able to defeat them. This is the stereotypical view, one as indebted to modern recasting of that historical sequence as it is to the Greek tradition itself. Herodotus wrote roughly two generations after the invasion, and his first six (of nine total) books build toward the cataclysmic confrontation. His account is suffused with cautionary tales of hubris and imperial overreach. Despite all the necessary caveats and qualifications – foremost among which is that we have no Persian sources whatsoever for the invasion – there is no doubt that Xerxes' invasion of Greece and the Greeks' reaction to it marked a turning point in the history of the western world. Some hyperbole is inevitable for such a momentous historical event.

According to Herodotus, when Darius died in 486 BCE, Xerxes took on the responsibility of retribution against Athens for their involvement in the Ionian revolt. After handling the more pressing problems in Egypt and Babylon (see discussion earlier in this chapter), Xerxes was able to turn his attention to a full-scale invasion of Greece. Herodotus relates that the preparations for this campaign, the assembling of manpower as well as the necessary supplies and logistical support, took four years. These preparations tell us as much about Persian military and administrative logistics as does the invasion itself – at least from a Greek perspective.

With his sense of drama, Herodotus sets the decision to invade Greece in a gripping debate at the Persian court. Mardonius, whom Darius sent on campaign to Thrace in the 490s, exhorts Xerxes to punish Athens, to finish the job that stalled in 490 at Marathon (7.5–6). Herodotus also includes a cast of Greek characters lobbying the King: Athenian exiles, aristocrats from northern Greece seeking support, and the exiled Spartan king, Demaratus. In contrast to Mardonius' headstrong and selfish motivation for glory, Xerxes' uncle Artabanus sounds notes of caution, but

Xerxes' ominous dreams forewarn him of disaster if he does not invade. As intimated by Herodotus during this lengthy excursus (7.12–19), even the gods impel the doomed Xerxes toward his fate.[5]

A military campaign understood as retribution fits nicely with Persian royal ideology, and that is generally how Darius' expedition against Marathon is interpreted. Xerxes' invasion was on a larger scale, and that retribution as the sole motivator seems unlikely, even if it may have been the main one. Persian campaigns in southeastern Europe and the Aegean Islands during Darius' reign foreshadowed Persian expansion in this region, and Xerxes' campaign may well have been a logical outgrowth of Persian expansionism. Mardonius' argumentation rings true that it was critical for the King to display his power: the overwhelming spectacle of the King's forces in full pageantry, the King receiving tribute and homage from subjects both old and new.

The scale of Xerxes' army arrayed against Greece, as relayed by Herodotus (7.184–187), defies reality. By the numbers: 277,610 men on 1,207 warships; 240,000 men on 3,000 transport ships; 1,700,000 infantry; 100,000 cavalry and charioteers; along with 300,000 men drafted from the Empire's European territories, who joined the expedition en route. This gives a grand total of 2,617,610 combatants, and Herodotus does not count the camp followers and other peripheral elements. Even if these numbers were factors of ten – assuming a tenfold exaggeration – the numbers still are too high for effective logistics. On the other hand, the greater the numbers of these "barbarian hordes" the greater and more glorious the Greek victory that Herodotus describes. With such wildly exaggerated numbers, it is no wonder that the motif of the army drinking rivers dry runs through Herodotus and later Classical accounts. Modern estimates range from 50,000 to 200,000 for the army and from 500 to 1,000 for the navy, and most realistic assessments tend toward the lower side of these ranges. Occasional references by Herodotus' younger contemporary Thucydides also support a lower number. Thucydides' work chronicles the war between Athens and Sparta in the late fifth century. Thucydides periodically mentions Xerxes' invasion, mainly in rhetorical contexts. But there is a common theme in these references. Thucydides points to the Persians' mistakes and their relatively small numbers as the main reasons why the invasion did not succeed.

Some other elements of Greek historiography must be mentioned here. The term "Persian Wars" is a label that reflects a Greek perspective. In any context that emphasizes a Persian perspective, a reversal seems more appropriate: the "Greek wars" or something to that effect. Also, Herodotus, Thucydides, and several other Classical writers refer to the Persians as "barbarians." This terminology, read at a superficial level in English translation, lies at the root of no shortage of misapprehension and stereotyping. The Greek term *barbaros*, whence the English term "barbarian," initially was used to refer to anyone who was not Greek, and who when speaking made sounds – to Greek ears – only like "bar-bar-bar-bar …" in other words, nonsense. From this the Greeks created the onomatopoeic word *barbaros*. In some Greek writings, the word certainly carried (and was meant to carry) a negative stereotype. The Greeks, ethnocentric as anyone else in that day, believed non-Greeks to be inherently inferior. But such a value judgment depends on one's perspective. The Persians were highly advanced, heirs to and innovators in civilizations that predated the Greeks by centuries. In any event, the Persians probably held similar views about the "barbarous" Greeks, the *Yauna* – differentiated only by geography and occasionally by their hats – to the Persians an insignificant, but troublesome, people on the far-flung edge of their empire.

MEDISM

Another important issue of terminology involves the Greek phenomenon of Medism. This term and its varying manifestations as verb and noun – "to Medize," "to go over to the Mede," "Medizer," etc. – referred to Greeks or others who supported the Persians, either by offering tokens of submission (earth and water) or by outright support. The term might apply whether the "Medizing" was compelled or voluntary. This is common but somewhat curious phraseology throughout the Classical accounts: we are dealing with Persians, of course, not Medes, though the latter were subjects of the Persian Empire. So, why "Medize" instead of "Persianize"? Scholars have struggled with this issue for a long time, and explanations vary.[6] Did the Greeks simply not differentiate between the culturally and linguistically related Medes and Persians? Did the Greeks simply see the Persian Empire as a continuation of the Median? Even though Herodotus uses the term "Medism" and its variants throughout his work, he clearly distinguishes the two peoples. One piece of evidence comes from a poet named Xenophanes, from the Ionian city of Colophon. Xenophanes was born circa 570 BCE and lived during both Lydian and Persian domination – or, as expressed in the following fragment – the Median domination.[7]

Such are the things to discuss by the fire in winter while reclining on a soft couch, well-fed, drinking sweet wine, snacking on seeds: Who are you, and from where among men? How many years have passed you by, good man? How old were you when the Mede came?

This is one of our earliest references to the Persian conquest of Ionia. Why does Xenophanes attribute it to "the Mede"? It is good to recall here that after the conquest of Lydia, according to Herodotus' account, Cyrus turned over operations in Anatolia to Mazares and then to Harpagus (see pp. 41–42). These two Medes must have left an impression. If they commanded Median (or even primarily Median) forces, it was thus the Median troops who conquered Ionia, even though they did it under Persian auspices. The conquered Ionians may not have given such distinctions high priority, at least not at first. Questions about the origins of the term "Medism" are certainly more complex, but in this early usage we find some explanation for the use of the term to designate the Persians.

EARTH AND WATER

Another recurrent motif in Herodotus is the Persian demand for earth and water as tokens of submission to the King. We find such requests first during Darius I's reign: made of the Scythians (4.126–132), of the Macedonians (5.18), and of the Athenian embassy to Artaphernes in 507 BCE (see p. 84), and especially in conjunction with the campaign that culminated in the Battle of Marathon in 490 BCE. Before that expedition, Darius sent heralds throughout Greece to ask for earth and water (Hdt. 6.48). There were not many city-states that refused. The implication is that the mere refusal to a formal request for earth and

water put one at odds with the King and that in itself demanded retribution. According to Herodotus' account, those Persian heralds sent
to Athens were thrown into a pit for condemned criminals, and those
visiting Sparta into a well, and they were told that they could seek their
earth and water there.

Before his campaign, Xerxes made the same request of Greek city-
states. Herodotus provides a list of specific city-states that offered earth
and water to Xerxes (7.132). The list cannot be specifically correlated
with the city-states submitting to Darius: no specific city-states are
named in that passage (6.48). When Xerxes sent out heralds before
his campaign, he purposely neglected sending them to either Athens
or Sparta because of their mistreatment of Darius' heralds. It seems a
safe assumption that a large number of city-states gave earth and water
to Darius and again to Xerxes some ten years later, but this is unverifiable. By the time Herodotus wrote, there was likely a fair amount of
revisionist history among some states about their fortitude in resisting
the Persians in 480.

The full significance of the giving of earth and water, especially
the symbolism associated with the actual elements themselves, is yet
debated. Were they meant to represent Persian possession of the (now
formally subject) territory? Was there some religious significance to
these elements? The request for earth and water appears closely tied to
Achaemenid imperial ideology, but its meanings for both parties, and
especially for the King, is harder to grasp. In context, it was clearly meant
as one ritual to establish the trustworthiness and loyalty of the contract-
ing party to the King.[8] But what specific obligations did it entail? That
is harder to answer. With the first evidence for such requests dating to
Darius' reign, one cannot help but be tempted to apply some religious
significance to earth and water in an early Zoroastrian, or Mazdaean,
context.

The Greek city-states that complied with the request acknowledged
the king's superiority in exchange for his protection and patronage. It is
notable that requests for earth and water disappear from the sources after
Xerxes' invasion – perhaps such requests were linked only to acquisition
of new territory – and with Persian expansion beyond the Aegean mostly
thwarted after 479. But Persian influence, in theory if not in applicable
practice, swept through much of Greece in the early fourth century, yet

no requests for earth and water are recorded in the sources we have for that period of Artaxerxes II's diplomatic triumph in 387/386 BCE (pp. 185–188). To assert that submission of earth and water was no longer relevant after Xerxes risks what historians call an argument from silence: simply because the sources do not mention a phenomenon does not mean that the phenomenon did not occur. Also curious, Herodotus preserves a fair amount of information from the reigns of Cyrus and Cambyses, both of whom were active in Ionia and the Aegean. Yet not once were either of these kings in Herodotus' account associated with requests of earth and water from conquered or potential subjects. If Cyrus or Cambyses requested it, it is a striking omission in Herodotus' account, but the perils of an argument from silence apply here also.

THE INVASION OF GREECE

Preparations for Xerxes' campaign, a display of Persian might and grandeur as much as a military expedition, were extensive. The force needed supplies, and earlier campaigns against Thrace, which also brought Macedon into the Empire, offered numerous depots for provisions along the planned route. A great pontoon bridge was constructed over the Hellespont at Abydos, a span that Herodotus measured at almost a mile. The first bridge was destroyed by a storm, and here Xerxes' hubris was put on display. The Hellespont was whipped and branded – branding served as a mark of ownership – with Xerxes ordering the following curse (7.35): "O Bitter Water, your Master, who has done you no wrong, inflicts this punishment upon you. But King Xerxes will cross you, whether you will it or not. It is right that no one among men sacrifices to you, a foul and bitter river."

The Phoenician and Egyptian engineers responsible for the first pontoon bridge were beheaded. The second bridging attempt was successful; one might note that the second group of engineers clearly had greater motivation to make the second bridge sturdier. How much of this is apocryphal and literary is impossible to discern. Among other possibilities: the whipping of the Hellespont may have been a ritual misconstrued by the Greeks.[9] Smaller bodies of rivers, for example the River Strymon in Thrace, also needed bridging en route. A far more

involved work of engineering took place at the easternmost finger of
the Chalcidian peninsula in the northern Aegean, the site of Mt. Athos.
There a canal was dug, roughly a mile and three-quarters long, the work
on which took three years according to Herodotus (7.22–24). He attributes one impetus for its construction to Mardonius' fleet having been
previously wrecked off Mt. Athos in 492 BCE and another to Xerxes'
wish (in his arrogance, of course) to leave a monument to his power –
rather than to rely on the more sensible plan of dragging the ships
across the isthmus instead. Arrogance perhaps, but Herodotus' cari-
cature of Xerxes here offers little historical insight. Kings frequently
expressed their piety – if not their egos – through monuments and
other construction works, and a parallel to the Mt. Athos project may
be found in Darius' work at Suez in Egypt (see p. 80). Practicality and
vanity are not necessarily mutually exclusive.

Infantry and naval forces were summoned from throughout the
Empire, and we may readily visualize royal dispatches requesting troops
and provisions according to each individual satrap's means. The forces
mustered in Cappadocia (southern Anatolia), with the infantry then
moving along the road through Phrygia to Sardis in Lydia. From there,
the road led to the Hellespont, at which point Xerxes himself offered
sacrifices in person. After crossing the Hellespont, the forces reassembled again at Doriscus, one of the Persian depots in southern Thrace.
Herodotus' detailed account gives the names of many of the commanders and delineates the individual ethnic contingents, highlighting their
appearance and equipment and the splendor of their jewelry and fine
clothing, especially of the Persians themselves (7.61–100). Such prestige items were not worn for their effectiveness in battle but were marks
of honor within the royal system.

The mere passing of such a host was memorable in itself, as revealed
by Herodotus' precise itinerary and the occasional aside, for example,
that the Thracians still held Xerxes' path in reverence during his time
(7.115). Much of Herodotus' account focuses on Xerxes as a tourist,
marveling for example at a particularly impressive gorge (7.128–130).
These vivid descriptions permitted Herodotus the ethnographer to
flourish in his own element. Herodotus juxtaposed his descriptions of
Xerxes' leisurely approach with divine omens that consistently prophesied certain doom for the expedition – just as he had done previously

with his portrayals of Cyrus and the Massagetae, Cambyses and the Ethiopians, and Darius and the Scythians. The themes of hubris and imperial overreach are everywhere; the Persians are, once again, violating the natural order of things. So masterfully is this arranged, one tends to forget that Herodotus was imposing his artistry on a historical event. None of the preceding should be taken to imply that this was not a serious campaign, even at greatly reduced estimates of the numbers involved. Of primary concern here is gauging Persian aims and perspectives and, where possible, gauging the Greek response as the Persians saw it. (See Map 5.1 for the progression of Xerxes' army.)

Once the Greeks decided to hold the strategic pass of Thermopylae in northern Greece, the first line of battle had been drawn. It was here that Xerxes' hammer would fall, accompanied by an attack on the Greek naval forces at nearby Artemisium. Thermopylae was well-suited for defense by a small number of men, in the end somewhere between 3,000 and 4,000, most famously the 300 Spartans who fought to the death under one of their kings, Leonidas. The narrow pass by the sea offered a bottleneck that would need to be forced. According to Herodotus, Xerxes' best troops were singularly ineffective despite multiple attempts (7.210–212): Medes, Elamites (Cissians), even the Immortals were repelled. The Greek forces had chosen well. Unable to force the passage head-on, Xerxes seized on an offer of treachery by a man named Ephialtes, a local Greek: to lead the Persians around the pass by way of an obscure mountain trail. By sending a force around the pass, the Persians were able to trap the remaining Greek forces, mainly Spartans, who fought to the finish while the others retreated.

This is one of the most celebrated battles in the western tradition, one that became equated with self-sacrifice and heroism, the stand of free men against tyranny. It has been told and retold countless times. And all retellings are indebted to Herodotus. Some take more liberties than others and add to an already weighty legend, with the result that the truth becomes even harder to discern. The symbolism and significance attached to the battle make it easy to forget that the pass was indeed forced. From the Persian perspective, Thermopylae was a victory. Despite heavy (exaggerated?) losses at sea, the Persians triumphed at Artemisium as well. That engagement is described in less detail by Herodotus. The Persians won mainly after news from Thermopylae

arrived: once the Persians had gained the pass there was no point for
the Greek fleet to wait there anymore, so they departed. These victories
opened the road to southern Greece for the Persian army. The Greeks
were not unified even at this point. Among those who chose to fight,
members of the so-called Hellenic League (most prominently Sparta
and Athens), there were incessant arguments over who would hold command and other strategic matters. Many Greek city-states, especially in
the north, medized: some by choice, others by necessity. The oracle of
Delphi had been depressingly pessimistic about the Greeks' chances;
careful and calculating, it operated on the assumption of a Persian
victory.

With Xerxes bearing down on southern Greece, many of the fis-
sures between city-states became more pronounced. The Spartans and
other Peloponnesians who yet fought argued strenuously that all their
efforts should be applied to defense of the Isthmus of Corinth, the narrow stretch of land that connected the Peloponnesian peninsula to the
rest of Greece. Many of the allies were unhappy with such a strategy.
Herodotus alludes to construction of a wall across the isthmus, fortifications to defend against a possible Persian attack there, but no archaeological evidence for such a wall has ever been found. Time and again,
characters in Herodotus' work offer Xerxes advice: Demaratus urges
Xerxes to exploit the Spartans (7.235); Artemisia advises him to ignore
Salamis and focus on the Peloponnese (8.68); the Thebans desired to use
Persian financial resources to encourage factional strife among Greek
city-states (9.2). Had Xerxes followed any of these courses he would
have caused a complete rupture among his enemies. These anecdotes are
also difficult to interpret. Are these accurate renderings of strategic considerations (however such may have been transmitted to Herodotus)?
Or are they simply manifestations of Greek hindsight common in the
later fifth century?

Athens remained the main goal of the expedition. Once the remaining city-states of Boeotia – on Xerxes' direct route toward Athens –
had medized (8.34), there was nothing to stop the Persians. The
Athenians decided to abandon their city, and the people removed from
Athens across the Saronic Gulf to Troezen and some of the nearby
islands, including Aegina and Salamis, the site of the later decisive
naval battle. The Persians sacked Athens and plundered and burned

its sanctuaries upon the acropolis (8.53). This act was cast as retribution for Athenian involvement in the Ionian revolt and the burning of Sardis. We may assume, if the Persians believed that the Athenians had formally entered into a treaty relationship with them – because of the offering of earth and water made in Sardis in 507 BCE – that this sack was also understood in Persian ideological terms as due punishment for a recalcitrant vassal. Herodotus emphasizes the significance of this victory to Xerxes by noting that he sent a special messenger to Susa to relay the good news to Artabanus, his uncle and regent (8.54). Athens was his.

The naval battle at Salamis in September 480 proved a turning point in the invasion. Herodotus attributes the Greek victory to the Athenian admiral Themistocles' tenacity and trickery. His manipulation of his Greek allies to fight in the narrow strait gave advantage to the Greek triremes, fast and maneuverable ships with metal bows for ramming. Themistocles sent a slave to feign desertion and convince Xerxes that the Greeks were about to disperse, and Xerxes was thus led to believe that the opportune moment was at hand. Xerxes' decision to attack played right into Themistocles' stratagem: to force the Persians to fight in the narrow and shallow waters that favored the Greek ships' maneuverability and speed over the more cumbersome ships in the Persian fleet. The clandestine, false message tricking the Great King makes great theater, but is it accurate? There is no way to know. Similarly, when Herodotus attributes the heavy Persian losses also to the Persian crews' inability to swim (8.89) we must ponder the likely interplay between fact, stereotype, and anecdote. The Greek victory may be attributed to superior tactics or Persian ineptitude (or both, as per 8.86). In such contexts, it is useful to recall the historian Thucydides' comments (e.g., 1.69 and 6.33) that it was Persian mistakes and misfortune that ultimately decided the day.

Xerxes watched the Battle of Salamis accompanied by scribes who wrote down the names of those who fought valiantly and otherwise. This too may seem anecdotal, but we do have references to Assyrian scribes of the seventh century tracking such details of battles, so that fitting rewards might be distributed thereafter. In this case there is a historical parallel that supports Herodotus' depiction. The Greek tradition suggests that the defeat at Salamis broke Xerxes. Herodotus tracks

him and his escort making an ignoble retreat to Sardis, abandoning
royal implements (such as the King's sacred chariot), and at times eat-
ing the bark off trees in their plight. Yet it is clear that more than one
version of Xerxes' withdrawal was available to Herodotus (cf. 8.115 and
8.118), which implies that at least two versions – likely more – were yet
circulating in the later fifth century. Furthermore, Xerxes left behind a
picked force under Mardonius to continue the campaign, so a pell-mell
withdrawal is hard to credit.[10] In the end, we do not know what motivated Xerxes to depart, but a significant Persian force stayed in Greece
for almost a year thereafter, with logistical support and aid from Greek
vassals and allies.

Mardonius encamped in Thessaly and the military maneuvering continued. The Greek fleet's attempts to separate some Aegean Islands from
the Persian cause, or to compel money from them for the war effort, met
with mixed results. Much time remains unaccounted for between late
fall of 480 and summer of 479. Herodotus and other sources offer little information for this critical interlude. Possibly the Peloponnesians
continued work on the wall across the isthmus (9.7–8). In the summer
of 479 Athens was again evacuated, before Mardonius invaded it a second time. Mardonius had previously sent Alexander I of Macedon (an
ancestor of Alexander the Great of the fourth century), a Persian subject
and friend of Athens, with an offer to the Athenians to join the Persian
side with no further penalty: resistance, Alexander said, was futile. But
he was rebuffed (8.143). The Athenians used this offer to compel the
Spartans, who were still trusting in their isthmus wall, to assist them
rather than watch the Athenians medize.

Once Mardonius had sacked Athens a second time, destroying all
that he could, he withdrew to Thebes: a friendly (medizing) territory
and a place more suited to Persian cavalry. The next and main infantry
engagement of the war took place at nearby Plataea. Herodotus attributes the Greek victory here to Greek superiority in armor: the hoplite
panoply versus light-armed soldiers on the Persian side. It is generally granted that there is some truth to this assessment, but we know
that not all Persian troops were light-armed. There is not enough data,
despite Herodotus' catalog of the Persian force en route to Greece, to
discern the facts. The clash at Plataea resulted in the death of several

noble Persians and of Mardonius himself, at which point the remainder of the Persian army under Artabazus withdrew from Greece. As tradition has it, on the very same day in late August 479 the Greeks also won a significant victory at Mycale in Ionia, considered by Herodotus proof that divine favor was supporting the Greek cause. The Persian navy was defeated at sea and, when the remnants disembarked on the beach, they were defeated there as well (9.99–102).

The Greek repulsion of Persian forces from Greece was the beginning, not the end, of the matter. Ionia immediately revolted again (9.104), and much of the rest of the fifth century saw shifting in the strategic situation on the Persians' far northwestern frontier. It was no longer an uncontested region but one in which the Persians were constantly forced to defend their territories and react against Athenian-led aggressiveness. On the other hand, the development of Athenian power was confined mainly to the Aegean world and occurred in the context of a constant Persian threat. In the immediate aftermath of Xerxes' defeat, it was more than a hypothetical question. Were the Persians going to come back? The frenetic military activity in the Hellespont and Ionia during the early 470s was not only for "Greek liberty" but should be viewed through a strategic lens as well: the projection of Athenian power and influence, and control of territory, was as much to create a buffer zone as it was for any imperialistic pretensions. The Hellespont was an Athenian lifeline; it was the main supply route that fed Athens – literally, as the main sea lane for via grain imports from the Black Sea region – as the fifth century progressed. Athenian military activity not only served their economic and political interests but also enabled them to challenge Persian control in that region and, if necessary, forestall any further Persian advances into Europe.

While Xerxes' defeat certainly imposed new challenges for the Persians in the northwest, we discern no impact on the Empire in its integrity or its stability. Some previous scholarly treatments attribute the downfall of Persia to Xerxes' defeat. But that "downfall" was 150 years in the making and, when cast in such terms, nonsense. Salamis, Plataea, and Mycale were not the first Persian setbacks in the field, nor were they the last. Xerxes' defeat in Greece and Alexander the Great's successful conquest of Persia are linked only in propaganda.

Dio Chrysostom, a Greek philosopher and orator of the first century CE, relays that the Persians rejected outright the Greek version of events and had their own take:

Xerxes invaded Greece and on the one hand defeated the Spartans at Thermopylae and killed their king, Leonidas, and on the other hand he captured the city of the Athenians and demolished it, and those who did not escape he sold into slavery. After he accomplished this he imposed tribute on the Greeks and returned to Asia. (11.149)

The reliability of this report must also remain open to question, as has been the case with Herodotus and other accounts datable much closer to the events. But it seems reasonable enough as a Persian perspective – it echoes in outline what one would expect from a royal inscription (such as Bisitun) about a successful campaign. In the final analysis it is correct to view Thermopylae and Artemisium as Persian victories: the Greeks were slaughtered or routed and the Persian advance continued. The punishment of Athens (sacked twice) was one point of the campaign, and Xerxes could view that mission as accomplished.

THE AEGEAN FRONT AND THE ATHENIAN PROBLEM

After the Battle of Mycale and into the year 478 BCE, Greek forces moved to push their advantage in Ionia and even to challenge Persian control in Cyprus. Initial Greek success in securing the Hellespont was soon bogged down by concerns and complaints about the Spartan general Pausanias, the leader of the expedition who had become flush with his own success and power and who, according to several sources, even made friendly overtures to Xerxes. This sort of treachery no doubt continued to feed concerns of another Persian expedition. The Spartans, always conservative and distrustful of foreign ventures, recalled Pausanias and gave way to Athenian leadership for the next phase.

The formation of what was initially called the "Delian League" was thus dominated by Athens, the League's premier power in terms of size and number of ships. The league took its name from the island of Delos, the original home to the league treasury until it was moved to Athens in 454. Under Athenian leadership, the League coerced several city-states in Ionia and southwestern Anatolia, in the territories of Caria and Lycia, to join them. These were Persian-held territories, and members of the League from those regions were, in effect, considered rebels by the King. There is no evidence that the Persians ever relinquished claim upon these territories.

Attacks against Persian interests and forts in the Hellespont and Thrace also were a high Greek priority. Herodotus preserves record of a Persian named Mascames, in charge of the important Persian staging point of Doriscus; he was highly honored by the King because no one was able to dislodge him. The implication is that Doriscus continued to be controlled by the Persians, an ongoing thorn in the side of Athenian military activities in this region. Another Persian, Boges, was lauded by the King for his bravery and sacrifice. Boges was the commander of a Persian fort at Eion (along the Strymon River in southern Thrace) who fought to the bitter end and committed suicide rather than be caught in failure (7.106–107). The high point of Athenian aggression came in the early 460s BCE, when Athenian forces won successive victories over Persian naval and infantry sources at Eurymedon in southern Anatolia. But any Athenian designs eastward were short-lived. The Delian League did not have the cohesion or resources to sustain a challenge to the Persian Empire on a broad scale.

Beyond these moves and countermoves in the Aegean – again, all traceable only from Greek sources – we know little of the rest of Xerxes' reign. A terse reference in a Babylonian astronomical tablet refers to the death of Xerxes at the hands of his son; the killer's name is not given. Details are not divulged in such texts, but there is no shortage of innuendo from Greek sources.

8 Anatomy of Empire

ROYAL CAPITALS

An empire of such scope as the Achaemenid Persian Empire could hardly have just one capital. The Persian kings had five, all in the center of the Empire (Map 8.1). Four straddled the Zagros mountain chain – Pasargadae and Persepolis in Fars (Parsa), Susa in Khuzistan, and Ecbatana in Media – and the fifth, Babylon, near modern Baghdad. Only the first two were new cities, founded by Cyrus and Darius, respectively, though not completed in their reigns. Susa and Babylon were centuries old. Susa is prominent in the Classical sources, but whether it was the capital at which the kings spent much of their time, or whether it was simply the horizon of most Greek experience, is unclear. Greek and Roman-era descriptions of these cities focus on the wealth and opulence of the King and his court. Few state archives from the capitals have been found; the main exception, the Persepolis Treasury and Fortification tablets, were discussed in Chapter 6. The main capital was, of course, wherever the King and his court happened to be at a given moment. They may have moved as much for the climate as for other reasons, such as the King's required involvement in certain rituals. Susa or Babylon in the low-lying plains appealed during the winter, Ecbatana in the mountains was attractive during the summer. The court on parade was a spectacle in itself, an awesome display of the splendor of the King, and this was no doubt one of the desired results.

Ecbatana

Ecbatana is the modern city of Hamadan, and large scale excavations there are impossible. The apparent capital of the Medes, it fell to the

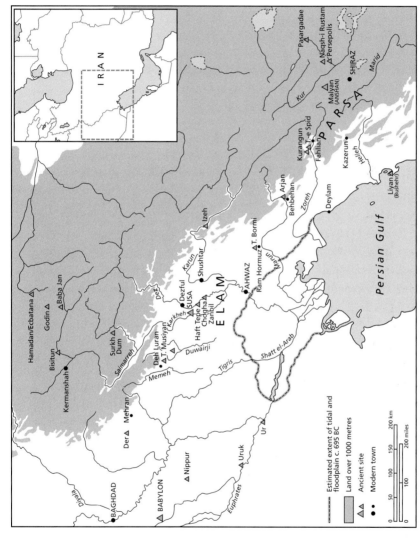

Map 8.1 Map of Western Iran and Mesopotamia, with Persian Capitals. After J. Álvarez-Mon, *The Arjān Tomb*, Plate 2 and P. de Miroschedji, "Susa and the Highlands," figure. 3.1.

Persians with Cyrus' conquest of Astyages. Its location astride the major east-west trade route in northwestern Iran (the forerunner of the Silk Road) attests to its strategic importance. Herodotus' description of Median Ecbatana seems mainly imaginative:

> [Ecbatana's] walls were built so that each circuit is higher than the one that circles it by the height of its ramparts ... There are seven circuits in all, within the last one are the palace and the treasuries. The largest of the walls is about the size of the wall around Athens. The ramparts of all the walls are painted in colors: those of the first circuit are white, while those of the second black, of the third purple, of the fourth blue, and of the fifth orange. But the final two walls have plated ramparts, one in silver, the other in gold. (Hdt. 1.98)

Ctesias attributes the legendary queen Semiramis with supplying irrigation works for the city. (Fragment F1b = DS 2.13.6). Despite the lack of excavation, a number of objects purportedly from Hamadan have circulated in modern museums, though whether that locale was the actual findspot or not is open to question. The tagline "from Hamadan" has been a favorite for illegally excavated materials (from whatever region in Iran) and, in some cases, forgeries.[1]

Babylon

Babylon had been an important city since the eighteenth century BCE and the time of King Hammurabi, he of the famous law code. It was the dominant city of southern Mesopotamia during most of the first millennium, the intellectual and cultural capital of the region. Babylon had undergone massive rebuilding during the Neo-Babylonian period, especially under King Nebuchadnezzar II in the early sixth century, and these remains dominate the excavated sections. Most of the Classical sources about the early Achaemenid kings and Babylon deal with conquest and revolt of the city, but it was fully incorporated into the Empire and served as a focal point for the blending of Persian and Babylonian traditions. The Achaemenid kings supported many of the important cults and shrines there, and they recognized the strategic and symbolic importance of the city. Darius II and his queen, Parysatis, had Babylonian mothers, and we have important evidence about the estates held in that region by many members of the Persian nobility during the late fifth and early fourth centuries (see pp. 168–171).

Susa

There is no evidence for major Achaemenid-period works at Susa before Darius I, but the magnitude of Achaemenid construction at Susa reflects its importance as a focal point of imperial expression. A number of inscriptions testify to Darius' building activities there, especially his great palace and the adjoining *apadana* (an Old Persian word often translated as "audience hall"); they offer many parallels to earlier Mesopotamian rulers' inscriptions, including the Cyrus Cylinder from Babylon. Darius aligned himself with that earlier tradition: his building and restoration works are contextualized with his establishment of order and the right to rule.

Darius the King proclaims: much that was out of place I put right. The lands were in an uproar, one was battling another. That which I have done I accomplished by the favor of Ahuramazda: one no longer battles another, each one is in its place. It is my law that they fear, so that the strong neither oppresses nor overpowers the weak. Darius the King proclaims: By the favor of Ahuramazda, there was much construction work done before which was in need of attention. That I accomplished.[2] (DSe §4–5)

An idealized version of the Empire emerges at Susa, in the roster of subject peoples assigned specific tasks in the (re)building efforts. The so-called foundation charter (DSf) from Susa survives in dozens of fragments of the original trilingual inscription. Groups of subject peoples are associated with a particular raw material or skill: Assyrians and Babylonian transported cedar timbers from Lebanon, Lydians and Bactrians brought gold, Sogdians (from the northeast) brought lapis lazuli, and several others are mentioned.

Pasargadae

In the tradition of previous conquerors, Cyrus founded a new capital, one with aspirations that matched his new world empire: Pasargadae (Elamite *Bakratatash*). Pasargadae is located in Fars, on a plain surrounded by high mountains. Herodotus, in his list of the six Persian tribes (1.125), describes the Pasargadae tribe as the noblest, a distant echo of the city's site and significance. The Greek geographer Strabo describes the site's importance to Cyrus:

Cyrus held Pasargadae in honor, because there he defeated Astyages the Mede in the final battle, transferred the rule of Asia to himself, founded a city, and built a palace as memorial to his victory. (15.3.8)

Archaeological work at Pasargadae has revealed the grandeur of the site, though the excavated remains make up only a portion of the whole settled area. The main features include two palaces, an elaborate gate, and a garden area. The chronology of Cyrus' building activity here is uncertain; there have been no archives yet found from Pasargadae that allow chronological demarcation. The capital was far from complete when Cyrus died, and construction continued there into the reign of Darius.

The remains at Pasargadae testify to Cyrus' willingness to adopt from his predecessors and neighbors, to make something uniquely Persian. Among many examples, the most striking is the famous guardian figure from a gateway in Palace R: a hybrid figure wearing an Elamite garment, with Assyrian-type wings and an Egyptian triple crown (Figure 8.1). This figure is stunning in its execution, symbolism, and internationalism. The inclusion of the Egyptian headdress is curious, because Cyrus did not conquer Egypt; perhaps the figure was finished or refashioned in the time of Cambyses or even Darius. Drawings of the guardian figure from the nineteenth century show a copy of an inscription attributed to Darius (labeled CMa in modern works, see discussion later in this chapter), the implication being that he finished those pieces or added the inscription subsequently.

Outside the central complex are two structures of note. One is a square tower roughly 275 yards to the northeast of the central complex. The tower, called the Zendan-i-Suleiman (the "Prison of Solomon"), is nearly 46 feet tall, and its purpose is uncertain. The other is Cyrus' plain but elegant tomb, roughly a half mile southwest of the palace complex (Figure 8.2). Cyrus' tomb itself measures roughly 44 feet by 40 feet and has a sloped roof, approximately 40 feet off the ground. The tomb sits on a monumental stepped platform of six tiers that calls to mind not only the stepped pyramids of Egypt but also, and more directly,

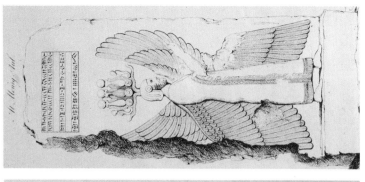

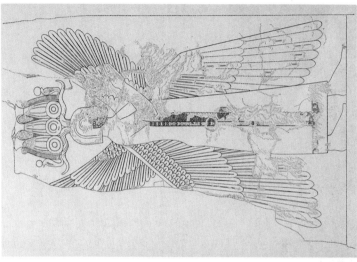

Figures 8.1a-c Winged Guardian Genius, Pasargadae. Figures 8a and 8b courtesy of David Stronach. Figure 8c from Sir Robert Ker Porter, *Travels in Georgia, Persia, Armenia, Ancient Babylonia*, Vol. I, 1821, opposite p. 492.

Figure 8.2 Tomb of Cyrus, Pasargadae. Photo courtesy of David Stronach.

the ziggurats (temple towers) in Mesopotamia and Elam. Tombs with similar tiers have been found elsewhere in Fars and even in Lydia and western Anatolia.

Already we see in Pasargadae's impressive garden and integrative sculptures parts of the new Persian vision. The Persians became renowned in particular for their gardens (Greek *paradeisoi*). Pasargadae also held an important place in a royal coronation ritual linked to the founder Cyrus. The Greek writer Plutarch reports (*Life of Artaxerxes* 3.1–2) on a royal rite administered by Persian priests, in which the King entered the sanctuary of the warrior goddess and donned the clothing that Cyrus wore before he became king. The new king then ate a cake of figs and some bitter leaves of a terebinth tree, and drank a bowl of sour milk. Plutarch implies there was more to the ritual, unknown to outsiders. The significance of these foods and their consumption in this context is unclear – perhaps a reminder of earlier, humbler days – but the link with Cyrus is telling. The ritual was clearly meant to establish the new king's connection with and continuity from the first ruler of their world empire. Despite being overshadowed by Persepolis, Pasargadae retained its importance.

Persepolis

Persepolis is Greek for Old Persian *Parsa* (Elamite *Parsha*), a word that could refer to the city itself and the surrounding region. Located roughly 20 miles southwest of Pasargadae and 30 miles east of Anshan, Persepolis dominated its portion of the Marv Dasht plain in Fars. When one speaks of Persepolis today, the reference point is usually the terrace, a complex of buildings raised on a platform (the walls of which are roughly 40 feet high) that covered 30 acres. It included monumental gates, the treasury, palaces, the so-called Harem, the Hall of 100 Columns (the Throne Hall), and the Apadana.

Much of the construction of the Persepolis terrace was initiated during Darius' reign, with significant portions added or completed by Xerxes and Artaxerxes I (Figure 8.3). Other evidence of buildings in the vicinity suggests urban areas and construction that occurred before Darius' reign. For example, 2.5 miles from the terrace were found the remains of foundations for a columned palace and platform, the Takht-i Rustam ("the throne of Rustam" – an Iranian hero), which shares structural elements similar to the base of the tomb of Cyrus. Persepolis was both an administrative and ceremonial center, a focal point for the King's displays of the royal ideology and of the scope and grandeur of Persian power. It is the enduring symbol of the Achaemenid legacy.

Diodorus Siculus provides vivid description of the city in context of describing Alexander the Great's sack of it in 330 BCE, an excerpt of which follows:

[Persepolis] ... was the richest city of all those under the sun and the private houses had been filled with all sorts of wealth accumulated over a long time ... many residences were filled with furniture and decorations of all sorts, much silver and no small amount of gold, loads of extravagant clothing ... its sprawling palaces renowned throughout the world. (17.70.1–3)

The main entrance to the terrace is through the Gate of Xerxes (sometimes called the Gate of All Nations) in the northwest corner, a monumental gate on the pattern of Neo-Assyrian ones from Nineveh and other cities in the eighth and seventh centuries. South of that gate are the main buildings that figure most often in discussions of Persepolis: the Hall of 100 Columns and the Apadana. Each of the four main

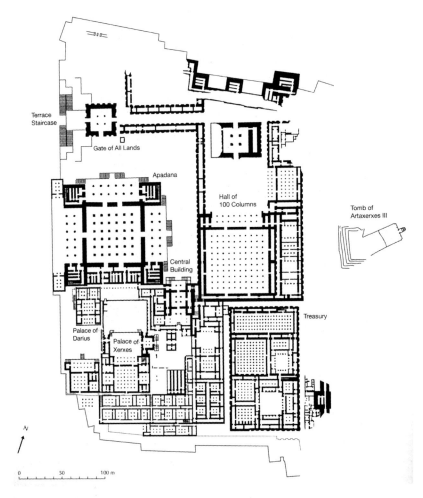

Figure 8.3 Plan of the Persepolis Terrace, courtesy of David Stronach.

doorways to the interior of the Hall portrayed a royal hero figure in combat with an animal – the same motif found elsewhere on the site (Figure 8.4). This image is an age-old apotropaic (i.e., protective) one, where the hero figure wards off the forces of chaos.

Moving south through the Gate of Xerxes one encounters the Apadana. This square hall measured almost 200 feet long on each side with 36 columns supporting a roof that was over 80 feet high. Also remarkable are the sculptures along the north and east staircase facades:

Figure 8.4 Darius as Royal Hero, Persepolis, Palace of Darius. Courtesy of the Oriental Institute of the University of Chicago.

a procession of Persians, Medes, and the subjects of the Empire bearing gifts to the King, a record in ornately sculpted stone representing an actual procession (Figure 8.5).[3] The various peoples of the Empire are led toward the center point, the stairway providing access to the Apadana's columned hall. Each delegation is depicted in that people's distinctive dress, and each delegation bears an offering (Figure 8.6). The delegations are not labeled, but by comparing the characteristics of each with similarly labeled portrayals on other monuments (e.g., those of Darius I's tomb), many are identifiable.

What messages were the portrayals of these subject peoples meant to send? The short-answer is: "many." Unlike their Assyrian predecessors, the Achaemenid kings did not portray in their monumental sculptures the violent subjugation of enemies. With the sole exception being the Bisitun relief of Darius I, subject peoples are not portrayed as humiliated or violently subdued. The message of the Apadana reliefs seems

Figure 8.5 Apadana, North Stairway, Persepolis. Courtesy of the Oriental Institute of the University of Chicago.

Figure 8.6 Scythians in Procession, Apadana, East Stairway, Persepolis. Courtesy of the Oriental Institute of the University of Chicago.

rather one of solidarity or inclusiveness between the King – to whom the procession and the gifts are directed – and his subjects. The nuances may be cast in a multitude of ways, but the underlying message is one of an order established and preserved by a benign king, the agent of Ahuramazda. Not surprisingly or accidentally this matches the rhetoric of the royal inscriptions. Even though the program at Persepolis may have been the most elaborate, its message was clearly not confined to this one place but was propagated throughout the Empire in word, image, and shared customs. There is little doubt that Persepolis is a stunningly effective portrayal of that message. But how successful that message was among the Persians' subjects is another matter. They may well have had an entirely different perspective.

Naqsh-i Rustam

Naqsh-i Rustam (in Persian "the picture of Rustam") is roughly 3.5 miles north of Persepolis. It is not a capital but rather the site of four royal Achaemenid tombs and the Ka'ba-i Zardusht ("the cube of Zoroaster"), a structure very similar in shape to the Zendan of Pasargadae. As with the Zendan, the function of the Ka'ba-i Zardusht remains unclear. Naqsh-i Rustam was a sacred place from the time of the Elamites through the Sassanian period; reliefs from each of the successive historical periods may be found there. The name Naqsh-i Rustam stems from the later association between these reliefs and the Iranian hero Rustam, as was the Takht-i Rustam mentioned earlier in this chapter.

At Naqsh-i Rustam the Achaemenid tombs are the main monuments, cut into the rock of the cliffside. One is dated by its inscriptions to Darius I (Figure 8.7). The others are generally attributed to Xerxes, Artaxerxes I, and Darius II. The tomb of Darius I has three registers, or panels, the middle one set roughly 60 feet above the ground. The entrance to the tomb itself is in the middle register, which is sculpted like the façade of an Achaemenid palace. There were three burials within, all empty when excavated in the 1930s CE. The upper register portrays the king on a plinth facing a fire altar (see Figure 1.1). Ahuramazda (the winged disk) hovers over the center of the scene, in the typical pose: the king raises one hand toward the god and in the other holds a bow. To the right of Ahuramazda is the symbol of a crescent moon.

The large platform is flanked on the side walls by reliefs of Persian courtiers. The two foremost among them, on the left side, are labeled: "Gobryas the Pateischorean, the spear-bearer of Darius the King" and "Aspathines, the garment-bearer, holds the bow case of Darius the King."[4] Gobryas is also named as one of Darius' helpers in the

Figure 8.7 Tomb of Darius I, Naqsh-i Rustam. Courtesy of the Oriental Institute of the University of Chicago. See also Figure 1.1.

Bisitun Inscription (§68) and also is prominent in Herodotus' account. Aspathines is not named in the Bisitun Inscription but is named in Herodotus' writings. Their positions are clearly of the highest honor, and the titles they bear likewise, even if their exact court functions are not fully understood. The entire platform is portrayed on the relief as held up by the various subject peoples of the Empire. At first glance this could be construed as a posture of humiliation, but the style in which the figures are portrayed suggests otherwise. Many modern scholars interpret this sculpture, and similar representations of the throne-bearer reliefs at Persepolis, as reflecting an inclusive ideology, one that emphasizes the subject peoples' important role in upholding – figuratively and literally – the King's power and thus the Empire's stability.

Even more, the thirty platform-bearer subjects are labeled by ethnicity, which allows comparisons with other portrayals of subject peoples, where they are not labeled.

ACHAEMENID ROYAL IDEOLOGY

Darius I expressed a cohesive ideology in his inscriptions, his construction works, and his sculptural program – in part to legitimize his newly won throne. This program was so pervasive and effective that it persisted for the remainder of the Achaemenid era, so much so, in fact, that even subtle differences in the formulae attract scholars' notice. Because Achaemenid royal ideology remained virtually unchanged for the next two centuries, it has been at times viewed as static or even stultifying. More recent interpretations of Darius' program, however, focus on its impact, the resounding success of its application.

The Bisitun Inscription served as the blueprint for a new Achaemenid royal ideology. Darius' royal titles and lineage (DB §1–4) give his descent, with emphasis on Achaemenes, for whom the dynasty is named. Darius does not provide his full lineage in subsequent inscriptions. Although he often mentions his father and occasionally his grandfather, he is always an Achaemenid. He also placed great emphasis on being Persian, which is somewhat curious. What else would he be? In two of his inscriptions from Naqsh-i Rustam and Susa (DNa and DSe) there is emphasis on being Iranian (from OP *Ariya*) as well; this emphasis also occurs once in one of Xerxes' inscriptions from Persepolis (XPh). A king's titles and epithets may vary in given contexts, but their use is never random. Some scholars have suggested plausibly that the marker "Iranian" serves to distinguish Iranian speakers from non-Iranian as, for example, when both Persians and Medes are frequently mentioned together in the Bisitun Inscription. This phenomenon is on par with the ethnocentrism one finds in the Greek world and is hardly unique. What is striking about Darius' emphasis is that it differs so markedly from Cyrus' use of the title "King of Anshan," which recalls an Elamite tradition. Darius' emphatic inclusion of his ethnicity may have served to distinguish his heritage, but the data sample is small. We are comparing Darius I's inscriptions from mainly Iranian sites with

Cyrus' inscriptions from strictly Babylonian ones. Further, as discussed previously, after decades (even centuries) of Elamite-Persian acculturation, attempts to strictly delineate between the traditions oversimplifies many complex issues.

Cyrus' capital Pasargadae was not complete when Cyrus died or during Cambyses' reign. Darius added many finishing touches and in doing so took full advantage to co-opt the founder's legacy and to strengthen his own legitimacy. Evidence for this comes mainly from two curious inscriptions found there. It is highly unlikely that Cyrus himself commissioned them, as they were installed near the end of the construction work sometime in the 510s BCE. Multiple copies of the two inscriptions were found on column remains of Palace S and Palace P (Figure 8.8). These trilingual inscriptions were originally attributed to Cyrus because of their content, and they are labeled in the scholarly literature CM for "Cyrus, Murghab" (i.e, a modern name for Pasargadae) with a lowercase letter designating the individual inscriptions.[5]

CMa: I am Cyrus the King, an Achaemenid
CMc: Cyrus the Great King, an Achaemenid

CMc is extant only in Elamite and Akkadian versions, on the garment folds of one of the figures from Palace P, but it is generally assumed that there was an Old Persian version as well, on parallel with CMa, which is inscribed in all three languages.

These two short inscriptions have caused no end of controversy within the field. On their face, they label Cyrus an Achaemenid, of the same dynastic heritage as Darius. Darius indirectly made the same implication in the Bisitun Inscription, by his assertion that Cambyses was of his family (DB §10). Darius also claimed to create the Old Persian writing system (DB §70), a claim that is irreconcilable with Cyrus having used Old Persian in any inscriptions at Pasargadae. Most scholars take Darius at his word on this particular issue, that is, that he was the one who first inscribed in Old Persian and thus was, in effect, its inventor. Old Persian inscriptions that purport to date before Darius, including CMa and CMc from Pasargadae, are all suspect.

There are other problems with taking the Pasargadae inscriptions at face value. A comparison with Cyrus' inscriptions from Babylonia reveals major differences. Variation in style may be attributed to the

Figure 8.8a Anta from Palace P, Pasargadae, with CMa at top. Courtesy of David Stronach.

Figure 8.8b Close-up view of CMa, inscribed in Old Persian, Elamite, and Akkadian. Courtesy of David Stronach.

different, Babylonian context. Variation in the dynastic line and royal titles are harder to reconcile. In the Cyrus Cylinder, Cyrus traces his descent in the Cyrus Cylinder from Teispes. Achaemenes is not mentioned. Cyrus uses the title "King of Anshan" in his inscriptions in Babylon but never the label "Achaemenid." It defies imagination why Cyrus would not use the title "king of Anshan" in the region of Anshan itself (the older name for *Parsa*), at his capital Pasargadae in that very region. The implications are clear enough. Darius not only finished the work at Pasargadae but he also added inscriptions in Cyrus' name that identified Cyrus as an Achaemenid. Darius thus retroactively transformed the illustrious Cyrus into one of his own ancestors and strengthened his own legitimacy.

Darius' main emphasis at Bisitun and thereafter is his special relationship with Ahuramazda, which provided him the legitimizing factor so central to all kings in Near Eastern history. The name of the deity is new to our eyes. Ahuramazda does not occur in any earlier written sources. That phenomenon is closely bound with questions about early Persian religion, which will be taken up later in this chapter. It is from Darius also that we find the first enumeration of certain qualities that the Persian king had to possess. These qualities are frequently emphasized in the royal inscriptions, and the foremost expressions are the inscriptions at Darius I's tomb: DNa and DNb, the second essentially copied by Xerxes at Persepolis (XPl). Reading these inscriptions is tantamount to reading a guide book on Achaemenid royal ideology. The King is the guardian of order as the divine agent, created by and supported by Ahuramazda (who created all else). Those who respect and support the will of Ahuramazda, and by extension the King, will prosper; those who do not will be destroyed. The King creates order out of chaos, and wars must be fought to do this, especially if it is a matter of protecting the King's integrity. The King places fundamental importance on what is right and, by extension, he is the antithesis of what is wrong.

The proper display of "kingly qualities" as relayed in DNb may be condensed, at the risk of oversimplification, to one word: balance.

Darius the King proclaims: By the favor of Ahuramazda, I am the type who is pleased by what is right. I am not pleased by what is wrong. (DNb §2)

And that is only the beginning. Darius continues with a long list of the appropriate royal attributes and behaviors. The King must respect the interests of all his subjects, strong and weak; he must protect what is right and thus strive actively against the Lie (drauga). The King controls his impulses and his temper, because he models intelligence, good thought, and calm in the face of threats. He is a paragon of order; he must reward good behavior and faithful service as well as punish disloyalty and wickedness — those things that are a threat to order. Beyond these attributes of good character and intelligence, the King himself is also effective in combat; this involved being an accomplished warrior on horse and on foot, with both bow and with spear. These qualities also appear in descriptions of the Persian kings in non-Persian sources, especially Greek. Xenophon's lengthy encomium of Cyrus the Younger relays the exact qualities mentioned above (*Anabasis* 1.9). Herodotus (1.138) emphasizes how important it was to the Persians to tell the truth, though later (3.72) he has Darius, of all people, advocate an outright lie when necessary.[6]

ACHAEMENID RELIGION

Any overview of religious traditions and practices – with emphasis on the plural – in the Achaemenid period must begin by setting parameters.[7] An overview of the wide array of religious practices across the scope of the entire Empire is one that would fill volumes by itself, because of the number and diversity of the peoples in it. In this book, the phrase "Achaemenid religion" (or "Persian religion") refers to the Achaemenid Persians themselves, especially the religious sentiments expressed in the royal inscriptions. As discussed earlier, Parsa (Fars), by the Achaemenid period, had undergone several centuries of Elamite-Iranian acculturation. This phenomenon is critical, but not always easily visible, to contextualizing numerous aspects of Persian culture, including cultic practices and ritual traditions. The persistence of Elamite practices and sacred places testifies to a rich and complex heritage, one that is especially traceable in both text and image of the administrative documentation from Persepolis. Study of the administrative documentation in particular is changing our understanding of Achaemenid religion in significant ways, a process yet at the nascent stages.

The Achamenids are often described as Zoroastrians. This is perhaps an apt characterization on the surface – especially if one focuses only on the ideology as expressed in the royal inscriptions – but one that does not do justice to the variety of evidence. Zoroastrianism is an age-old religion in its own right that reached its floruit during the Sassanian period (c. 250–700 CE), and it was never static. Based on teachings of the prophet Zoroaster (the Greek name of Zarathustra), over time Zoroastrianism became strongly dualistic – light against dark, good against evil – with emphasis on the cosmic struggle between Ahuramazda and Ahriman (or Angra Mainyu). Zoroastrianism, like its Indian counterpart Hinduism, has Indo-Iranian origins, but the development of Zoroastrianism took place in an Iranian milieu. Zoroastrianism's most central texts – among them Zoroaster's hymns, the *Gathas* – were passed down orally for centuries before they were written down: chronology therefore is not an insignificant problem.

The *Gathas* form the core of a much longer work, the Avesta. The Avesta is a complex collection of works of which the earliest extant copies date several centuries after the Achaemenid period. There is no evidence that Avestan – the language of the text – was used outside the religious context, and the language (and wider tradition, for that matter) was thus one transmitted mainly by the Zoroastrian priesthood, the magi. Because of the manifold problems in assessing this material's relevance to the Achaemenid historical period, it is difficult to use it as a source. On the other hand, there is much relevant material gleaned from Achaemenid royal inscriptions, iconography (both monumental and personal), Classical sources on the Persians, and, as indicated earlier, the administrative documents from Persepolis.

The date of Zoroaster himself is still debated, with estimates ranging from c. 1800 to the sixth century BCE, the latter contemporary with Cyrus the Great. Thus Zoroaster's relevance to Achaemenid history as a living person is dependent on one's assessment about when he lived. The early dating is based on Zoroaster's surviving hymns, the *Gathas*, and their presumed age based on linguistic analysis of the words in their Indo-Iranian context; written copies date centuries later than the hymns are assumed to have been composed. The late date for Zoroaster stems from a Greek tradition that dates Zoroaster 258 years before Alexander the Great, which could mean 258 years before Alexander's birth or before his overthrow of the Persian Empire. The last option, which has achieved acceptance by many scholars, has significant ramifications for our understanding of Zoroastrianism and the early Persian Empire. For many other scholars, such questions of date are meaningless; they doubt that Zoroaster ever existed, or see him as a literary creation that lent credibility to an evolving belief system.

Another approach to dating Zoroaster essentially splits the difference: locating Zoroaster circa 1000 BCE by incorporating the linguistic arguments into a historical context and setting Zoroaster in the wave of Iranian migrations into northeastern Iran at the turn of the second millennium. Later Zoroastrian tradition locates Zoroaster's homeland and activity in that region. The Achaemenids' ubiquitous references to Ahuramazda in the royal inscriptions obviously provide pieces to the puzzle. But a central problem in establishing a mid-first-millennium historical context for the Avesta is that none of the texts therein contains clear reference to the Medes or the Achaemenid Persians. However one defines a Zoroastrian stream of tradition, the Achaemenid kings were instrumental in shaping it. Instead of forcing the Achaemenids into a preconceived Zoroastrian system, we should consider the Achaemenids' impact on a still nascent and evolving tradition.

There are many Zoroastrian, or Mazdean, elements to be found in the religious traditions of the Achaemenid period.[8] Among others, these include the ubiquity of Ahuramazda in the royal inscriptions, especially as a creator god; the antipathy toward the Lie (see discussion earlier in this chapter); and the central place of fire in certain rituals. Greek writers emphasize that the Persians did not have temples. Remnants of what are presumed to have been fire altars have been found in excavation, and they are also identified in sculpture, for example on Darius I's tomb facade.

Herodotus' brief survey (1.131–132) of Persian religious practices has served for a long time as one of our main sources, and it is a mixed bag.

I know that the Persians employ the following customs. It is not their custom to dedicate statues, temples, or altars, but they assail as folly those who do so, and so it seems to me, that they do not think of their gods as humanized in the fashion that the Greeks do. They worship Zeus by ascending to the loftiest places to make offerings, they call the entire circle of heaven Zeus. They sacrifice to both the sun and to the moon, as well as to the earth, to fire, to water, and to the winds. At first they sacrificed to these only, but subsequently they learned from both the Assyrians and Arabs to sacrifice to Heavenly Aphrodite. The Assyrians call Aphrodite Mullissu, the Arabs call her Alilat, and the Persians Mithra. The Persians make sacrifice to these deities in this way. When they are about to sacrifice they neither construct altars nor light fire; they do not use libations, reed pipes, garlands, or barley. (1.131–132.1)

The passage continues to describe, in some detail, the Persian procedure for sacrificing an animal and emphasizes that a magus must be present. Herodotus mentions fire altars, and we do have many depictions (e.g., on seal impressions) of worship before divinities. The name Zeus presumably refers to Ahuramazda, a Greek syncretism common not only in Herodotus. His descriptions of sacrifices to the celestial bodies and the elements are in some ways harder to reconcile with our knowledge of Persian religious practices. Worship of the sun may be equated with Mithra, and if one considers that the Persians sacrificed with fire and water instead of to them, Herodotus may be given some credit. Sealings from the Persepolis Fortification archives are replete with divinely-associated astral imagery.[9] Worship of Heavenly Aphrodite (Ourania) is generally believed to refer to Persian Anahita — as later Classical writers noted — but many non-Greek female deities are associated with Aphrodite, so Herodotus' meaning here is ultimately unclear. Assyrian Mullissu was at times synchronized with Ishtar, another deity with whom Anahita shares several attributes. Mithra is a male god in Persian and Indo-Iranian tradition.

The plural *magi* comes from singular Latin *magus*, taken directly from Greek *magos*, which in turn is a loan word from Old Persian, *magush*. The word has broad application in Greek and Roman texts: from its primary usage to refer to the priests of the Persian kings to a pejorative used for charlatans of the sort who foretell the future; it is from this latter sense that we get the word "magician." In the Achaemenid period, the magi are generally understood as priests, but that does not do full justice to the range of functions they fulfilled. Magi were the transmitters of Iranian lore and traditions, not just religious ones, and they both performed rituals as well as served as dream (and other omen) interpreters. For example, in Herodotus they interpreted Astyages' ominous dreams about his daughter Mandane and the birth of Cyrus (1.107–108), and they recur as functionaries performing sacrifices and warding off evil omens, such as when Xerxes is marching against Greece (Hdt. 7.113, 7.191, etc.). Parallels to their function and influence may be found in the cadre of scholars that surrounded the Assyrian and Babylonian kings, the Persians' predecessors.

Herodotus names the Magi as one of six Median tribes (1.101). Historians still do not know what to make of this. Does it imply that these priests or learned men were exclusively from one Median tribe? That does not seem to be the case during the Achaemenid period, though it is impossible to confirm. As noted previously, the Medes seem to have held a special place in the Persian Empire's hierarchy – politically, militarily, and culturally – more so than any other ethnic group besides the Persians themselves. Forging a connection between this and the presumed Median origins of the magi may make sense but is not definitive.[10] Scholars are also divided on the extent to which practices and rituals attributed to the magi may be considered truly Zoroastrian or not, but attempts to delineate this run the danger of becoming circular, a caveat that applies to the entire study of Achaemenid religious beliefs. Some take the magi as the original Zoroastrian priests, others see them as the antithesis, as the *daiva*-worshippers attacked by Xerxes. That they were key state functionaries is beyond doubt, and they certainly left an imprint on the Greek imagination.

Zoroaster himself is not mentioned in any extant Persian text from our period. The names of many Achaemenid elites clearly come from Zoroastrian tradition. Darius I's father Hystaspes (Old Persian *Vishtaspa*), for example, shares his name with Zoroaster's patron Vishtaspa in the Avesta. Few scholars think this is a coincidence, though fewer still uphold an exact correlation between the two. That is, few hold that Darius' father was the same person as Zoroaster's patron, a key assertion for supporters of a late (sixth century) date for Zoroaster himself.

Most twentieth-century discussions of Achaemenid religion focus on reconciling the strong assertions of piety in the royal inscription with no evidence that the Achaemenids forcibly compelled worship of Ahuramazda among their subjects. This seeming dichotomy led to extreme approaches, either attributing religious significance to everything the kings did or emphasizing a religious tolerance totally removed from the ideology expressed in the royal inscriptions. Either of these approaches is tricky to apply consistently. Persian royal inscriptions typically lack specificity – the Bisitun Inscription notwithstanding – and specific historical events are usually only recorded in non-Persian sources. Evidence for Persian reprisals against religious sites or groups is often ambiguous. The severity and extent of Cambyses' purported actions against Egyptian temples remain unclear, and because that information is filtered through a hostile source (the Egyptian priesthood) via

Herodotus there is much room for skepticism. In any event, there is no traceable instance of compulsory worship of Ahuramazda. The expressions of the king's piety in the royal inscriptions are, as has been noted, standard for kings in the ancient Near East. An important corollary is the overwhelming evidence that the Achaemenid kings' emphasis on Ahuramazda did not displace older or local gods. The Persepolis Fortification archive indicates that well over a dozen Iranian, Elamite, and Mesopotamian deities were worshipped in the core of the Empire, testimony to the continuity and compatibility of several traditions.

9 Empire at Large: From the Death of Xerxes to Darius II

The reign of Xerxes, and especially his invasion of Greece in 480–479 BCE, has always been viewed as a watershed for Greek history as well as Achaemenid historiography – the former emphasizing a historical narrative and the latter studying the historical sequence. This is not surprising, because they both involve many of the same sources. The study of subsequent Achaemenid history typifies the methodological problem so prevalent in studying Xerxes' invasion of Greece: a disproportionate reliance on Greek source material. Royal inscriptions become fewer, shorter, and more stylized. Economic and administrative archival materials from Near Eastern sources retain their paramount importance, but the material (with a few exceptions) is more sporadic and less richly detailed than the Persepolis Fortification tablets.

PALACE INTRIGUE AND THE ASSASSINATION OF XERXES

A Babylonian tablet contains reference to Xerxes death: "on the 14th day of Abu, Xerxes' son killed him." The terse reference is to the point and relatively precise on the time of death – by our calendar sometime in late July or early August in 465 BCE.[1] For a narrative account, we must turn to the Classical tradition. Ctesias, Diodorus Siculus, and Justin all point to a plot hatched by one of Xerxes' courtiers, a certain Artabanus (Artapanus in Ctesias), who was abetted by other high officials. No reason for the plot is given, although Justin relates a stereotyped view that Xerxes' defeat in Greece – fifteen years earlier than his

death – was somehow responsible for a serious decline in both Xerxes'
and the Empire's fortunes, a view contradicted by more than 130 years
of continued Persian rule.

Xerxes had (at least) three sons: Darius, Artaxerxes, and Hystaspes.
Artabanus managed to convince Artaxerxes that Darius was responsible
for the assassination. Darius was brought before Artaxerxes, who put
Darius to death. Artaxerxes then foiled Artabanus' plan to kill him as
well; Artabanus was slain instead. Some scholars interpret the entire
Artabanus story as an elaborate cover-up. After all, the Babylonian evidence states that Xerxes' own son killed him. In such instances one
may look to the ultimate winner for responsibility, in this case the next
king, Artaxerxes. But with the record so confused, the truth cannot be
ascertained.

Artaxerxes I's inscriptions follow the previous patterns. An inscription on a silver drinking bowl lists the standard titles: great king, king
of kings, and king of lands. The main emphasis is on descent within the
Achaemenid line: Artaxerxes is the son of Xerxes, who was the son of
Darius and, of course, an Achaemenid. Fragmentary trilingual inscriptions from Persepolis cite the same titles and, as one would expect,
emphasize continuity in the building work at Persepolis. Artaxerxes
finished a palace started by his father Xerxes (A^{1}Pa). This is not only
filial piety but such works were expected of any king.

Ctesias recorded a challenge from the satrap of Bactria, "another
Artapanus," whom Artaxerxes defeated (Fragment 14 §35). It is unclear
whether the phrase "another Artapanus" is to be understood as someone
sharing the name of Xerxes' assassin (as relayed in the Greek tradition)
or whether the satrap styled himself as another usurper bearing that
name. Diodorus notes that Hystapes was the satrap of Bactria; Ctesias
lists Hystaspes as one of Xerxes' sons but offers no information on his
official role. If the rebellious satrap was indeed Artaxerxes' brother,
Hystaspes, it is unclear why Ctesias would not have identified him by
name. The sporadic source material does not facilitate clear historical
reconstruction here. In light of the violence that marred the transition,
Artaxerxes I's recitation of his Achaemenid descent in his own inscriptions may not have simply been rote, as per standard royal ideology, but
perhaps necessary. It reinforced Artaxerxes' credentials in the confused
aftermath of Xerxes' assassination.

REIGN OF ARTAXERXES I

The major problem that confronted Artaxerxes I in his early reign was a revolt in Egypt, dating from 464 to 454 BCE. Diodorus attributes the Egyptian revolt to the chaos surrounding Xerxes' death. The rebellion was led by one Inaros, a dynast from the western Delta in northern Egypt. A demotic inscription from the Kharga oasis region that dates to Inaros' second regnal year labels him "Prince of the Rebels" – an odd designation suggesting that Inaros did not take, or was not granted, the standard royal titles. Other evidence demonstrates that Inaros' claim was not accepted everywhere. An inscription by an Egyptian official from Koptos in the Wadi Hammamat (modern Qift) is dated to the fifth year of Artaxerxes, "King of Upper and Lower Egypt" (the standard royal title), that is, the year 461, while Inaros' revolt was underway. The dedicator names his parents: a father with a Persian name and a mother with an Egyptian one, a signal of the acculturation of the elite in the provinces.

For narratives of the rebellion, we rely mainly on Diodorus, Thucydides' brief account, and Ctesias. Thucydides labels Inaros the son of Psammetichus, which was also the name of the king defeated by Cambyses in 525 as well as of an earlier king (from the late seventh century) who reunified Egypt after expelling rulers from Nubia (the Sudan). The filiation here may be a manufactured one, similar to the various challengers during the crisis of 522, who assumed names and filiations from illustrious predecessors to increase their legitimacy. The revolt posed a significant challenge to Artaxerxes. Inaros secured territories in northern Egypt (the Delta region) and, for roughly five years beginning in 460 or 459, received help from an Athenian naval fleet of 200 ships that had been campaigning in Cyprus. With the help of this fleet, the rebels defeated the Persian force under Artaxerxes' uncle Achaemenes, captured territory around the northern capital of Memphis, and besieged the defeated Persian forces in a stronghold called by the Egyptians the "White Wall" and by the Greeks the "White Castle."

A new Persian force was gathered in Cilicia and Phoenicia under the command of Megabyzus, son of Zopyrus. This army broke the siege of the White Castle and put the rebel forces to flight. The Athenian naval force became trapped on an island called Prosopitis in the western

Delta. By using canals to drain the river around the island, the Persian forces were able to storm the island on foot. According to both Diodorus (11.71.3–6 and 11.77.1–5) and Ctesias (Fragment 14 §36–38), the victorious Persians allowed the Athenians a safe withdrawal from the island and from Egypt. But Thucydides' account differs. Thucydides refers to a momentous defeat in which most of the Athenian forces were destroyed. An Athenian relief force of fifty ships, unaware of the reverse in the rebels' fortunes, was also wiped out on their arrival in the eastern Delta (1.109–110). Thucydides' account is given greater credence. The specific impact on Athens in the 450s is difficult to track, but this defeat effectively brought an end to their ambitions on Persian territory beyond Ionia and the Aegean, with the exception of one ill-fated expedition against Cyprus in 451. Inaros was betrayed and impaled, which brought a formal end to the rebellion. Other rebels held out in the western Delta – in an area where it was difficult to maintain effective control – but Persian rule of Egypt was stabilized.

Ctesias' account of this period focuses mainly on one member of the Persian nobility: Megabyzus, son of Zopyrus and grandson of Megabyzus who was one of the Seven against Bardiya in 522.[2] By the time Ctesias wrote (c. 400 BCE), only a few decades after Megabyzus' life in the mid-fifth century, Megabyzus had become a legend in his own right, as he repeatedly proved his resilience and his nobility in the face of numerous challenges. Pained by suspicion that his wife Amytis, the daughter of Xerxes, was an adulterer, Megabyzus was nevertheless instrumental in saving Artaxerxes from Artabanus' continued plotting after the assassination of Xerxes. Megabyzus was also instrumental in ending Inaros' revolt by promising terms to the rebel Inaros and his Greek supporters. Yet Artaxerxes contravened Megabyzus' promises and had Inaros put to death. Megabyzus' distress at the King's betrayal of his word caused him to withdraw to Syria, where he subsequently rebelled. Megabyzus defeated two armies sent against him, and only thereafter – and after much negotiation – came to terms with the King. The reconciliation was short-lived, however. During a lion hunt Megabyzus struck and killed a lion before the King – a grave offense – and Artaxerxes in his anger ordered Megabyzus beheaded. Megabyzus then fled into exile and only returned, in disguise, five years later, to once more be reconciled with the king and made a table companion (Ctesias Fragment 14 §40–43).

How to make sense of this account? Megabyzus' revolt is not recorded in other sources. We thus have no sense of its length or magnitude. Ctesias' allusions to armies in the hundreds of thousands follow typical exaggerations and are not credible. But if the general report of rebellion may be relied on – a question that remains in doubt – a revolt by a prominent noble, a descendant of one of the Seven, may have posed a threat to Achaemenid control.

EZRA AND NEHEMIAH: DISCONTENT IN THE LEVANT

The missions of the Hebrews Ezra and Nehemiah to Jerusalem, in the Persian province of Yehud (i.e., Judah), are sometimes read as evidence for a revolt in the Levant, but a number of methodological problems call that assumption into question. A mid-fifth-century date for these missions is subject to debate, partnered with questions about the sources' reliability. Some scholars question not only the traditional composition dates of the biblical Books of Ezra and Nehemiah but also the historicity of the characters and situations portrayed therein, wondering for example, whether the circumstances portrayed are anachronistic projections into the fifth century BCE.[3]

The Book of Ezra begins with reference to a proclamation from Cyrus sometime after the conquest of Babylon in 539 BCE. Jewish exiles from Babylonia returned to Jerusalem and rebuilt the temple that had been sacked by the Babylonian king Nebuchadnezzar II in 586. References in the Books of Haggai and Zechariah indicate that the temple was dedicated early in the reign of Darius I. Governors of Judah may be traced through most of the fifth century, but the social and religious context that precipitated Ezra's mission is unclear.

Ezra, bearing a royal letter, was sent to Jerusalem under the imprimatur of King Artaxerxes in his seventh year (7.12–26). If this was Artaxerxes I, that year was 458, although some see the passage as referring to Artaxerxes II and thus date the mission to his seventh year, 398. The authenticity of this letter (the so-called "Artaxerxes Rescript") is debated. It includes instructions to the royal treasurers of the province to provide Ezra silver and supplies with which to arrange proper sacrifices like those performed before the temple's sack. Another component of Ezra's mission was the charge to appoint judges and officials who would enforce "the laws of your god" (7.25–26). Most scholars take this to mean the Mosaic law code, even if they differ on the extent of its implementation. Did it apply only in Judah? Or did it apply to all Jews living in the satrapy of Trans-Euphrates? (That region was also called "Beyond the River" – the regions west of the Euphrates.) Ezra's mission provides a compelling example of local autonomy under the aegis of the King's law. The former could be granted as long as it did not contravene the latter.

Cyrus' edict may contain echoes of a building inscription, one marking the reconstruction of the temple and including the repatriation of the original temple vessels plundered by Nebuchadnezzar (Ezra 1.7–11). The reasons for the exiles' return and the attendant grants are unclear. Some modern works trumpet Achaemenid tolerance of other belief systems. Such tolerance may well have been actual practice, but it was contingent on submission to the central political authority. Some view Cyrus' initial move in strategic terms. In returning the Jewish exiles to Jerusalem, Cyrus may have been establishing a base for operations against Egypt. Other motives could be postulated. In any event, one result of the return was a significant increase in the number of priests and the development of a citizen-temple community in Jerusalem, one that developed a quasi-independence from both the local provincial authority and the imperial one. At the risk of understatement, this led to problems.

Nehemiah held an official position within the Achaemenid hierarchy, that of governor (Hebrew *peḥā*), subordinate to the satrap who was probably based in Damascus. In 445, Nehemiah was dispatched to deal with a number of serious problems in Jerusalem and surrounding areas. The cause of these problems is not known, although if Ezra's mission may be dated before Nehemiah's, then some of the problems were likely related to the context of Ezra's mission. Armed with several royal dispatches, Nehemiah was able to garner supplies for his own use and to implement major projects: a citadel and the fortification of the city walls (2.1–10). Nehemiah established a garrison, conducted a census, and supported efforts to restore the temple rituals. In 433, after twelve years, he returned to the King. During his mission Nehemiah was accompanied by one Pethahiah, identified as a royal commissioner.

Nehemiah was clearly trusted, but an extra level of bureaucracy – in the person of Pethahiah – helped to ensure adherence to the King's commands.

Unsurprisingly, the King's commands involved maintaining the political and social order. Nehemiah's establishment of fortifications at royal behest has generated a variety of interpretations in modern scholarship. Were these meant to reassert Persian control, in conjunction with a garrison, as perhaps a reaction to internal strife? Or were they reflective of the city's increased size and status? It seems clear from the Book of Nehemiah that the people were immersed in a bitter internal conflict. What brought the province to such straits is never explained, although allusions to usury and a high level of indentured servitude imply a widening social gap. Internal instability, left unchecked, might magnify and spread. Nehemiah appears to have been chosen as the King's agent to resolve these problems, but he encountered resistance from vested interests in the province.

When the social unrest manifest in the Book of Nehemiah is juxtaposed with the garbled accounts of a revolt by Megabyzus (see discussion earlier in this chapter), a correlation of the two is tempting, even reasonable. Yet there is no shortage of problems even beyond the chronological difficulties. The biblical material offers no indication of a widespread revolt, as Ctesias recounted. In light of the (relatively) rich documentation, this is surprising. It is no simple task to connect Megabyzus' revolt to the internal squabbles between Judah and its immediate neighbors.

REVISITING THE NORTHWESTERN FRONT: PERSIAN-GREEK INTERCHANGE

Given the continued Athenian success in the Aegean for several decades, and the thin historical record, it is easy to lose sight of the Persian threat. It was revealed occasionally by the activities and ambitions of the satraps in Asia Minor, especially at Sardis (Lydia) and Dascylium (Hellespontine Phrygia). How long did the question that must have dogged them after 479 BCE – "Are the Persians coming back?" – continue to do so?

In 451 the Athenians sent an expedition to Cyprus, the particulars and point of which remain unclear. Any long-term Athenian designs on the island seem unlikely, because Athens did not have the resources for sustained imperial pursuits. Perhaps we should simply attribute the campaign against Cyprus to the Delian League's stated purpose, which was, according to Thucydides, to ravage the King's territories (1.96) and thereby afflict some retribution for the Persian invasion of Greece. Thucydides' account of the expedition (1.112) is here, as elsewhere for the years between 480–430, extremely terse. The Athenian Cimon won battles at sea and on land, but his death, together with supply problems, forced Athenian withdrawal. Diodorus' account has more detail but is also more problematic: the Cypriot cities of Kition and Marion were taken, but the siege of Salamis was unsuccessful (12.3.2–4). Diodorus ties the end of the expedition not to logistical problems but to a peace treaty with Persia.

This treaty, called the Peace of Callias after the Athenian ambassador sent to Susa to negotiate it, is one of the most contentious historiographic problems for the mid-fifth century. Its date, its terms, and its very historicity are all questioned. The particulars of the treaty are mentioned in various late sources and preserved by Diodorus.

A treaty was made by the Athenians and their allies for peace with the Persians, the main points of which were the following: all the Greek cities throughout Asia were to be autonomous, and the satraps of the Persians were not to come closer to the sea than a three days' journey, nor was any war vessel to sail within (the waters between) Phaselis and Cyaneae. If the King and the satraps keep these terms, the Athenians will not campaign into the territory that the King rules. (12.4.5)

Phaselis was a coastal city in Lycia in southwestern Anatolia, and Cyaneae (or Kyaneai) at the northern end of the Bosporus, where it enters the Black Sea. Such markers would effectively have barred any Persian military ship from the entire Aegean Sea; the Hellespont, Propontis, and Bosporus; and anywhere west of the southernmost points of the Anatolian peninsula. On land, a stricture of three days journey from the coast included a lot of Persian territory, including Dascylium, the capital of Hellespontine Phrygia, within about 20 miles of the Propontis coast. To note that it was unlikely that the Persians would have made such concessions is an understatement.

It is difficult to make sense of the treaty's terms as preserved by Diodorus. Our two main sources for fifth-century Greek history – Herodotus and Thucydides – are silent on the peace, which is startling. Herodotus does mention an Athenian embassy to Artaxerxes I, led by Callias (7.151) but makes no mention of any formal peace. Thucydides has nothing about an embassy of Callias or a Peace attributed to him. Arguments from silence are rarely compelling, but such a flagrant omission in both authors gives most modern scholars pause. A fourth-century BCE historian, Theopompous, in fact denies the historicity of the Peace altogether. Some modern scholars view the Peace as a patriotic fiction, one promulgated in the fourth century to recall the height of Athenian glory from a century earlier as a counter to the humiliating peace imposed on them by Artaxerxes II in 487/486 BCE (see pp. 186–187). Reduced Athenian ambitions in the eastern Mediterranean may have coincided with some agreement – or even an informal détente – if not simply from a scaling back of their ambitions.

The attitude of the King and his satraps is another matter. There are several instances of Persian activity that would contravene the terms of the peace given by Diodorus, the most significant of which is the active involvement of the satrap Pissouthnes of Sardis in a revolt by one of Athens' most important allies, the island of Samos in the Aegean in 441–440 (Thuc. 1.115–117). After an Athenian intervention on their island, some Samians arranged an alliance with Pissouthnes. With his support, they gathered 700 mercenaries, returned to Samos, and took power. The Athenian garrison stationed there, along with its commanders, was delivered to Pissouthnes. The Athenians subsequently quelled the revolt, but what they did about their captured garrison is unknown. Through this episode and similar references in a number of Greek inscriptions, it is clear that Athenian-Persian tension (and, at times, outright conflict) persisted in the very zone that was supposedly declared off-limits by the Peace of Callias.

It is difficult to reconcile Pissouthnes' active involvement in the Samian revolt with the formal Peace as described by Diodorus. Some scholars have ingeniously reconciled joint Athenian and Persian claims on much of western Anatolia by assuming that the city-states in question paid tribute not only to Athens – which is attested to varying degrees through the latter half of the fifth century – but also to the Persian satrap. In other words, a double tribute was paid by many city-states, faced with the reality that both parties – Persian satraps and Athens – had made claims and could compel payment. How this was justified, how it worked in practice, as well as the wider ramifications of such arrangements are impossible to track in the extant sources. Attempts to fit a formalized Peace of Callias into a persistent Athenian-Persian conflict in the eastern Aegean are bound to be problematic. In general, it is safe to assume that the King never relinquished his claim on his Ionian holdings, and that the satraps were given freedom – indeed, probably were expected – to contest Athenian inroads there at every opportunity.

There is, of course, no question that Persia had diplomatic relations with Athens and other frontier states. Here too, Greek sources provide a wealth of evidence. After Xerxes' invasion, requests for submission of earth and water cease. Subsequently, Persian-Greek treaties usually were cast in Greek terms of *philia* ("friendship"), a fluid and wide-ranging concept that applied not only to interpersonal relationships but also to the diplomatic realm. One example of Persian diplomacy demonstrates their ingenuity. Sometime during the Egyptian revolt in the 450s BCE, a Persian mission was sent to Sparta (Thuc. 1.109). This embassy offered to fund a Spartan invasion of Athens. Of course, the Persians were well versed in Greek affairs – in this case the enmity between Athens and Sparta – and this mission reveals an attempt to create a strategic distraction: a Spartan invasion of Athens might have compelled the Athenian forces in Egypt to withdraw. But the Spartans rebuffed the offer. Later in Artaxerxes I's reign, when tensions between Athens and Sparta (and their respective allies) came to a head – the outbreak of what we call the Peloponnesian War – both sides expressed hopes for alliances with Persia (compare Thuc. 1.82 and 2.7) to further their own ends in what became, for the Greeks, a long and destructive internecine war for hegemony in the Aegean. The Persians were prepared to exploit these divisions among rivals on their northwestern frontier in order to reconsolidate their holdings in Asia Minor.

Persian-Greek interchange occurred at many levels. The consistent back-and-forth of diplomats and their retinues, not to mention long-standing trading networks throughout the eastern Mediterranean and into the Near East, offered ample opportunity for cultural exchange. Especially from Athens there is abundant evidence that Persian influence left its mark on the literature, architecture, and culture of Classical

Greece.[4] Examples are many, and a prominent one is the famous building program of the Athenian general and statesman Pericles in the mid-fifth century. This was undertaken at the height of Athenian domination of the Aegean world, through its leadership of the Delian League. As a hegemon with imperial ambitions, Pericles and Athens' other leaders had to look somewhere for models of imperial expression. The only true model was Persia.

Comparisons between the famous Parthenon of Athens and the Apadana at Persepolis yield interesting parallels. The original Parthenon on the acropolis was destroyed during Xerxes' invasion; Pericles commissioned a new and improved model in the 440s. In particular, the procession on the Parthenon's interior frieze – depicting a procession perhaps of the Panathenaic Festival, which under Pericles took on trappings of imperial grandeur through required tribute from Athens' subjects – parallels the similar procession of the subject peoples portrayed on the Apadana. Of course, the Parthenon is a uniquely Athenian expression, but the metaphor and the meaning are quite similar. Another structure was the so-called Odeion, built under Pericles' direction on the south slope of the acropolis. At its time, it was the largest covered building in the Greek world. The Odeion was modeled on the tent used by Xerxes during the invasion of Greece. Despite some scholarly uncertainties about its form, its "Persian look" is well-established. Debate continues about its function and the Athenians' response to it in the midst of their city. Primarily, its value was symbolic. It was a visible manifestation of Athens' status and glory, a monument to the victory that led to its own empire – one modeled, consciously or not, on their much larger rival to the east.[5] That this and similar imperial expressions - in architecture, sculpture, modes of dress, drinking and tableware, especially (though not exclusively) cultivated by the elite – participated in a complex relationship, simultaneously one of loathing and admiration, is a well-studied phenomenon and one certainly not unique to Athens' reception of objects and ideas Persian.

FROM ARTAXERXES I TO DARIUS II

Artaxerxes I died after a reign of forty-one years (465–424 BCE). There is no indication of a violent death, though the succession itself was violent. Ctesias' *Persica* indicates that Artaxerxes I and his wife Damaspia, who is otherwise unknown, died on the same day. Their only son, Xerxes II, took the throne. He ruled only forty-five days before he, drunk and unconscious in the palace, was assassinated by his half brother Sogdianus and Sogdianus' coconspirators Pharnacyas and Menostanes. Sogdianus was one of Artaxerxes I's many sons by secondary wives and concubines, Menostanes a high-ranking military commander, and Phranacyas a palace eunuch. Another half brother, Ochus (Akkadian *Umakush*, the future Darius II), satrap of Hyrcania, immediately challenged Sogdianus.

Ochus managed to secure the allegiance of several high-ranking Persians, first and foremost Arbarios, who had been Sogdianus' cavalry commander. Others who joined Ochus include Arshama (Arsames), satrap of Egypt, and a certain Artoxares who had been exiled to Armenia by Artaxerxes I because of Artoxares' support for Megabyzus' rebellion (see discussion earlier in this chapter). Relying on trickery instead of battle (at any rate, no battle is recorded) Ochus convinced Sogdianus, who had been ruling as king for six months, to give himself up. Sogdianus and his supporters were soaked in alcohol, then cast into a pit filled with glowing hot embers. Ochus took the throne name Darius, and thus became Darius II.

There is no record of either Xerxes II or Sogdianus as kings in Babylonian documentation, which immediately raises questions about the accounts of Ctesias and other Greek writers. But a number of the rival claimants' supporters named by Ctesias are found in Babylonian documents, so his account is not entirely lacking in credibility. That neither Xerxes II nor Sogdianus is mentioned as king in Babylonian documents can be interpreted to mean that the reigns of these two were not formally recognized in Babylonia and that they overlapped with the recognized reign of Darius II.

THE MURASHU ARCHIVE – LAND MANAGEMENT PRACTICES IN ACHAEMENID BABYLONIA

One important component of the Babylonian documentation for this period is the Murashu archive. The Murashu were a family of businessmen with wide-ranging commercial interests involving the management of landed estates around the Babylonian city of Nippur. The archive consists of more than 700 tablets dating from the reigns of Artaxerxes I and Darius II (dating from 440 to 416 BCE). The Murashu and similar contractors managed estates, or farms, for their tenants, among whom were members of the highest levels of Persian administration. Darius II's queen Parysatis, the satrap of Egypt (Arshama), and other notables are mentioned in texts from the archive. Some of the estates that the Murashu managed (especially larger ones that were gifts of the King) were state controlled, granted to various individuals for their use, and in some cases profit, in return for services to the King. The practice was not unique to Babylonia. The word "tenant" rather than "owner" is used to describe the grant-holder, because these estates were royal grants and thus, technically, still royal property.

These tenants turned over the management of the estates to managers like the Murashu. The tenants could draw farm produce or borrow money from the Murashu against future harvests. The Murashu in turn sublet the land to farmers, who did the actual agricultural work and were allowed to keep a percentage. Any surplus produce would be sold on the market for silver and credited to the tenant's account for future use; from this the Murashu would also receive a percentage. The Murashu and similar firms also engaged in other economic activities, such as banking and tax collection.

Although the Murashu family's type of land management business was commonplace, it stands out because of the size of their organization and the number of texts available for study. A further example is found in a small archive dating from 438–400 BCE, from Babylon, which catalogues the work of one Belshunu. He was at first a governor answerable to the satrap of Babylon and then apparently a satrap himself of the province Trans-Euphrates ("Beyond the River"), Syro-Palestine. This Belshunu has been identified with the Greek Belesys who was involved in the civil war between Darius II's sons Artaxerxes II and Cyrus the Younger. Belshunu's archive provides information about his private business activities as well as his public duties; one text relays Belshunu's role in adjudicating a case of a temple theft in Dilbat, a city near Babylon.

These archives shed light not only on members of the elite. They are also critical sources for social history, for understanding how the Empire literally worked. How did the Empire obtain labor, military service, or other service from its subjects? The Murashu archive helps us understand how military obligations were fulfilled. These were arranged by what is called the *ḫaṭru*-system. This system consisted of what are called "bow-lands" (or "bow-fiefs") in the modern literature – Akkadian *bīt qašti* in the singular, referring to a bow (*qaštu*) as a piece of military equipment. This was, in other words, a land-for-service system: grants of land were given by the crown in return for services on demand. These bow-lands were organized in groups, each of which had a supervisor. A complete definition is found in a seminal study based on analysis of the Murashu archive:

> (T)he *ḫaṭru* was in effect a small-scale fiscal district; the institution was a means of producing and extracting fees for the Achaemenid state. At the same time, it was a means of insuring and extending agricultural production, the basis from which state revenues were drawn. And, not least, it was a means of supporting a standing military reserve, a local garrison force, and cadres of state-controlled workers.[6]

This basic system included most socioeconomic groups. The amount of land granted to each person was commensurate with that person's socioeconomic status and the amount of services expected in return. Bow-lands themselves may be traced back to the time of the Babylonian Nebuchadnezzar II and provide another example of continuity with the Neo-Babylonian period; in fact, at its most basic level the land-for-service system was centuries old. Precise records allowed careful regulating and accounting of these lands and their associated obligations. That such records do not provide us with narrative history is unfortunate, but these are the very kinds of records least likely to do so. Very helpfully, though, they do contradict the stereotypical picture of the Achaemenid Empire as a laissez-faire organization that persisted thanks to inertia.

Several of the main participants in the succession crisis after Artaxerxes I's death had estates managed by the Murashu, and some of these appear also in Ctesias' *Persica*, providing a fascinating confluence of Babylonian and Greek evidence. Arbarios, Sogdianus' cavalry commander who joined Ochus' rebellion, has been identified as the Arbareme who held the equerry's estate in Babylonia. Artoxares, a prominent supporter of Ochus (Darius II), has been identified with the Artahsharu who was granted the estate of Sogdianus' supporter Menostanes, who is the Manushtana of Murashu texts.[7] Through these records we are able to discern critical information about the economic lives of these members of the nobility. In the case of Artoxares and Menostanes, the Murashu texts show us how Darius II punished his enemies and rewarded his supporters. A grant of land may be unsurprising in itself, but it is infrequent enough in Achaemenid history to permit us to track the King's consolidation of power and the installation of his supporters in prominent positions, as described in Near Eastern sources.

EXCURSUS: ACHAEMENID THRONE NAMES

Ochus' adoption of the throne name Darius (II) is the first, clearly attested use of a throne name by an Achaemenid ruler, but whether this was really the first instance is a matter of debate. The use of throne names is age-old but not always easy to track in extant sources. For example, in the Neo-Assyrian period, the designated heir to the throne was given a new name, his throne name, once he was formally declared crown prince. Was it different in the Achaemenid period?

Compounding the problem for the earliest kings is that the etymologies of the names of Cyrus and Cambyses are uncertain. Unlike the clearly Iranian names of Darius I and his successors, neither Cyrus' nor Cambyses' names are readily etymologized as Iranian. Many scholars are inclined to attribute an Elamite etymology to Cyrus' name ("He who bestows care"), with the implication that Cambyses' name may also be Elamite. The question of the linguistic heritage of Cyrus' name persists as does the question of whether it was Cyrus' birth name or throne name. Testimony from the Greek author Strabo indicates that Cyrus originally had an Iranian name: "There is also a river Cyrus, flowing through so-called 'hollow' Persis near Pasargadae, from which the king took his name, taking the name Cyrus in place of Agradates" (15.3.6).[8] Is this report accurate? Where did Strabo get this information? Why do we find no comparable reference in earlier works that treat Cyrus so extensively, such as Herodotus or Xenophon? Intriguingly, Herodotus calls him Cyrus throughout his account, but he notes more than once in relaying stories of the young Cyrus that that was not yet his name (1.113–114). In light of earlier tradition, it would not be surprising if all Achaemenid kings took throne names upon succession or designation as crown prince, but this cannot be confirmed.

DARIUS II AND DYNASTIC CONTINUITY

As a throne name, "Darius" was a compelling choice. In taking this name, Ochus identified himself with one of the foremost kings of the Empire's history. Ochus could not have done much more to solidify his dynastic credentials. In the context of the confusion and jockeying for position after Artaxerxes I's death, it is notable that all claimants had one thing in common: direct descent from the Achaemenid line. According to Ctesias, Darius II was faced with another rival: his full brother Arsites, the son of Artaxerxes I and the Babylonian concubine Cosmartidene. Artyphios, the son of Megabyzus, rebelled as well. Both these threats were quelled, and both Arsites and Artyphios were thrown into burning embers. Ctesias records another revolt against Darius II, that of Pissouthnes, the satrap of Sardis. Details are sparse, and the chronology is wholly uncertain. As a consequence some scholars connect it to a revolt by Pissouthnes' son Amorges, in the late 410s. Tissaphernes, a Persian who becomes prominent in the Greek sources for the next two decades, was instrumental in quelling the rebellion and as reward was given the satrapy of Lydia to govern (Fragment 15 §52–53).

The inscriptional record for Darius II is thin. Two copies of a building inscription come from Susa and contain the requisite titles (great king, king of kings), lineage (son of Artaxerxes), as well as the all-important favor of Ahuramazda. While formulaic, such proclamations contain some urgency in light of the contested succession. There were obviously other and, on the face of it, equally qualified Achaemenid claimants: sons of Artaxerxes by women other than his primary wife, Damaspia. On a gold tablet from Hamadan, the authenticity of which (like others from the same area) has been disputed, Darius II traced his lineage more explicitly, father to son, back to the important link with Darius I.

OPPORTUNITY ON THE NORTHWESTERN FRONT

Beginning in 431 BCE, much of the Aegean world was involved in the war between Athens and Sparta and their respective allies. Both sides appealed for Persian support throughout the war. One such occurrence dates to the end of Artaxerxes I's reign: the Athenians at Eion on coastal

Thrace captured a Persian named Artaphernes who was bearing a message from the King to the Spartans. The main point, as expressed by Thucydides, was that "... the King did not understand what they [i.e., the Spartans] wanted. For while many (Spartan) ambassadors had come, they never said the same thing." (4.50) In other words, if the Spartans had specific proposals in mind, they should send men capable of making them. The Athenians decided to send ambassadors instead, but upon reaching Ephesus in western Asia Minor they learned that Artaxerxes had recently died, so they returned home. Because of the structure of Thucydides' narrative, scholars thus thought for a long time that Artaxerxes died in the year 425/424; however, Babylonian documentation indicates that Artaxerxes' death occurred in 424/423.[9]

Beginning in the late 420s, there is a gap in Persian-Greek political relations for roughly a decade. The war between Athens and Sparta was on hiatus but not over. A disastrous Athenian expedition against Sicily from 413 to 411 encouraged many of Athens' subjects in Ionia to rebel, and Sparta and its allies took advantage as hostilities recommenced. Persia – mainly through its financial resources – then assumed a much larger role in the war. From the Persian perspective, order and stability in the Empire was an expectation: the northwestern territory of Yauna (Ionia) did not fit this expectation. With Athens reeling, the Persian satraps in Anatolia saw opportunities to reassert Persian authority in Ionia.

Pharnabazus in Hellespontine Phrygia and Tissaphernes in Lydia not only sought stability but also increase in their own prestige, and they occasionally were at odds in pursuing their own agendas. Both actively sought Spartan military aid to rid themselves of the Athenian presence in their territories but the Spartans initially chose to help only Tissaphernes. Thucydides notes (8.57) that Tissaphernes' aim was to keep the two sides (Athens and Sparta) equal, with the hope that this might prevent them from interfering in his satrapy, which included Ionia.

Persian-Spartan coordination was ensured through a treaty negotiated between the King (through his representative Tissaphernes) and the Spartans and their allies. Thucydides preserves actually three treaties, which some scholars consider to be separate drafts, or stages, of the negotiations. An acknowledgement of Persian control of western

Anatolia was paramount.[10] The rest of the first agreement (Thuc. 8.18) is straightforward. Both parties would prevent Ionian cities from sending money to Athens; both parties would jointly wage war against Athens; neither would make peace with Athens unless both parties agree; and the Persians and Spartans would consider any rebels of their treaty partner as their own enemies. The second (8.36–37) and third versions (8.58) modify the first in diplomatic nuance and in logistics, which reflected changing conditions. For example, the insistence on stopping Athens' collection of tribute is modified to emphasize that the Spartans would not collect tribute either – that was the Persian prerogative. The issue of pay for Spartan forces was a major one, reflected in these further modifications: Spartan forces operating in the King's territory and for the King's aims – that the Spartans did not view their involvement that way was another matter entirely – were to be supported by Persian money. Tissaphernes subsequently spent a great deal of effort trying to stall or circumvent these incredibly expensive obligations, which at least initially would have been from his own resources. His actions in delaying payment may be considered bad faith (a Spartan perspective) or good strategy (a Persian perspective).

The third treaty draft finds an echo in an interesting but fragmentary inscription from Xanthos in Lycia (southwestern Anatolia). Thucydides relates that the third treaty was made at Caunus, along the Lycian-Carian frontier, which is identified in the Xanthos inscriptions as the site of a treaty between Tissaphernes and the Spartans. The inscription is found on the side of a funerary pillar that celebrates the accomplishments of the dynast Kheriga (Greek *Gergis*) buried there. It has two versions in Lycian and a short summary in Greek. In the inscription Tissaphernes is called the son of Hydarnes. Hydarnes is not an uncommon name, but the temptation is strong to connect this Hydarnes with the family name of one of the Seven, thus linking Tissaphernes to a prominent family who supported Darius II's rise. Hydarnes' support was rewarded by marriages to Darius II's children. Not all scholars accept this link for Tissaphernes, however.

Continued Spartan ambivalence about their negotiating partner Tissaphernes led them to consider cooperating with another satrap, Pharnabazus, in Dascylium. Athenian control of the strategic shipping route through the Hellespont, through which the city was supplied with much of its food, was slipping. Pharnabazus, like Tissaphernes, was prepared to exploit Athens' difficulties. In 411, perhaps dissatisfied with Tissaphernes' failure to pay them (Thuc. 8.80), the Spartans accepted Pharnabazus' offer to fund a Spartan fleet operating in the Hellespont. Within two years, thanks to renewed Athenian success in the Hellespont, Pharnbazus was making terms with the Athenians instead.

The ebb and flow of Persian support between Sparta and Athens, on the part of two different satraps, make for a confusing historical period. One wonders how the King and his court officials interpreted the vacillating fortunes and negotiations – of which the King would have been informed – of his two satraps in western Asia Minor. One sign of Darius' thoughts was the dispatch in 408 of his younger son Cyrus with special powers that superseded those of both satraps. This Cyrus is usually called "Cyrus the Younger" in modern texts to differentiate him from Cyrus the Great, the founder of the Empire. Xenophon, whose *Hellenica* becomes our main source for this period, uses the title *karanos* for Cyrus' position, but it is unclear what exactly that term meant.[11] Cyrus' arrival proved crucial in the Greek conflict. His unwavering support for the Spartans was decisive in ensuring the Spartan victory over Athens in 404.

10 Maintaining Empire: Artaxerxes II and Artaxerxes III

THE DEATH OF DARIUS II AND THE ACCESSION OF ARTAXERXES II

From the historian's perspective, the last years of Darius II are notable mainly for the events that led to the civil war between Darius II's successor, Artaxerxes II (Arses), and his younger brother Cyrus. It soon became clear that Cyrus' aim in trying to hasten the end of the Peloponnesian War was to prepare a Greek mercenary army to help him overthrow his brother. Cyrus' expedition and the defeated Greek mercenary army's return westward were immortalized by the Greek writers Ctesias and Xenophon as well as by Plutarch in his *Life of Artaxerxes*, which relied heavily on Ctesias' and Xenophon's accounts. Xenophon was a participant in Cyrus' expedition and thus well-placed to offer a Greek insider's perspective. While we have a rich trove of Greek sources to tap, we have relatively little Near Eastern material to supplement or correct them.

The final years of Darius II are mostly opaque. Trouble in Egypt around 410 BCE may presage its full secession between 401 and 399. A terse reference in Xenophon's *Hellenica* (1.2.19) implies a rebellion in Media in 408, but no details as to its seriousness or extent are given. Xenophon also alludes to Darius on campaign against rebellious Cadusians (somewhere south of the Caspian Sea, *Hellenica* 2.1.13) in 405, but no context is provided. An oblique reference in a Babylonian economic tablet dated to 407 appears to imply, based on similar occurrences of the rare phraseology used in the text, that a state of siege existed in the city of Uruk in southern Babylonia, but one hesitates to read too much into an isolated reference. It is impossible to discern if these episodes were significant problems beyond the routine troubles any imperial power would face.

Darius II with his wife Parysatis had two sons, Arses and Cyrus, with Arses as the designated successor. Arses, sometimes spelled Arsaces, took the throne name Artaxerxes II. Plutarch (*Artaxerxes* 2.3) suggests that the succession was up for grabs until the end of Darius' life. Parysatis purportedly preferred Cyrus and wished for him to become king, so she summoned him from his command in Asia Minor in hopes of arranging the succession for him. That Darius II would have waited until his deathbed to proclaim a successor stretches credibility, however. The careful and ritualized preparations of the designated crown prince were not a last minute phenomenon. That Cyrus may have returned when his father's death was imminent is believable enough, but he would not have done so with hopes that he would be named successor.

Xenophon (*Anabasis* 1.3) and Plutarch (*Artaxerxes* 3.3–5) both report that Cyrus planned an attempt on Arses' life during the coronation ceremony at Pasargadae. This was not the work of paid assassins but rather planned as an ambush by Cyrus himself. Tissaphernes revealed the plot, and only Parysatis' intervention saved Cyrus' life. He was sent back to his post in Asia Minor. That is a surprise, and one is right to be skeptical, but the incongruity may stem from the sources: details may have been conflated or exaggerated in light of Cyrus' open rebellion later.

THE WAR BETWEEN THE BROTHERS

Cyrus' support of the Spartans in their war against the Athenians thus came to be viewed as motivated by his own agenda. Cyrus mustered his Greek mercenary forces in Thrace and the Hellespont, areas presumably less likely to attract imperial attention. But the ostensible reasons for his campaign would be more important than any attempt to keep the mustering itself a secret. Garrison commanders were initially told that preparations were being made against Tissaphernes, thus cast as an episode in a rivalry. This is told from a Greek perspective. Any such conflict would have been construed by the King as an act of insubordination, if not rebellion. As the muster continued, Cyrus then claimed that he was preparing a campaign against the Pisidians in central Anatolia. Neither

Tissaphernes nor Pharnabazus was deceived. Tissaphernes doubted that such a large force was aimed at nettlesome tribesmen (Xen. *Anab.* 1.2.1–4). Pharnabazus learned the truth of the matter from an Athenian exile and sent a special dispatch, as early as 404, straight to the King (Diodorus 14.11.2–3). These reports suggest that, whatever Cyrus told his followers and however carefully he disguised his intentions, the coming rebellion could not have taken Artaxerxes by surprise.

Xenophon's *Anabasis* contains a consistent theme that highlights the precariousness of Cyrus' army: Cyrus' Greek followers were not informed of the true goal of the expedition. Time and again their suspicions were raised, until either further deception or an increase in pay was applied to keep the men on the march. The truth was revealed – along with a promise of a huge bonus – only when they were in northern Syria. Despite Xenophon's clear admiration for Cyrus, it is notable that relatively few high-ranking Persians were to be found in Cyrus' camp. Stripped of its Greek veneer and considering Xenophon's perspective as a participant, what we have in the *Anabasis* is an adventure story: a rogue royal whose charisma and deep pockets presented a clear danger to the King. It is an open question what level of support Cyrus might have generated had he successfully killed his brother. Xenophon does provide the names of some Persian supporters, but both his and Ctesias' vague references to large numbers defecting to Cyrus are unsubstantiated. One example of resistance occurred while Cyrus was still in central Anatolia. He there plundered the territory of Lycaonia because it was hostile (*Anab.* 1.2.19), by implication, because the inhabitants refused to support Cyrus with provisions.

Of particular note are those who worked against Cyrus. The Achaemenid system – focused on loyalty to the King – proved effective. As noted above, both satraps in western Asia Minor, Tissaphernes and Pharnabazus, warned the King about Cyrus' preparations. Another high-ranking Persian, Orontas, described by Xenophon as a member of the Achaemenid extended royal family, acted as a double agent (*Anab.* 1.6.1). A subordinate of Tisasaphernes, Orontas initially acted against Cyrus from Sardis, but subsequently went over to Cyrus and offered his services. Gathering some of Cyrus' cavalry, Orontas then sent to Artaxerxes a message that professed his loyalty and promised to come to the King with cavalry. But Orontas was in turn betrayed, and the message delivered to Cyrus instead, who then executed him after a secret trial. While Cyrus' forces were marching through Cappadocia in central Anatolia, Cyrus executed a certain Megaphernes – whom Xenophon calls a royal scribe – and another important man among Megaphernes' lieutenants (*Anab.* 1.2.20) on the charge of plotting against him. Xenophon provides no other details, but apparently Megaphernes also remained loyal to the King. The local ruler of Cilicia, whom Xenophon calls Syennesis (the name is actually a title), was compelled by the threat of Cyrus' army to offer aid, but he simultaneously sent messages to the King assuring his loyalty.

The confrontation occurred at Cunaxa, northwest of Babylon along the Euphrates River. Xenophon (*Anab.* 1.7.10–13) states that Cyrus' army consisted of 10,400 hoplites and 3,500 peltasts (light-armed infantry), along with 100,000 barbarians (non-Greeks). Of the King's army of 1,200,000 infantry, 200 scythe-bearing chariots, and 6,000 cavalry, only(!) 900,000 infantry and 150 chariots took part in the battle. This was because one of Artaxerxes' commanders, Abrocomas, arrived from Phoenicia too late for the action. Plutarch's account (*Life of Artaxerxes* 7.4–6) echoes Xenophon's, no accident because Plutarch mentions Xenophon explicitly. Both speak of 900,000 men, a typical exaggeration in Greek sources that – as a very approximate rule of thumb – may be assumed to be exaggerated at least tenfold. For the drama of the battle, and the unsurprisingly valiant and effective efforts of Cyrus' Greek contingents, one may turn to the pages of Xenophon or Plutarch. And, of course, Cyrus' own bravery is lionized, even while fighting at 10 to 1 odds, as he sought out and engaged his royal brother. Cyrus in fact wounded the King but was then struck by a javelin and died shortly thereafter.

But the battle was not done. Various Persian contingents regrouped but were still unsuccessful attacking Cyrus' Greek troops, even though the Greek mercenaries now had no point in being there. Their purpose – Cyrus – was dead on the field. Persian forces had meanwhile plundered the Greek camp and taken many of their provisions. Cyrus' deputy, the Persian Ariaeus, was induced to leave the Greek forces to their fate and return to the King. The Greek mercenaries then offered to enlist with the King for a campaign against rebellious Egypt but were summarily rebuffed. At a parley after the battle, Tissaphernes arranged the capture of almost all the Greek generals, an act of supreme clever-ness or abject treachery that depends on one's perspective. The remain-ing Greek forces were left unmolested, though shadowed by Persian forces, to make their arduous journey homeward.

AFTERMATH OF THE REBELLION

Because Plutarch chose to dedicate one of his *Lives* to Artaxerxes II, we have many insights into the aftermath of Cyrus' rebellion and into court intrigues. Parysatis' grief and wrath at Cyrus' death exacted a heavy toll on the wider royal family. In the Classical literary tradition, she thus became a paradigm of the caprice and licentiousness of the Persian court, which – in the stereotype reliant Greek view – revolved around the machinations of powerful royal women and eunuchs (see pp. 94–96). According to both Ctesias and Plutarch, there was also great tension between the queen mother Parysatis and her daughter-in-law, the queen herself, Stateira. Stateira was the daughter of a high-ranking Persian noble, Hydarnes, whose support had been essential in Darius II's seizure of the throne.[1] The rivalry culminated in Parystis' clever poisoning of Stateira. As Plutarch relays it (*Life of Artaxerxes* 19) the two women distrusted each other so much that when they dined they ate the same portions from the same plate. Parysatis arranged a meal of a tiny bird, a delicacy so light that the Persians believed it lived on air and dew. The knife used to slice it was coated with a deadly poi-son, only on one side. The poisoned portion was given to Stateira, who died horribly a few days later. Artaxerxes in his rage and grief executed the table servants and banished his mother to Babylon. Greek sources reveal Parysatis' mother's Babylonian origin, and documents from the Murashu archive show that Parysatis held vast estates in Babylonia – her sojourn there was certainly not in a foreign land. She and Artaxerxes were later reconciled.

When considering these tales of vindictive vengeance and cruel torture, the caprice of tyrants may offer sufficient, if clichéd, expla-nation. But these stories are also about the integrity and survival of the Achaemenid dynastic principle. The Achaemenids' emphasis on endogamous marriage was not simply a monstrous perversion of the natural order, as some Greeks believed, but rather a dynastic safeguard. While Ochus (Darius II) was struggling for the throne, intermarriage with another prominent, Persian family – in this instance the family of Hydarnes – was not only acceptable but desirous. But a prestigious family was as much potential rival as ally. In consideration of Darius II's own less than straightforward path to the throne, the link with Hydarnes' family may have expanded the potential pool of successors too much.

Darius and Parysatis, as children of secondary wives or concubines of Artaxerxes I, could both claim Achaemenid descent. So could others, such as Arsites and Pissouthnes (see p. 172). Once Darius II was secure on the throne, there was less hesitation – and perhaps more incentive – to reinforce the dynastic principle. The poisoning of Stateira represented also the complete annihilation of that rival branch to the royal line. Regardless of circumstances or pretext, that reinforced Achaemenid primacy. It is possible in such a context to view Parysatis' fierce actions, mainly on behalf of her husband or children, as a dynastic virtue motivated by her desire to preserve her own line, the Achaemenid line, unchallenged. It is easy to apply a moralizing perspective to horrific acts, but a superficial reading of these accounts misses many key matters of power – the accumulation or maintenance thereof – and prestige. The stakes were high: the control of a world empire.

ROYAL INSCRIPTIONS OF ARTAXERXES II

The extant royal inscriptions from Artaxerxes II's reign are associated mainly with finds from Ecbatana and from his construction works at Susa. One inscription was found in four copies on the bases of columns (A²Sa), in which Artaxerxes provided the standard titles and lineage traced, father to son, back to Darius I and, interestingly, one more generation to Darius I's father Hystaspes. Hystaspes' inclusion is a curiosity, over a century after his death, because he did not rule as king – at least, not as the Achaemenid king of kings.

In light of Cyrus' rebellion the chance for Artaxerxes II to broadcast his lineage, and thus his legitimacy, was no doubt a welcome one. He further reinforced the link by direct reference to his restoration of an *apadana* built by Darius I, one that had been destroyed by a fire during Artaxerxes I's reign. Persian kings were expected to undertake such restoration work, just as their Assyrian, Babylonian, and Elamite predecessors emphasized similar projects in their royal inscriptions. That this work involved building on, literally and figuratively, one of Artaxerxes II's most illustrious predecessors' works was no doubt also intentional. Another trilingual building inscription records a similar restoration project at Ecbatana, modern Hamadan (A²Ha). In addition, Artaxerxes built at Susa a large, new palace (roughly 10 acres, A²Sd) set among lavish gardens, a paradigmatic example of an Old Persian *paradayadam*. That Old Persian word is understood as the origin of Greek *paradeisos*, thus "paradise," but that translation and meaning are disputed. Beyond philological arguments, the garden setting makes one confident that the beauty and tranquility of the place, a "pleasant retreat" as some modern scholars translate *paradayadam*, was meant to be emphasized.

What is most striking in Artaxerxes II's building inscriptions is the mention of the gods Anahita and Mithra alongside Ahuramazda in the invocation formula, for example in A²Sd §2: "May Ahuramazda, Anahita, and Mithra protect me and what I have built from all evil." The inclusion of Anahita and Mithra is new, but the reasons for their inclusion are unclear. Explanations abound in modern scholarship, and there is little agreement. Both Mithra and Anahita are Iranian deities, and Mithra is prominent in the Vedic tradition as well: a warrior god and associated with the sun. Specific mentions of sacrificing to Mithra in an Achaemenid context occur in a much later source, Athenaeus (10.434e), in which Mithra's worship is associated with drinking and dancing. According to this later tradition, the festival of Mithra was the only time that the King got drunk.[2] He also performed a specific dance, unhelpfully labeled the *persica* ("Persian things"), though what sort of dance that was is unexplained.

Anahita was a fertility goddess, associated with water and the heavens. She was identified with a number of other deities: Greek Athena, Artemis, Aphrodite, and Babylonian Ishtar, a goddess of sexual love (fertility) and war. Syncretism between various traditions was commonplace in antiquity. In the Persepolis Fortification Tablets, numerous gods received sacrifice in the wider area of Persepolis itself, a phenomenon that may be assumed to apply throughout the Empire. Plutarch (*Art.*

Figure 10.1 King Approaching Anahita on a Lion, from a Fourth Century Cylinder Seal. Courtesy of The State Hermitage Museum, St. Petersburg.

27.3) implies that there was a shrine to Anahita in Ecbatana. One of the most famous representations of Anahita appears on a cylinder seal scene dated to the fourth century. The goddess is standing on a lion, symbolism closely related to that of Ishtar, and the king (wearing a distinctive crown) approaches her with hands outstretched in worship. Aelian (*On the Nature of Animals* 12.23, perhaps taken from Ctesias) describes a shrine of Anahita, whom he calls Anaitis, in Elam that housed tame lions, animals that again emphasize the Ishtar connection.

The king in Figure 10.1 is not labeled, but most scholars assume it is Artaxerxes II. Mithra and Anahita are listed, after Ahuramazda, consistently in Artaxerxes II's extant inscriptions. In other words, they are not anomalous to one inscription, so his devotion to them is clear. The Babylonian Berossus credited Artaxerxes with the introduction of Anahita's cult and the stipulation that she be worshipped by his subjects (Fragments 11–12). If accurate, it is safe to say that such a proclamation did not exclude worship of other deities. For whom was the proclamation meant? Berossus' listing of specific places matches the main administrative centers of the Empire: Persepolis and Pasargadae, Babylon, Susa, Ecbatana, Bactria, Damascus, and Sardis. (Notably,

Memphis in Egypt is not mentioned, a tacit acknowledgement that it was beyond Persian control at the time of this edict.) Based on this, it has been assumed that the Persians in the provinces were the target of this stipulated devotion to Anahita, especially the Persian satraps and their staffs. Why Artaxerxes chose to promulgate worship of Anahita among the Persians abroad is another matter, but one presumes he meant to use it as a binding mechanism, a reminder of royal power under the aegis of the gods. Because Anahita effectively disappears from Artaxerxes III's inscriptions – meaning that she is not mentioned in them – many questions linger.

PERSIA TRIUMPHANT: THE NORTHWESTERN FRONT

During the 390s BCE, continued squabbling among the Greek cities of the mainland allowed Persia to reassert its territorial claims in Ionia and the Hellespont, and even to influence affairs among the city-states of Greece proper. At least from the diplomatic perspective, Artaxerxes II was able to achieve in Greece what Xerxes had not – Persian domination. Because of the help that the Spartans gave to Cyrus in his revolt in 401, they were considered enemies of the King. The situation that prevailed in Greece for most of the last decade of the fifth century – Persian support of Sparta that enabled the defeat of Athens – was effectively reversed within a decade.

Artaxerxes awarded to Tissaphernes Cyrus the Younger's old command in western Anatolia (Diodorus 14.26.4 and Xen., *Hell.* 3.1.3). Tissaphernes' job was to reconsolidate Achaemenid holdings in Ionia, not an easy task. Not only did many Ionian cities resist, Greek sources indicate ongoing rivalry between Tissaphernes and his counterpart, Pharnabazus, the satrap of Hellespontine Phrygia. In 396, the Spartan king Agesilaus raided Pharnabazus' territories in the Hellespont. The following year he advanced as far as Sardis and destroyed Tissaphernes' *paradeisos* in the countryside, along with a Persian force contesting him. (Diodorus 14.80.1–5).[3] This defeat may have been a significant one, or at least tried Artaxerxes' patience, because it resulted in Tissaphernes' removal from command. Artaxerxes dispatched a Persian replacement named Tithraustes, about whom we know little, neither exact title nor family connection. With the aid of the same Ariaeus who had defected from Cyrus (and had obviously returned to Artaxerxes' good graces), Tithraustes took Tissaphernes prisoner and sent him to Susa. Several sources implicate Parysatis' implacable anger against Tissaphernes – for his part in Cyrus the Younger's eventual defeat and death – for the turn in Tissaphernes' fortunes.

In the interval, and with the King's imprimatur, Pharnabazus outfitted a new navy and appointed an Athenian admiral named Conon as the commander. This Persian fleet decisively defeated the Spartan fleet at Cnidus in southwestern Anatolia in 394. The situation in Greece itself in the mid-390s had deteriorated, with Sparta's hegemony there threatened by an alliance of its erstwhile allies and enemies: Athens, Argos, Corinth, and Thebes. Persian money supported this alliance, another instance of a successful policy to keep the Greek city-states unbalanced and diminish their threats to Persian interests. This situation impelled the authorities in Sparta to recall Agesilaus (Xen. *Hell.* 4.2), so the Spartan king's grand plans for an "anabasis" against the King were untenable – and probably not very realistic from the start. Artaxerxes and his satraps had the stronger hand.

Pharnabazus then took the offensive and removed Spartan governors throughout western Asia Minor. Pharnabazus apparently used a lighter touch this time, freeing Ionia with Conon, a Greek face, at the head of his navy and trumpeting the Ionians' own (internal) autonomy. In 393 Pharnabazus then carried the war much closer to Sparta itself. He reasserted Persian command of the sea in the Aegean, even up to the islands off the southern coast of the Peloponnesus itself. A garrison was left in Cythera, an island just off the coast. These were major Persian accomplishments: a reversal of Spartan hegemony in the Aegean.

A flurry of diplomatic activity followed. Spartan representatives led by Antalcidas – who became Sparta's main ambassador to Persia – negotiated with a certain Tiribazus (Xen. *Hell.* 4.8.12–17), who is described as the King's general in Anatolia. Antalcidas expressed willingness to cede formally all of Asia Minor to the King, with the Aegean Islands left autonomous. Other Greek city-states objected, as they had territories and interests in these regions. Tiribazus, for reasons not revealed, decided to support the Spartans secretly: he gave money to Antalcidas to support a fleet against the resurgent Athenians, who were still acting as

Pharnabazus' agents. The situation – as Xenophon depicts it, at least – became suddenly complex. Despite Tiribazus' authority in Asia Minor, he could not make a peace treaty on his own, so he himself traveled (or was summoned) to the King. The King's response was telling.

Artaxerxes replaced Tiribazus with a certain Struthas who was "to manage affairs on the coast" (Xen. *Hell.* 4.8.17). What does this mean? As many interpret it, the imprecise phrasing indicates only that Struthas replaced Tiribazus as satrap of Lydia. Alternatively, this wording implies that Struthas was given a special appointment, one whose command approximated that of Cyrus the Younger's. The imprecise phrasing may imply authority on par with, if not greater than, that of the regional satraps, but it remains an open question. A Greek inscription usually dated 392/391 BCE records a certain Strouses' arbitration, on the King's authority, of a border dispute between Miletus and Myous, cities in southwestern Anatolia.[4] This Strouses is understood to be the Struthas of Xenophon's account. Here is as good example as any of the actual application of Persian authority in this region of the Empire. Notably, the quarreling parties did not seek Athenian or Spartan adjudication of the matter.

Struthas was not dispatched to continue Tiribazus' policy. On the contrary, he pursued a strongly pro-Athenian policy, on par with what Pharnabazus had been advocating (and applying) for most of the previous decade. This impelled the Spartans to dispatch forces into Asia Minor, and the fighting – mostly skirmishing at this stage – was renewed. An anecdote related by Xenophon (*Hell.* 4.8.24) reveals the chaos in Ionia. The Athenians, just then supported by the King, had sent a flotilla of aid to the rebellious king of Cyprus, Evagoras; the Spartans, who were at odds with the King, captured and destroyed that Athenian fleet.

Diplomacy continued, and the Spartan ambassador Antalcidas carried the day with the King. By 387/386, the year of the so-called King's Peace – also sometimes called the Peace of Antalcidas – the situation had come to a head. Antalcidas was accompanied homeward by Tiribazus, who resumed his position in Lydia and whose return marked another change in policy: a return to the pro-Spartan stance the Persians had championed at the end of the fifth century. The King was prepared to ally himself with Sparta and go to war if his peace terms were rejected. And there was additional incentive: Antalcidas commanded an overwhelming naval force, supplemented by Persian support, with which he was able to seize control of the shipping routes through the Hellespont. Control of that sea lane threatened Athens' grain supply; it was the same tactic that helped Sparta emerge victorious during the Peloponnesian War. Ships and funding from the satraps of Lydia, Tiribazus, and of Hellespontine Phrygia, Ariobarzanes, augmented Antalcidas' force. The previous satrap of Hellespontine Phrygia, Pharnabazus, had been called to the interior so as to marry the King's daughter Apame (Plut. *Art.* 27.4). Some scholars identify Ariobarzanes as Pharnabazus' son, but his filiation is not given in Xenophon.

Athens was cowed, wary of the sudden change in Persian support that swung naval dominance to Sparta. All the Greek cities, Sparta included, were weary of the back-and-forth that characterized the so-called Corinthian War of the 390s in Greece. Persia's direct involvement on Sparta's behalf, even the threat thereof, once again changed the calculus. Memories of the last decade of the Peloponnesian War would still have been fresh in the minds of many. The change in Persian policy was a major boon, if not outright coup, for the Spartans. Spartan willingness to abandon claims to the King's Ionian territories was a compelling point in their favor.

The terms of the King's Peace of 387/386 read more like an edict than a treaty. Representatives of the Greek cities were summoned before Tiribazus, presumably in Sardis, where he showed them the letter with the King's seal and read out the terms:

King Artaxerxes holds it just that the cities in Asia be his along with Clazomenae and Cyprus of the islands. And the other Greek cities, both large and small, should be left autonomous, except for Lemnos, Imbros, and Skyros. These, just as in the past, should belong to Athens. And if either of the two parties does not accept this peace, I will make war upon them, along with those willing to abide by these terms, both by land and by sea, both with ships and with money. (Xen. *Hell.* 5.1.31)

The few specific places named reflect some of the underlying negotiations. Clazomenae in western Anatolia had previously been controlled by Athens, but Artaxerxes specifically included it in his domain. The Aegean Islands left to Athens were closer to the Greek mainland than to Ionia and were thus, apparently, not of sufficient concern to the King.

Cyprus was probably only mentioned to encourage the Greeks to cease their meddling there while the Persians brought the Cypriot rebels to heel.

The application of the King's Peace, especially the King's explicit threat to wage war against those who refused to accept it, has been debated ever since. Many scholars reject as unrealistic the likelihood of Persian military action on the Greek mainland. But in 393 Pharnabazus, one of the highest ranking Persians in the west, had recently arrived with his fleet at the Isthmus of Corinth; perhaps the thought of another Persian campaign in Greece was not so far-fetched after all. Despite the Peace, the bitter infighting and squabbling among Greek city-states continued unabated. Later sources indicate that Artaxerxes insisted on reaffirmation of the terms of the Peace in 375 and 371 BCE.

CYPRUS AND THE EGYPTIAN PROBLEM

Because of its strategic location off the Phoenician coast, control of Cyprus was the prerequisite for control of the eastern Mediterranean seaboard. This in turn was necessary to any successful Persian reconquest of Egypt, especially because the Egyptian rebels were primarily based in the Nile delta region. Like Greece, Cyprus consisted of several independent city-states, the rulers of which were in constant competition. One of these rulers, Evagoras of Salamis, had wider ambitions to control the entire island. His career is mixed and often difficult to track. Some scholars postulate that he aided Cyrus the Younger in his revolt, but there is no evidence to confirm that. In 398, Evagoras did support the Persians' efforts against the Spartans in Asia Minor. Ctesias' *Persica* alludes to friction between Evagoras and Artaxerxes (Fragment 30 §72), but the context is lost. Diodorus relates Evagoras' defeat at sea in 386 and a Persian siege of Salamis (15.3–4 and 15.8–9). Persian authority was restored within a few years. A broken reference in a Babylonian astronomical text dating from 382/381 implies a reconquered Salamis.[5] Interestingly, Evagoras was allowed to continue as king in Salamis but was to pay the expected tribute and obey Artaxerxes, the King of kings.

EGYPT IN REVOLT AND THE ARSHAMA ARCHIVE

The most significant foreign crisis that we can track during Artaxerxes II's reign is the revolt of Egypt, a sporadic affair that involved several Egyptian rulers (mostly from the Delta in the north) and that effectively removed Egypt from Persian control for the first half of the fourth century. Egypt was able to resist full reincorporation into the Empire until Artaxerxes III's reconquest in the late 340s BCE. Many of Egypt's kings' reigns in the fourth century were of short duration, a reflection of Egypt's own internal struggles. The initial stages of this rebellion may be tracked during the transitional period from the reigns of Darius II to Artaxerxes II.

An important corpus of sources from Egypt partially overlaps this period of unrest: the so-called Arshama archive, named after the Persian satrap of Egypt in the late fifth century. Arshama is Greek Arsames, the name of several prominent Achaemenids, among them Darius I's grandfather and one of Darius I's sons by Artystone (daughter of Cyrus), a half brother of Xerxes and the commander of the Arabian and Ethiopian forces during the invasion of Greece (Hdt. 7.69). Any connection to the Persian satrap Arshama is unclear – perhaps he was a grandson of Darius' son Arsames? This is often assumed, but unproven.

In this archive's varied documentation we find reference to Arshama's satrapal responsibilities juxtaposed with great concern for his personal holdings. Topics range from the distribution of rations to slaves to transfer and maintenance of property. One of the more striking letters contains the satrap's admonishment to his subordinate Nakhtor to take advantage of unrest in Egypt itself to bolster Arshama's own holdings (A6.10).[6] That Arshama and other satraps were concerned to maintain their own positions and economic security is hardly surprising, but it is not often that we are able to track it directly. From Babylonian documentation we learn that Arshama also held estates in Babylonia, like many other notables of the time. The Arxanes whom Ctesias identifies as the satrap of Egypt, who aided Ochus (Darius II) in his bid for the throne, has been identified with this Arshama. If that is correct, Arshama was satrap in Egypt by or before 425. Extant documentation indicates that he served as satrap until at least 407.

Amyrtaeus of Sais, in the Delta, rebelled against the Persians and was recognized as king sometime in 404/403, according to the Egyptian writer Manetho. Amyrtaeus' rebellion seems to have been confined to the Delta region. His name suggests a dynastic link, whether real or fabricated, with the Delta kings who had rebelled during Artaxerxes I's reign in the 460s. The progression of the revolt through southern Egypt is not entirely clear. Some of the Aramaic documents from Elephantine continued to be dated to Artaxerxes II reign until 402 or 401, but the significance of that is debatable. By 399 at the latest Egypt must be considered outside Persian control, but warring factions within Egypt itself led to instability. Amyrtaeus was deposed in 398/397 by Nepherites I, whose own reign (c. 398–391 BCE) ended in an Egyptian succession crisis – one of several in this turbulent period – that produced one of the longest ruling of the rebel kings, Akoris (391–378 BCE).

After the Aegean front was stabilized in the early 380s (see discussion earlier in this chapter), Artaxerxes apparently applied a more sustained focus on Egypt but one that was in the short-term unsuccessful. The Athenian orator Isocrates alludes to a massive Persian campaign against Egypt in the late 380s, but there is no reference to such a campaign in other sources. Isocrates portrays Persia's inability to reconquer Egypt as a sign of weakness (*Panegyricus* 140). Isocrates made a career of agitating for a pan-Hellenic campaign against, as he describes it, a weak and doddering Persian Empire – his characterization is exaggerated.

In the 370s, Pharnabzus, previously the satrap of Hellespontine Phrygia, was charged with retaking Egypt, now ruled by Nectanebo I. Diodorus relates Pharnabazus' need to resort to ship transport to circumvent elaborate defensive fortifications (15.41–43.4). Pharnabazus' failure to follow his Greek mercenary commander Iphicrates' advice to take the undefended capital Memphis in a quick strike, while the Egyptian rebels were still stationed in the Delta, doomed the campaign to failure. That miscalculation and subsequent Egyptian successes ultimately forced a Persian withdrawal. Diodorus' stylized Hellenocentric approach – which generally elevates the Greeks and denigrates the Persians, as in the case of Iphicrates and Pharnabazus' differences – makes the particulars of this account difficult to gauge. The true course and strategy remain uncertain, but scholars tend to accept the general outline of a significant but failed attempt to recapture Egypt by force in the mid-to-late 370s.

In the late 360s, Tachos (coruler and then successor of Nectanebo I) launched a major campaign into Phoenicia, an area in which Egypt had long had an interest. During the campaign, Tachos' nephew rebelled against him and seized the throne under the name of Nectanebo II. Various late sources suggest that Tachos' nephew's rebellion was a consequence of Tachos' defeat by a Persian army in Phoenicia. Whatever the truth of the matter, Tachos fled, of all places, to Persia. There he was welcomed by Artaxerxes, who planned another attempt at the reconquest of Egpyt. But that campaign was ultimately left to Artaxerxes III.

Scattered references dating to the last decade of Artaxerxes II's rule remind us that the Aegean and Egyptian fronts were not the only concerns of the King. An entry in one of the Babylonian astronomical diaries refers to a campaign in 369 against a place called "Razaundu," the location of which is uncertain. Opinions vary but a location somewhere in northwestern or north central Iran seems most likely; the fragmentary entry does not preserve details of the campaign. It has been linked to a reference in Plutarch (*Art.* 24.1) to Artaxerxes' campaign against Cadusians in the north. Another Babylonian astronomical diary entry indicates that in 367 the King met an unspecified threat somewhere in (northern?) Mesopotamia.

REVOLTS IN ANATOLIA

Other threats to Persian stability developed in Anatolia in the late 360s BCE. In modern treatments, the so-called Great Satraps' Revolt has often been put forward as a harbinger of the end of the Empire. That somewhat melodramatic assessment has been called into question, and what has resulted is a classic historiographic case study on the nature and interpretation of our evidence for the Achaemenid Persian Empire in the fourth century. There are fundamental problems in the chronology and reliability of the ancient accounts that allude to this revolt – or, better put, revolts – and many scholars are unprepared to accept a unified effort by several satraps that was carefully orchestrated against the King. Diodorus is the main source for the portrayal of an empire on the brink (15.90), at least in its western holdings. A number of satraps in Anatolia, aided by the Spartans and in conjunction with a major offensive by Tachos of Egypt, threatened Artaxerxes. The satraps included Ariobarzanes of Hellespontine Phyrgia, Mausolus of Caria (he of the famous Mausoleum of Halicarnassus), Orontes of Mysia, and Autophradates of Lydia.

To contextualize the revolts as a whole, Classical sources contemporary to the events are, unfortunately, of little additional help. Athenian orators such as Isocrates and Demosthenes include or omit, embellish or gloss, details about the King's troubles for their rhetorical purposes. Their job was to persuade an Athenian audience. On matters Persian, their speeches read like selections from a political campaign. This is not to imply that the references to revolts against the King are fabricated, but the details are on the whole unreliable. Some sources contradict Diodorus' much later account.[7] For example, Xenophon (in one of his minor works entitled *Agesilaus* 2.26) indicates that the rebel Ariobarzanes of Hellespontine Phrygia was defeated by royal forces commanded by none other than Autophradates, satrap of Lydia – Diodorus lists both as involved in the same revolt. That the King faced challenges in his territories is nothing new. That these challenges may occasionally have come from satraps' rebellions is also not new. But a revolt coordinated by many satraps simultaneously would definitely be new, at least with our extant documentation. The varying traditions in the Athenian orators' speeches, in Diodorus, and in other sources likely reflect real problems in Anatolia, but the particulars are in doubt.

FROM ARTAXERXES II TO ARTAXERXES III: ANOTHER SUCCESSION CRISIS

Our most detailed source for the history of this period, Diodorus, mentions the transition from Artaxerxes II to Artaxerxes III only briefly (15.93.1), and he got the chronology wrong. Babylonian texts indicate that Artaxerxes II ruled forty-six years (405–359 BCE), not the forty-three of Diodorus, and that Artaxerxes III ruled for twenty-one years (359 to 338 BCE), not the twenty-three of Diodorus. In reading Diodorus, one could get the impression that the transition occurred without incident, but other sources give a different impression.

Plutarch in his *Life of Artaxerxes* portrays Ochus – Artaxerxes III's name before he took the throne – as a bloodthirsty, conniving rogue. Artaxerxes II and Stateira had three sons: Darius (the eldest), Ariaspes, and Ochus himself.[8] Darius was designated crown prince (*Art.* 26–28), but nevertheless his schemes, ambition, and desire (for one of his father's favorite concubines, no less) led him on a convoluted path to rebellion. When the plot was revealed, Darius, several courtiers, and fifty of his illegitimate half brothers, along with their entire families, were killed. Then, through veiled (and fabricated) threats that Ochus orchestrated as though they came from the King himself, Ochus drove his brother Ariaspes to grief and, ultimately, suicide. Artaxerxes' favorite illegitimate son, Arsames, then gained stature at court, only to be killed by a noble Arpates, son of Tiribazus, at the instigation of Ochus. This series of scandals was apparently too much for the old king Artaxerxes II, who died shortly thereafter.

This whole story reads like high romance, probably inspired by Ctesias' *Persica*, so its validity is immediately cast into doubt. To add to the salaciousness of his account, Plutarch portrays Ochus as having been encouraged by his lover, a half sister named Atossa. Atossa was the youngest daughter, and also a wife, of Artaxerxes II, thus making her Ochus' stepmother as well. Rather than asking if all these details could possibly be true, it is better to ask if any element might square with what we know is reliable. These stories about Ochus, who took the throne name Artaxerxes (III) are a mother lode of Greek stereotypes about Persian rulers and their families. According to a first century CE Roman writer, Valerius Maximus (4.2.7), Ochus buried his lover Atossa alive and also locked his uncle and 100 other relatives in a courtyard and had them shot down by arrows. As described by Plutarch, his character stands in stark contrast to the mild Artaxerxes II because Ochus "surpassed all others in cruelty and bloodlust" (*Art.* 30).

INSCRIPTIONS AND REIGN OF ARTAXERXES III

Artaxerxes III's own royal inscriptions are more in line with what we have come to expect from his predecessors, yet they also have some notable elements. Their archaizing language, coupled with a number of grammatical peculiarities, suggest a conscious hearkening back to the past. Inscriptions riddled with grammatical mistakes always arouse suspicion, but because these were found *in situ* at Persepolis, their authenticity is not in question. In this case, the errors are believed to reflect a use of the script and language that strove for an archaizing effect. In so doing, a sense of antiquarianism is fostered, one that adds to the inscription's authority, similar to the use of archaic sign forms in Cyrus' brick inscription at Ur (see p. 50).

An inscription in four copies from Persepolis testifies to Artaxerxes' building activity, reflecting the Near Eastern tradition of the king as builder and restorer (A^3Pa). Notable is Artaxerxes' lineage therein, a precise accounting through Darius I to his father Hystaspes and grandfather Arsames. This enhanced antiquarianism is curious, especially because Artaxerxes III – regardless of circumstances surrounding the royal succession – was a legitimate son of his predecessor. It may have been included for the archaizing effect just described.

The inscription opens with a standard invocation to Ahuramazda as the creator god, and he used the same phraseology Darius I used in his tomb inscriptions (DNa and DNb): "A great god is Ahuramazda, who created this earth, who created that sky, who created man" (A^3Pa §1). It closes with a standard blessing formula invoking Ahuramazda and also mentions Mithra as well. That is not so surprising, in light of Mithra's introduction in Artaxerxes II's inscriptions, but where is Anahita? Just as we have no reason offered for her and Mithra's inclusion in Artaxerxes II's inscriptions we have no reason given for her exclusion from Artaxerxes III's.

We revert to the classical tradition, mainly Diodorus, for a narrative of Artaxerxes III's reign. Even here the record is slim, though he reigned for twenty-one years. The early 350s BCE are mostly a blank, but the main foreign policy preoccupation continued to be Egypt. As is frequently the case with Diodorus, the chronology is confused; related campaigns and descriptions of their preparations are conflated into much shorter time spans than would have been necessary. Isocrates (*To Philip* 101) and Diodorus (16.40.3) allude to a failed attempt to retake Egypt dating to 351, but no details are known. Around this same time – before, during, or after makes a difference, but the sequence cannot be determined – Artaxerxes faced a crisis in the Levant in the form of revolts by some Phoenician cities, notably Sidon, and Cyprus.

Diodorus implicitly links all this trouble with the Egyptian problem. The Phoenicians and Cypriots rebelled "imitating the Egyptians" and in contempt of Artaxerxes (16.40.5).

The chronological range for these revolts is between 351 and late in 345. The latter date is confirmed by a Babylonian chronicle entry that refers to prisoners taken from Sidon to Babylonia and Susa. This evidence supplies a welcome certainty given the chronological difficulties inherent in the Classical accounts. Diodorus' implication is that Persian officials' oppressive behavior drove the people to revolt. This is understood by modern scholars to mean the Persians' demands during the ongoing war against Egypt.

Careful preparations are described, but Diodorus attributes Artaxerxes' victory in Phoenicia to the treachery – arranged by Artaxerxes beforehand – of a certain Tennes, the ruler of Sidon, who became overawed at the size of the approaching Persian force (16.45). The treachery motif is a stock one, which does not make it any less plausible, but its recurrence in Classical sources tends to overshadow more compelling questions of Persian strategy and logistics. Artaxerxes wanted to make an example of Sidon, so it was completely destroyed, according to Diodorus. But its full destruction must be an exaggeration, because within twenty years (at the time of Alexander the Great's invasion) it was again a large and thriving city. Cyprus was also compelled to return to the Empire, though the timing (before or after the capture of Sidon? – Diodorus indicates the latter) is unclear. In any case, with these areas back firmly under Persian control, the path toward Egypt was open.

Egypt had been beyond Persian control for roughly sixty years. To facilitate the invasion in 343/342, Artaxerxes III had summoned a large cadre of mercenaries from Greece. Diodorus offers, as usual, an outsized role to these forces in Artaxerxes' successful campaign. Diodorus' account (16.46.4–51) is unsatisfactory in other ways. One of his first remarks about the invasion is how Artaxerxes lost part of his army in the marshes of the eastern Delta because of his ignorance of the lay of the land. This is difficult to reconcile with reality. The Persians were familiar with the territory and approach into Egypt, having traversed it several times since Cambyses' invasion in 525 BCE. After securing the Delta region, presumably the main strongholds of the rebel kings, Artaxerxes' forces moved systematically south, up the Nile, toward

Memphis where his adversary, Nectanebo II, had withdrawn – but not for long. Afraid of the defection of other cities to Persia – which would have been described by the Persians as reaffirmation of loyalty to the Persian king – Nectanebo fled to Ethiopia and took refuge there. Later tradition elaborates several outrages committed by Artaxerxes as he laid waste to Egypt, some of which – for example the killing of an Apis bull (Aelian, *Varia Historia* 4.8) – echo those purportedly committed by Cambyses during his invasion in 525–522. It is difficult to give this credibility, but of course it makes for a neat literary parallel.

Diodorus finishes his account with a simple acknowledgement of Artaxerxes' victory and the appointment of a satrap named Pherendates. What Persian control of Egypt really looked like in the ten years before Alexander's invasion is unclear. An otherwise unknown Egyptian king called Khababash may have ruled in the early 330s BCE. His control over substantial parts of Egypt is implied by inscriptional material, but he does not appear in any extant Egyptian king list.[9] One other important development during Artaxerxes III's reign was the rising power of Macedon in the northwest, an issue that drives the narrative of the next chapter.

11 Twilight of the Achaemenids

THE DEATH OF ARTAXERXES III, REIGN OF
ARTAXERXES IV, AND ACCESSION OF DARIUS III

The death of Artaxerxes III and the period of transition to Darius III's accession is marked by treachery and violence – in other words, at least according to the Classical tradition, the norm. It may be more appropriate, if less dramatic, to grant that the circumstances of the succession remain elusive. A Babylonian astronomical tablet contains the laconic note that Umakush (the Babylonian name of Artaxerxes III) "went to his fate" (Akkadian *ana šimtišu illik*). This is standard Babylonian wording for a death often understood to be from natural causes, though that understanding here stems mainly from the direct contrast to the wording used on the same type of tablet for Xerxes I's assassination by his son (p. 157). Artaxerxes III died sometime between late August and late September of 338 BCE, and he was succeeded by his son Arshu, the Arses of Classical sources who took the throne name Artaxerxes IV.

The terse reference in the astronomical tablet stands in stark contrast to Diodorus (17.5.3–6), who indicates that Artaxerxes III was murdered. Bagoas, a eunuch and a chiliarch (a high-ranking military official), poisoned Artaxerxes, because the king "behaved forcefully and violently toward his subjects." Bagoas then elevated Artaxerxes' youngest son, Arses, to the kingship. Bagoas did not stop there: he slaughtered the young king's brothers with the intent of isolating Arses and making him easier to control. Arses, not surprisingly, reacted negatively to Bagoas' power play, so Bagoas killed the new king and his family during his third year of reign (336 BCE). Because the royal house was bereft, Bagoas installed as king one of Arses' "friends" – in reality, a second cousin of Arses – who became Darius III. Bagoas subsequently turned on Darius as well and poisoned his drink. But Darius got wind of the plot and invited Bagoas to drink first, as a token of his friendship, and thus the conniving eunuch met his end.

There are a number of problems with Diodorus' account. The consistent stereotype in Classical sources of the powerful eunuch gives one pause to consider what level of literary license Diodorus (or his source) may have taken with this sequence. It is hard to accept Bagoas as a king-maker, especially one who had a hand in the death of two kings over four years and attempted to end the life of a third. A Babylonian text, however, complicates a glib dismissal of Diodorus' account. Written in the style of a prophecy, the text lists major events that occurred during the reigns of Achaemenid kings.[1] For the reign of Artaxerxes IV there is a fragmentary reference to the murder of the king by a *sha reshi* official, the Akkadian term that has been frequently translated as "eunuch." This text provides a potential link to Diodorus' Bagoas, although the Babylonian text does not provide the official's name or any other details. The prophecy then says that a prince will seize the throne, and it accurately relays Darius III's five-year reign in Babylonia, from 336 until Alexander the Great's capture of Babylon after Gaugamela.

To return to the Classical tradition, both Diodorus (17.6.1–2) and Justin (10.3.2–5) trace the future-king Darius III's name and reputation to his good service and bravery during Artaxerxes III's war against the Cadusians in northern Iran, during which he slew one of their champions in single combat. Justin names him "Codomannus," and from the context it is clear that this Codomannus is the future Darius III; that name is sometimes used in modern works to identify him as Darius Codomannus. Babylonian documentation suggests that Darius III's original name was Artashata. We know little more about him before he became king, beyond the small but significant detail that he was from another branch of the royal line. He was the son of Arsanes, the son of Ostanes, who was a brother of Artaxerxes II. Justin further indicates that Codomannus was a satrap in Armenia, which, if accurate, indicates that the future Darius III had military forces at his immediate disposal. Justin omits entirely the reign of Artaxerxes IV from his account; therein Codomannus became Darius III right after Artaxerxes III died.

There are no surviving royal inscriptions attributable to Artaxerxes IV or Darius III, and the telescoped account in the Classical tradition reminds us again of the precarious nature of much of our knowledge.

MACEDON RISING

The history of the kingdom of Macedon, north of Greece, is obscure before the mid-fourth century BCE. In the late sixth and early fifth centuries, the Macedonian king, having given earth and water to Darius I, was a Persian vassal (see p. 83). Macedon's status vis-à-vis Persia after Xerxes' invasion, when Persian holdings in Europe were reduced, is unclear. Macedonians were not Greek, although the ruling family and elites were thoroughly Hellenized, and they shared cultural and political ties with Greek city-state neighbors to the south. Macedon, however, was not a city-state but rather a kingdom, one with extensive natural resources and manpower.

In the mid-fourth century, the dynamic and aggressive Philip II (reigned 359–336 BCE) expanded Macedonian power in southeastern Europe through alliance and conquest. Philip reformed the Macedonian army based on Greek phalanx warfare, an improvement over the militias that Macedon had relied on in the past. Members of the highly trained phalanx wore armor and helmets and carried a small shield and short sword. The greatest effect came from employment of the *sarissa*, a long spear or pike that could measure more than sixteen feet. Macedonian cavalry was a force with which to be reckoned, but it was the phalanx that Philip employed to overcome his Greek enemies and that Alexander subsequently used in Asia. Over the course of the 350s and 340s, Philip extended his influence into Greece proper. Athens and other Greek city-states were determined to resist him, despite Philip's greater numbers and resources. Ironically, that meant seeking Persian assistance; parallels with the situation on the eve of Xerxes' invasion are many. Philip, however, was already at Greece's doorstep. With his victory at the Battle of Chaeronia in 338, Philip became master of Greece. While we have massive amounts of Greek material charting Philip's activities there, we cannot track Persian reactions to Philip's rise – although the Persians would have monitored his activities closely.

The slim evidence we do have for Persian-Macedonian interaction during this period is often problematic, a function of the paucity of sources and their biased nature. One often cited example is found in Arrian's *Anabasis* (2.14). In the aftermath of Darius III's defeat by Alexander at Issus (see discussion later in this chapter), Darius purportedly sent Alexander a letter that alluded to the friendship and alliance between Artaxerxes III and Philip, mentioned an unspecified injustice that Philip committed against Arses (Artaxerxes IV), and accused Alexander of not renewing the alliance but instead invading Asia. Alexander's indignant response lambasted Darius for Persian military aid given to the city of Perinthus, a Persian force sent by Artaxerxes III into Thrace (considered by Alexander and Philip to be Macedonian territory), and Persian support for the plot that resulted in Philip's assassination. Any of these would be big news if confirmed, but the whole exchange appears to be a piece of Macedonian propaganda. Most of the assertions in the letter exchange must be treated with skepticism – as parts of a rhetorically charged context – given that the only verifiable accusation is Persian support for Perinthus in 340/339 BCE.

Perinthus was located on the northern (European) shore of the Propontis, an Athenian allied city that had resisted Philip's expansionism in Thrace and thus found itself besieged. Some speculate that Philip eyed this city and others nearby, such as Byzantium (modern Istanbul), as strategic holdings from which he could threaten Athens' grain supply. When word of the siege reached Artaxerxes III, the king sent instructions that provided Perinthus with troops and supplies (Diodorus 16.75). This may be considered the first verifiable clash between Macedon and Persia. In 339 BCE, Artaxerxes III would have considered this another flare-up on the far northwestern fringe of the Empire. The situation soon escalated. In 337, Philip called on the Greek city-states to provide contingents for an attack on the Persian Empire, according to Diodorus (16.89.1) because Philip "wished on behalf of the Greeks to launch a war against the Persians and to take vengeance upon them for their transgression against the temples." This was a not-so-subtle reference to Xerxes' destruction of the temples on the Athenian acropolis in 480 BCE, itself cast – according to the Greek tradition – as retribution for Athenian involvement in the burning of the Cybele temple in Sardis in 499. And so the propaganda cycle continued.

Reprisal against Persia was as good a pretext as any for a war. Philip's true motivation is much discussed in the modern literature. Perhaps it was nothing more than an expansionist power, flush with recent successes, setting its sights on larger and more tempting targets: the northwestern satrapies of the Persian Empire. This of course leads to larger questions: How far did Philip intend to go? What was the extent of his plans? Similar questions about aims and strategy are raised about Alexander's progress over the course of his invasion (Map 11.1). Similar questions – with similar uncertainties – have been posed also about Cyrus the Great's conquests more than 200 years earlier.

In 336 BCE, Philip sent a force of 10,000 men under his generals Attalus and Parmenion across the Hellespont, a campaign cast as the liberation of the Greek city-states of Ionia.[2] One target was Abydos on the Hellespont, which later became the staging area for Alexander's crossing, in 334. In 336–335, however, Persian forces under the commander Memnon, an Ionian Greek mercenary, were able to check the advance of Philip's forces at several points. At the time of Philip's death in the summer of 336, there was thus open war between Persian and Macedonian forces in Hellespontine Phrygia. This was the war that Alexander inherited. Alexander was twenty years old when he became king, having been tutored by the philosopher Aristotle and groomed for kingship by governing Macedon while his father was on campaign, when Alexander was not campaigning with him. Between 336 and 334, Alexander consolidated Macedonian power in Thrace and in Greece. He promulgated two clear messages: he would brook no challenges and he planned to continue his father's military operations in Asia.

SOURCES AND PROBLEMS

The historiography of Alexander is gigantic, suitable for a man that so captured the imagination of his own time and ever since. Alexander brought with him several writers and chroniclers to record his deeds, perhaps with an eye on the magnitude of what he meant to do. Not one of the works by writers contemporary with Alexander has survived to our day, but they were extant through much of antiquity and were used by later writers. These are now our main sources. The reader has

Map 11.1 Alexander's Route through the Persian Empire. After
Cambridge History of Iran, Vol. 2, 1985, map 17.

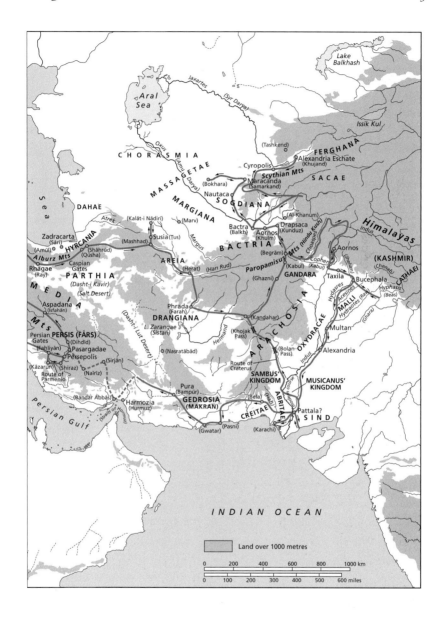

Lake Balkhash

Aral Sea

Jaxartes

(Syr Darya)

Issik Kul

CHORASMIA

Oxus (Amu Darya)

MASSAGETAE

(Tashkend)

FERGHANA

Cyropolis

Alexandria Eschate (Khujand)

Scythian Mts

MARGIANA

Nautaca

Maracanda (Samarkand)

(Bokhara)

SOGDIANA

SACAE

Margus

(Al-Khanum)

(Marv)

Bactra (Balkh)

Aornos (Khulm)

Drapsaca (Kunduz)

Himalayas

Indus

DAHAE

Caspian Sea

Atrek

(Kalāt-i Nādiri)

Susia (Tus)

BACTRIA

Paropamisus Mts (Hindu Kush)

Aornos

(KASHMIR)

Zadracarta (Sári)

(Āmil)

HYRCANIA

(Mashhad)

(Shāhrūd) (Qūsha)

AREIA

(Begrām)

Copher

(Kophen)

(Kabul) (Kabul)

Chenab

Alburz Mts

(Herat) Hari Rud

GANDARA

Taxila

CATHAEI

Rhagae (Ray)

Caspian Gates

PARTHIA

(Dasht-i Kavir) (Salt Desert)

(Ghazni)

Bucephala

Hydaspes (Jhelum)

Hyphasis (Beas)

MEDIA

Aspadana (Isfahān)

Mts

ARACHOSIA

MALLI

Acesines

Hydraotes (Ravi)

(Chara)

PERSIS (FĀRS)

Persian Gates

(Fahliyān)

(Dihdid)

Pasargadae

Phrada (Farah)

DRANGIANA

(Kandahar)

OXYDRACAE

Multan

Persepolis

(Kāzarūn)

(Shiraz)

(Sirjān)

(Naïrīz)

Route of Parmenio

(Dasht-i Lut Desert)

L. Zarangae (Sistan)

(Khojak Pass)

Helmand

(Nasratābād)

Route of Craterus

(Bolan Pass)

Alexandria

Indus

SAMBUS' KINGDOM

MUSICANUS' KINGDOM

Persian Gulf

Harmozia (Hurmuz)

Pura (Bampūr)

GEDROSIA (MAKRAN)

(Bela)

CREITAE

ABRITAE

(Nab)

SIND

(Bandar Abbās)

Straits of Hormuz

Pattala?

(Pasni)

(Gwatar)

(Karachi)

INDIAN OCEAN

Land over 1000 metres

0   200   400   600   800   1000 km

0   100   200   300   400   500   600 miles

already encountered Diodorus Siculus and Plutarch, to whom we now add Arrian, Quintus Curtius, and Justin, each of whom has been cited only occasionally thus far. All of these later writers date between two and four centuries after Alexander's death. Arrian, Quintus Curtius, and Justin are sometimes called the "Alexander historians." Of these, Arrian is generally considered to be the most reliable; he used and cited writings of Alexander's admiral Nearchus and other high-ranking military commanders. Reflecting the scope and scale of Alexander's march, these sources shed some light on the Achaemenid Empire's eastern provinces, which had hitherto been mostly neglected by earlier Greek writers.

THE INVASION BEGINS: BATTLES OF GRANICUS (MAY 334 BCE) AND ISSUS (NOVEMBER 333 BCE) AND ALEXANDER'S OPERATIONS IN ASIA MINOR

Macedonian control of Abydos served as a bridgehead for Alexander's forces to cross into Anatolia. Alexander's army numbered between 30,000 and 40,000 – a combination of the Macedonian phalanx, cavalry and royal guard, and Greek allies. Arrian (1.12.8–10) emphasizes the strategic discussions among the various Persian satraps and commanders in Anatolia, foremost among whom was Arsites, the satrap of Hellespontine Phrygia, in whose territory the Battle of Granicus occurred. The Greek mercenary commander Memnon's advice to his employers – do not engage the Macedonian phalanx but rather deprive them of provisions via a "scorched earth" policy – was rejected by Arsites, who refused to countenance any damage to property or harm to the people in his charge. In contrast to Arrian, Justin's account of the preliminaries (11.6.8–10) provides little information on the thinking or preparations of the commanders but focuses on Darius' attitude. According to Justin, Darius sought a straight-up fight (with no trickery) and even permitted the Macedonians to invade, because it was more honorable to repel them in a battle than to prevent them from landing.

Scholars debate the difference in tone of these two accounts. Justin's seems more apocryphal and romanticized. Of course Darius was apprised of the situation and in communication with his commanders, but the gist of any specific orders he may have given beforehand is unknown to us. The commanders would have had discretion as to where and how to prepare for battle on the ground. The Macedonians held Abydos, on the Asian side of the Hellespont, and the Persian fleet was not deployed – for reasons unclear to us, although it was later evident in full force around Miletus. So there was no attempt to prevent the Macedonian army's crossing, and the Persian force could only go about preparing to meet them in battle. Whatever the case about the preliminaries, the end result is clear. Alexander triumphed on the bank of the Granicus River in northwestern Anatolia, near Troy. The Persians focused on killing Alexander himself, and almost succeeded in hard fighting: Alexander barely escaped death thanks to a fellow Macedonian slicing off the arm of a Persian delivering what might have been a killing blow (Arrian 1.15.8). The Persian cavalry was trapped and slaughtered, the infantry fled, and Memnon's mercenary force was overwhelmed. The satraps' forces were scattered, and Alexander then had a free hand in western Anatolia, at least in those places that chose not to resist.

One place that did not resist was Sardis, and its loss was a key blow to the Empire. Spithridates, the satrap of Lydia, died at Granicus. Sardis' garrison commander, Mithrenes, voluntarily surrendered the city to Alexander. Why would a Persian commander freely surrender a satrapal capital so early in the fight against Macedon? Even with Alexander's victory at Granicus, he controlled only one corner of a vast Empire, and in the summer of 334 BCE the outcome of his invasion was far from certain. Indeed, based on the Persians' long history of conflict with recalcitrant Greeks – Macedonians were probably not viewed as much different – Darius III and his advisors likely had full confidence that Alexander's foray, like Agesilaus' in the 390s BCE, would be foiled or simply run its course. But even if the surrender of Sardis was a simple matter of Mithrenes and the Sardinians trying to save their own skins, their surrender was unlikely to have been spontaneous; there must have been negotiation with Alexander's agents.

In dealing with Mithrenes and Sardis, Alexander thus gave notice of his approach as conqueror. Achaemenid officials who surrendered were not only spared but might keep their position and status. Alexander needed the Persian imperial bureaucracy – headed mainly by Persian elites – to have any chance at maintaining a successful conquest. Sardis in 334, beyond a change in ruler and allegiance, looked no different than it had before Alexander arrived: local rule and local institutions continued. More than 200 years of Achaemenid rule would have "Persianized" it to some extent, especially among the elites. That component would not have troubled the new ruler, whose main concern going forward was a compliant imperial center behind him.

Alexander's progress through the rest of western Asia Minor followed a similar pattern: those cities that gave themselves up willingly were "liberated" from Persian rule and subjected to Macedonian rule with no dramatic changes in their civic affairs. Several cities chose that path, but many resisted, and Persian officials initiated counterattacks. Miletus held out thanks to Persian naval power. Alexander had disbanded his own fleet shortly after the Battle of Granicus to focus on the land campaign; his plan was to deprive Persian naval forces of bases and supplies, and thus ultimately to nullify their advantage. Resistance also persisted at Halicarnassus. Alexander was unable to dislodge the defensive forces gathered in the citadels. Meanwhile, Memnon was dispatched north along the Ionian coast to recapture cities that had submitted to Alexander. He met with much success until he was killed in a siege of Mytilene on the island of Lesbos during the summer of 333. Command passed to a certain Autophradates along with Memnon's nephew, Pharnabazus, who continued operations in Ionia and even the islands – testimony to the Persians' intent to contest every inch of Alexander's progress.

During the first part of Alexander's invasion, the action therefore occurred simultaneously on many fronts in Anatolia. Through the late summer of 334 BCE, Achaemenid forces were active in defending territory in Ionia and the Aegean, efforts that persisted into 332. Leaving the siege of Halicarnassus to deputies, Alexander turned east and during a difficult winter campaign – again facing significant resistance from many cities – took control of the coastal regions of Lycia and Pamphylia, while the Persians employed countermoves. Alexander's progress was inexorable, however, and the Persians soon lost the Phrygian satrapal capital Kelainai. The city of Gordion in central Anatolia (roughly 50 miles southwest of modern Ankara) was also taken, and Alexander spent several months there during the spring of 333, as he received reinforcements from Macedon and Greece.

Darius III himself was not idle. He massed forces in preparation for the second pitched battle against Alexander, this one at Issus in southeastern Anatolia. Several modern scholars attribute Darius III's failure to stop Alexander to Darius' dilatory approach to marshaling his army. The mustering of large Achaemenid forces was never a rapid process. Darius and his officials were in fact broadly engaged in defensive efforts as noted earlier in this chapter. Inexplicably, Darius failed to defend sufficiently the so-called Cilician Gates (a pass through the Taurus Mountains about 25 miles north of Tarsus), and by the summer of 333, Alexander had taken them and then continued on to conquer Tarsus, the capital of the satrapy of Cilicia. Alexander's and Darius' armies passed each other, within 100 miles, and wheeled about to meet at Issus, along the Pinarus River (identified with the modern Payas River) near the modern town of Iskenderun. Meanwhile, Persian commanders in Ionia – still fighting – coordinated their efforts with the Spartan king, Agis. The Spartans were determined to resist Macedonian rule, and cooperation with Persia was a logical choice. But before these efforts could bear any fruit, the Persian defeat at Issus changed the calculus. Thereafter the Persians abandoned any thought of operations in Greece, and Pharnabazus, the commander in charge, sped back to Ionia to deal with the consequences of this latest defeat.

The sources describe Darius III's army at the Battle of Issus (November 333 BCE) as momentous, and similarly the consequences of its defeat. Accounts vary. The Persian right wing apparently smashed the Macedonian left, but a full-out assault by Alexander and his cavalry on the Persian middle caused it to collapse and Darius to flee – a sequence so compellingly portrayed in the so-called Issus Mosaic (Figure 11.1). From the perspective of the Greek accounts on which we must rely, Issus was a complete catastrophe for the Empire. By any measure the battle had important consequences, although Persian forces remained battling in central Anatolia well into 332. Darius fled to a city called Thapsacus, along the Euphrates River. The defeat at Issus meant that the way to Phoenicia was now open, and this gave Alexander access to the Persians' main naval facilities based in the cities of Phoenicia.

During the winter of 333/332, Alexander captured the imperial treasury at Damascus, thanks to the treachery of its governor who went over to Alexander. Damascus was a critical center and, as it turned out, the

Figure 11.1 Roman Mosaic of Alexander and Darius III, Pompeii, First Century CE, Naples Archaeological Museum. Art Resource. Photo Credit: Erich Lessing/Art Resource, NY.

place where many prominent Persian families had gathered: those of the Persian elite and, most importantly, Darius' own family and household. Alexander thus found himself the captor of Darius' wife, mother, and several children: a disaster for the King and a gift for Alexander. The Persian defeat found exaggerated expression in the famous mosaic from Pompeii that portrays an energetic, brave Alexander, without a helmet, driving against a despairing, overwhelmed Darius III. This image encapsulates a Greco-Roman perspective of the weak and cowardly peoples of the Orient, an inaccurate stereotype visited time and again in the source material that has so colored subsequent tradition.

Issus was followed by further Macedonian successes, as the important Phoenician cities of Byblos and Sidon surrendered to Alexander. Only a decade earlier, Artaxerxes III forcibly reincorporated Sidon into the Empire after the city's revolt. Conversely, the Phoenician city of Tyre resisted Alexander for more than a year, ready for a long and expensive siege that Alexander had his soldiers pursue with relentless ferocity. Diodorus portrays the siege of the city and its fall in epic terms. He attributes the Tyrian resolve to their desire to remain on good terms with Darius and to their hopes for great rewards for their loyalty (17.40.2–3). With few exceptions, by the summer of 332 BCE, the Persians had lost control of their northwestern territories in Anatolia and also much of the eastern Mediterranean seaboard. This brought not only the Phoenician and Cypriot fleets to Alexander, but also several other contingents from Rhodes and other important bases along the southern coast of Anatolia. This meant the end of Persian naval superiority.

THE LOSS OF EGYPT, THE BATTLE OF GAUGAMELA, AND THE SURRENDERS OF BABYLON AND SUSA (332–331 BCE)

While Darius III mustered another army, thanks to the extent of the Empire's reach and resources, Alexander continued to drive south to take Egypt. Batis, the Persian official in charge of Gaza, which served as the access point to Egypt, had readied his forces to withstand a lengthy siege. Arrian relates that even after the city was breached, after two months of siege, the inhabitants of Gaza continued fighting, essentially street by street (2.27.7). Quintus Curtius (4.6.26–29) adds a striking anecdote about Alexander playing the part of Achilles, his ancestor and model. Alexander tied Batis, who refused to bow to Alexander as king even in defeat, to his chariot and dragged him, still alive, around the city, as Achilles had done with the corpse of Hector (*Iliad* 22.395–404).

With his fleet, Alexander then made a triumphant entry into Egypt. The Persian satrap Mazaces surrendered the satrapy of Egypt to its new overlord. Arrian notes that Darius had recently appointed Mazaces as satrap there, because the previous satrap Sabaces had been killed at Issus. Arrian's description of the surrender follows Greek stereotypes: Mazaces scorned Darius' flight at Issus and was therefore ready to welcome Alexander (3.1.2). In the same passage, Arrian notes that Alexander now controlled Phoenicia, Syria, and much of Arabia. That critical fact and Mazaces' apparent lack of manpower and resources put him in an untenable position, regardless of his personal feelings toward Darius.

The ease with which Egypt was taken by Alexander remains the
subject of intense debate in modern scholarship. If Mazaces was truly
unable to muster effective resistance, his surrender is not surprising, but
beyond Arrian's glib remark there is a dearth of detail about the situation. Egypt had only a decade before been reintegrated into the Empire
by Artaxerxes III, and we are uncertain about the extent of successful
control achieved. In any case, one cannot help but contrast Batis' fierce
resistance at Gaza and Mazaces' immediate surrender of Egypt without
a fight. That the satrapy of Beyond-the-River (Trans-Euphrates) was
not fully secured is illustrated by a revolt in Samaria against Alexander's
appointed governor there, Andromachus. Alexander reacted swiftly
by executing the perpetrators and installing a new governor. Quintus
Curtius (4.8.9–11) also links this episode to a purge of local, Persian-
supported rulers who yet remained in the Aegean – a message not only
to Samaria's population but also to his own Greek and Macedonian subjects that he was indeed in command of the situation.

Alexander's march through Samaria toward Mesopotamia set the
stage for the last set battle at Gaugamela (October 1, 331 BCE), just
east of the old Assyrian capital Nineveh on the Tigris River, where
Darius had amassed his army. Diodorus (17.53) describes an enormous
and well-equipped Persian army in splendid array and led by the most
excellent commanders – 800,000 infantry and more than 200,000 cavalry – along with scythed chariots, whose function was perhaps more of
shock than any real tactical advantage. From a Greek writer's perspective, the larger and more fearsome that Darius' army was the better, to
magnify Alexander's victory.

The Classical accounts about the Battle of Gaugamela are replete
with details about Alexander's feelings and anecdotes of high drama. For
example, Darius is described as making another approach to Alexander,
offering him the territory west of the Halys River in Anatolia, 30,000
talents of silver, and the hand of one of his daughters in marriage. The
last would have made Alexander, in effect, Darius' coruler. Alexander
rejected this offer and, with grandiose pomposity, compared an empire
with two kings to that of a world with two suns, a violation of the natural order of the earth (Diodorus 17.54.2–6). This is wonderful stuff,
but how much is history and how much hyperbole? Darius' offer to cede

half the Empire seems far-fetched to say the least, since there is no precedent in Achaemenid history or no component of their royal ideology
to help us imagine such a thing. On the other hand, Darius was dealing
with a new situation, an unprecedented threat. Any earlier assumption
that Alexander's expedition would come to naught would have been
long since abandoned, and there no longer would have been any under-
estimation of Alexander's capability or determination.

Darius' preparations – careful defense of river crossings, a scorched
earth policy along Alexander's line of approach, choice of battlefield to
maximize Persian cavalry – proved insufficient. The Battle of Gaugamela
itself hung in the balance for some time, but the Macedonians were
ultimately victorious. Darius fled the field, regrouped at nearby Arbela,
and then withdrew to Ecbatana in Media, where he intended to muster
yet another army from the Upper Satrapies – the phrase Diodorus uses
(17.64.1) for the territories of the Iranian plateau and beyond – with
which to challenge Alexander. A fragmentary Babylonian astronomical
tablet refers to the Persian defeat at Gaugamela, the desertion of at least
some of Darius' troops, and his withdrawal into "Gutium" – an archaic
term for the northern Zagros Mountains. It here refers to Media.

Darius' decision to withdraw to Media left the way open for Alexander
to march on Babylon and, from there, east across the Mesopotamian
alluvium to Susa. Once at Susa, the route south toward the Empire's
greatest prizes – Pasargadae and Persepolis – lay before him. Why
would Darius choose such a move? His withdrawal to Ecbatana in effect
ceded the core of the Empire, four of the five main capitals (exclud-
ing Ecbatana), to the enemy. The reasons typically given allow varied
interpretation. The centrality of the King himself – around whom the
entire Achaemenid system revolved – should not be overlooked. One
reason was strategic: according to Arrian (3.16.2) Darius thought that
Alexander would take the route to Babylon and Susa, and Darius therefore avoided that route. This was no doubt a difficult decision, but it
gave him time to organize another army in the north. If part of Darius'
calculations rested on the assumed loyalty of his satraps, that assumption proved ill-founded in the cases of Babylon and Susa.

Alexander's reception into Babylon in October of 331 BCE, as
related by Arrian (3.16.3–5) and Quintus Curtius (5.1.17–23), follows

the pattern of Alexander's reception at Sardis and, subsequently, at Susa – all cities that surrendered voluntarily. Both Arrian's and Quintus Curtius' accounts emphasize ritualistic acts that symbolize an orderly transfer of power. Alexander's entry into Babylon followed a discernible pattern for which there are several earlier historical examples. The most immediate and germane parallel was that of Cyrus' conquest of the city in 539 (pp. 44–46). After a hard-fought battle and decisive victory at Opis against the forces of the Babylonian king Nabonidus, Cyrus was received into the city of Babylon without a fight. This was a carefully choreographed entrance that belied the violence that preceded it. Cyrus arranged not only his entry into Babylon but also the messages associated with his assumption of power.

Arrian's and Quintus Curtius' accounts describe a similar sequence. The Persian satrap Mazaeus delivered the city to Alexander, and he was subsequently reappointed to that office. The Babylonians lined the walls and the streets to greet their new king, and the entry was a grand parade. A fragmentary Babylonian astronomical diary also relates this event.[3] The surrender of the city only occurred after negotiations between Alexander and the Babylonians assured a peaceful transition and, by extension, a traditional reception for Alexander. The reception culminated in Alexander paying respect to the Babylonian god Marduk (Bel) and his temple, a necessary part of the exercise. This peaceful entry belied the violence of the Battle of Gaugamela, the battle that paved the way, just as Cyrus' victory did at Opis in 539. In the astronomical diary Alexander is called "King of the World" (Akkadian *šar kiššati*), the same title used to describe Cyrus in the so-called Verse Account of Nabonidus. The title *šar kiššati* had a long history of use by Assyrian and Babylonian kings. The application of this traditional title to Cyrus was not accidental, nor to Alexander. In the latter's case, its use implies a continuity of imperial tradition and supplies a connection to Cyrus, highlighted by their similar welcomes into Babylon. Alexander received a similar reception from Susa in December of 331 BCE (Arrian 3.16.6–7). After negotiations, the satrap of Elam, Abulites, sent his son Oxathres to meet Alexander on the road to the city and to offer him a formal welcome. This culminated in the surrender of Susa and delivery of its treasury to Alexander.

THE DEFENSE OF PARSA

The next step was not so easy. In the first few months of 330, Alexander faced a difficult road from Susa to Persepolis. The Uxians, who dwelled in the Zagros Mountains, were only passed after extremely hard fighting, which was compounded by the difficult terrain. Alexander subsequently split his forces. His group continued traveling through the difficult mountain paths, Parmenion's group kept to the main road, which was more suitable for wagons, toward Fars.

A Persian army of 40,000 infantry and 700 cavalry, commanded by Ariobarzanes, held the so-called Persian Gates – an east-west pass through a river valley in the northern part of Parsa (Arrian 3.18.2–9). The main Persian forces waited behind a wall, and Alexander thus found his Macedonians in the role of the Persians at Thermopylae in 480 BCE with a narrow and fortified pass held against them. The Classical accounts abound with parallels, and it is therefore difficult to discern which elements are historical, which literary. Arrian's account relates a group of locals, prisoners, who led the attackers by night over mountain paths behind the defending forces. Unlike the heroic Greeks at Thermopylae, though, the cowardly – according to Arrian – Persian forces attempted to flee. Ariobarzanes with his remaining forces managed to break through the Macedonian line and made for Persepolis, with Alexander in close pursuit. Arrian draws no explicit parallel to Thermopylae, but of course he did not need to. It would have been as familiar to any Greek or Roman reader as a contrast between cowardly Persians and brave Macedonians. A high-ranking official at Persepolis, Tiridates, sent a letter to Alexander promising to deliver the city to him if he got there before Ariobarzanes did. Alexander caught, defeated, and killed Ariobarzanes and the remainder of his forces, and took control of Persepolis in mid-January 330. Gobares, who controlled Pasargadae, surrendered that city and its treasury to Alexander as well. Alexander ordered the mass removal of the contents of the treasuries mainly to Susa – according to Diodorus (17.71.2–3), because he was thoroughly suspicious of the inhabitants of Persepolis and he intended to destroy the city.

The sources are sparse about the next several months, with Alexander encamped in the heart of the Empire. It appears that Alexander had to expend a great deal of effort, and with mixed results, to quell resistance in the outlying regions of Fars. A visit to Cyrus' tomb to pay his respects to the Empire's founder culminated in the continuation of the traditional sacrifices performed there, but both Diodorus and Quintus Curtius (5.7.1–4) suggest continuing hostility from the inhabitants of Fars. In May of 330, much of the Persepolis terrace was burned. Alexander's motives for this are still debated, though most agree that it was a calculated act rather than a drunken impulse (Diodorus 17.72). Arrian casts the destruction (3.18.11–12) as Alexander's retribution for the Persians' burning of the Athenian acropolis and all the other harms done to Greeks – a recurrent motif. This makes a good story, but there was more to it. Even Arrian comments that he disagreed with the logic of Alexander's retribution. Most modern scholars supply much significance to the act: Persian rule was no more, and continued resistance was futile. Alexander thereafter turned his forces north on the direct route from Fars to Ecbatana, to continue his pursuit of Darius III.

Darius had not been idle, but his situation had become precarious. The sources do not reveal if conscripts summoned from the Cadusians and Scythians had not yet arrived or if they had abandoned the King. In any case, Darius' forces were becoming insufficient to his needs. After emptying Ecbatana's treasury, Darius departed the city before Alexander arrived (Arrian 3.19.4–5). The news of Darius' departure was brought to Alexander by none other than Bisthanes, a son of Artaxerxes III, who cast his lot with the invader. As the action progresses, abandonment of Darius becomes a recurring theme. Quintus Curtius portrays Darius as increasingly despondent, as those around him lost faith (5.9.13–17). Keeping with our sources' Hellenocentric bias, a certain Artabazus and a group of Greek mercenaries take on a prominent role in keeping the Persians' flagging spirits up. To compound Darius' grim situation, the satrap of Bactria, Bessus, along with Nabarzanes the chiliarch and other accomplices carried out a plan to capture the King for their own ends. Their strategy in turn, which we may assume was Darius III's actual strategy, was to employ the resources of Bactria and the eastern satrapies to forestall Alexander's advance, and from there to win back the Empire. In the end, Bessus and his accomplices attempted to kill the King with Alexander hot on their heels. They mortally wounded Darius and then fled.

Another interpretation of this episode has been put forward that fits well in a Near Eastern context. It is controversial, however. In Quintus Curtius' account (5.9.8 and 5.12.15–20) Nabarzanes attempts to persuade Darius to allow Bessus to take his place as king "for a time" (the Latin word *interim*), until the enemy withdrew. In other words, Darius would be replaced temporarily until the danger, made manifest by several bad omens, had passed. In this reading, the conspirators – who were not really conspirators, but loyalists – only apparently abandoned Darius. They removed his royal garb and paraphernalia, bound him in gold fetters, and placed him in an unremarkable wagon – all so that Darius would not be recognized by anyone. This description matches the portrayal in Classical sources of Darius forlorn and abandoned, suffering one disgrace after another as his death approaches. But this portrayal may instead be read as part of the substitute-king ritual of Near Eastern tradition (see p. 75), a divinely-inspired attempt to circumvent horrible omens and the coming disaster that was Alexander. The anguish and dismay of Darius is in this reading viewed as ritualistic behavior in a time of crisis and as a part of the ritual itself. With the perspective of hindsight, it is easy to contextualize such a ritual, if that is the correct interpretation, as a desperate attempt to forestall Alexander's victory. It is impossible to tell how much of a genuine ritual might have underlain this crisis, but the parallels to the substitute-king ritual provide a compelling counter-narrative. That Bessus and Nabarzanes killed Darius in the end – so the Classical tradition relays – suggests that the substitute-king interpretation is incorrect, that it went awry, or that the situation changed.

When Alexander arrived on the scene, somewhere in northern Iran on the route to Bactria, the last Achaemenid king had died, and the King was the Empire. Alexander did not hesitate to turn this to his advantage as well. Alexander treated Darius' body with utmost respect and sent it to Persepolis for burial befitting the King. Alexander took upon himself the role of Darius' avenger and thus his successor. Alexander continued the pursuit of Bessus, who had in the meantime proclaimed himself king with the name Artaxerxes. But the Achaemenid Empire was, for all intents and purposes, finished, although Bessus remained a threat to Alexander and his claim to Achaemenid rule could not be ignored. Even after Bessus' capture and execution – before which his nose and ears were cut off (Arrian 4.7.3–4, cf. 3.30.4–5), reminiscent of the punishments meted out by Darius I to the liar-kings (pp. 64–65) – Alexander continued to face heavy resistance in the eastern satrapies until early 327 BCE.

Alexander's "Persianization" also, not coincidentally, became more pronounced via his adoption of elements of Achaemenid kingship and the incorporation of Persian and Iranian elites into his entourage. Alexander's attitude and approach were bitterly unpopular with many of his Macedonian cohorts. These and other important aspects of Alexander's rule, however, are part of another (hi)story. It is at this point that we transition from Achaemenid history to the so-called Hellenistic period, in modern periodization starting with Alexander's successful conquest of Persia, especially the burning of Persepolis and the death of Darius III. Alexander was both transformative and transitional. If he was to have any chance at holding his conquests together, he had to model much of his rule on Achaemenid norms. Even with appropriate emphases on continuity, Alexander was obviously not an Achaemenid. Despite his amazing success, his rule was short-lived, and the Empire Alexander conquered did not long survive his death in 323 BCE.

12 Epilogue

Alexander cast himself in the role of Darius III's avenger. As he consolidated and expanded his conquests, it was necessary to put the Empire on a stable footing as he prepared for the future. Just as the Persians were "new" conquerors two centuries earlier under Cyrus, Alexander was likewise. But there were many differences, not least of which was familiarity. The Persians had lived in close proximity with the neighbors whom they conquered, in the core regions of Iran and Mesopotamia, for centuries previous. The Macedonians were an entirely foreign element to the region. And what Cyrus built almost from scratch Alexander conquered as a mature, unified entity. Cyrus' task had been to build; Alexander's was to prevent dissolution.

Alexander's fusion policy – the joining of Iranian and Macedonian elites – is debated in its particulars. Alexander recruited Iranian troops from throughout the eastern satrapies, including a specialized troop of 30,000 young men who were to learn Greek and to train in Macedonian tactics (Arrian 7.6.1 and compare Quitus Curtius 8.5.1). In 327 BCE Alexander married Rhoxane, the daughter of Oxyartes, an Iranian nobleman who was appointed as a satrap. Whatever other reasons motivated Alexander, this act secured allegiances among the eastern Iranian nobles. After his return from the Indian campaign in 324, Alexander also married the Achaemenid princesses Stateira (daughter of Darius III) and Parysatis (daughter of Artaxerxes III). At the same time he staged a mass marriage ceremony at Susa between members of his Companions (his own elite Macedonian corps) and Iranian noble women. This act recalls Darius I's marriage to Cyrus' daughters, but Alexander took the symbolism to an entirely new level by including dozens of his own nobility in the same process. The mass marriage in particular reveals Alexander's large-scale plan to integrate the Iranian and Macedonian elite, to form effectively a new ruling class.

Was Alexander simply being a pragmatist? Or was he intending some sublime synthesis of east and west, a new *oikumene* of which he would be the glorious founder? The first certainly applies, because of the obvious necessity of the continued involvement of the Persian governing class. The Macedonians had neither the experience nor the credibility, at least at first, to govern this sprawling empire. Answers to the second question, which is dramatically phrased, are more subjective. The image that Alexander chose to project took him beyond both Macedonian and Persian norms, and interpretations are as varied as they are fascinating. The subsequent development of the ruler cult, the deification of rulers during the Seleucid period, is not incidentally traced to Alexander's program.

Alexander's Persianization – regardless of its motivations – was bitterly resented by many of his Macedonian cohorts. It is an open question how well his fusion policy would have worked in the long run. But in the end Alexander had less than ten years, much of that time on campaign, to implement his plans. The splitting of the Achaemenid Empire among his successors into the Antigonid, Seleucid, and Ptolemaic monarchies (the so-called Hellenistic kingdoms) dominated the next three centuries of Near Eastern and Greek history, until the Roman conquests and the rise of the Parthians. Achaemenid imagery and traditions lived on not only in these eastern kingdoms – especially the Seleucid kingdom and some Hellenistic monarchies of Anatolia – but in the Persians' successors in Iran itself: the Parthians and Sasanians. The histories of these kingdoms have often been perceived as secondary, overshadowed by the Hellenistic kingdoms and then Rome, though their import was no less. This has been understood for some time, even if often overlooked.

Especially it seemed to the writer that the picture of the world during the Roman period, commonly put before students in "Histories of Rome," was defective, not to say false, in its omission to recognize the real position of Parthia during the three most interesting centuries of that period, as a counterpoise to the power of Rome, a second figure in the picture not much inferior to the first, a rival state dividing with Rome the attention of mankind and the sovereignty of the known earth.[1]

A recurring theme in this book has been the necessary reliance on Greek sources to write a narrative of Achaemenid Persian history, and all the problems that that entails. The poet Aeschylus' embellished portrayal of Xerxes – in a literally dramatic context, a play performed in 472 BCE in Athens – is paradigmatic of the west's portrayal of this monarch, seen for example in Xerxes' bitter lamentation after his disastrous defeat of his expedition against the Greeks:

Alas! Unfortunate I am, beset by an unfathomable fate, how brutally some god has trodden upon the Persian race. (*Persae*, lines 908–912)

As discussed, we have no Persian side of that story, but a Persian perspective – extrapolated from the ideology manifest in Xerxes' inscriptions, for example – would have been significantly different. The unavoidable reliance on Greek sources is not entirely negative, thanks to its rich and varied material. And it is being balanced by increasingly accessible data from Near Eastern sources, textual and archaeological, though much remains to be done. Not until the Roman Empire at its height did a supra-regional state again have the organizational capacity and similar capability to project its power as did the Achaemenid Empire. The Achaemenid Persian Empire served as both model and foil for its successors. Its legacy persists.

Appendix A – Timeline

c. 900–609:	Neo-Assyrian Empire
830s:	Earliest references to Persians in written texts (the annals of the Assyrian king Shalmaneser III)
c. 640:	Cyrus, King of Parsumash, pays obeisance to Ashurbanipal, King of Assyria
c. 640–550:	Height of Median power
c. 626–539:	Neo-Babylonian Empire
612:	Sack of Nineveh and fall of Assyria (until 609)
550:	Cyrus the Great defeats Astyages, King of the Medes
540s:	Cyrus conquers Lydia
539:	Cyrus conquers Babylonia
530:	Death of Cyrus in battle and succession of Cambyses
530s?–510s:	Main construction at Pasargadae
525–522:	Cambyses invades Egypt
522:	Death of Cambyses in April; reign of Bardiya (6 months) and usurpation of Darius I
520–519:	Engraving of Bisitun relief and inscription
510s:	Founding of Persepolis
510s:	Darius I's campaigns into Europe (Scythians) and India
499–493:	Ionian revolt
490:	Battle of Marathon
486:	Death of Darius I and accession of Xerxes; revolt in Egypt
484:	Revolt in Babylonia
480–479:	Xerxes' invasion of Greece
465:	Assassination of Xerxes and accession of Artaxerxes I
464/463–454:	Egyptian revolt

424:	Death of Artaxerxes I; accession and assassination of Xerxes II
423:	Accession of Darius II
408:	Cyrus the Younger dispatched to Anatolia with a special command
405:	Death of Darius II; accession of Artaxerxes II
401:	War of the Brothers: Cyrus the Younger revolts against Artaxerxes II, Battle of Cunaxa
401–343/342:	Egypt in revolt and effectively outside of Achaemenid control
387/386:	King's Peace (Peace of Antalcidas) imposed upon Greece
359:	Death of Artaxerxes II and accession of Artaxerxes III
343/342:	Artaxerxes III's reconquest of Egypt
338:	Death of Artaxerxes III and accession of Artaxerxes IV (Arses)
336:	Artaxerxes IV assassinated; accession of Darius III
334:	Alexander, King of Macedon, invades the Persian Empire; Battle of Granicus
333:	Battle of Issus; much of Darius III's family captured at Damascus
331:	Battle of Gaugamela; Alexander welcomed into Babylon and Susa, invades Fars
330:	End of Empire: Burning of Persepolis terrace and death of Darius III
320s:	Alexander campaigns in eastern Iran and India, adding the eastern domains of the Achaemenid Empire and consolidating his conquests; Alexander dies in 323 in Babylon

Appendix B – Chronological Chart of Achaemenid Persian Kings

Cyrus the Great, 559–530
Cambyses, 530–522
Bardiya, 522
Darius I, 522–486
Xerxes I, 486–465
Artaxerxes I, 465–424
Xerxes II, 424–423
Darius II, 423–405
Artaxerxes II, 405–359
Artaxerxes III, 359–338
Artaxerxes IV (Arses), 338–336
Darius III, 336–330

Appendix C – Lineages of the Achaemenid Royal Family

The following represents a condensed version of the lineages of the wider Achaemenid royal family. In general, only individuals who are prominent in this book are noted. The charts are not exhaustive. Dotted lines indicate that the mother is uncertain.

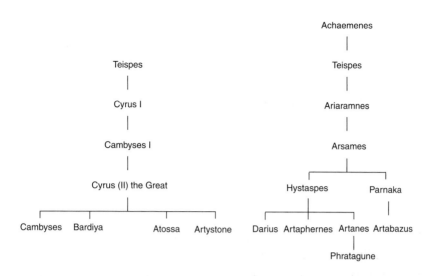

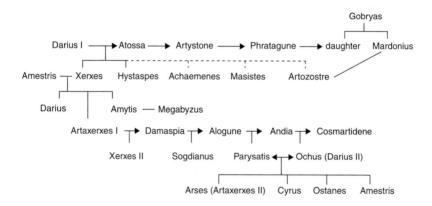

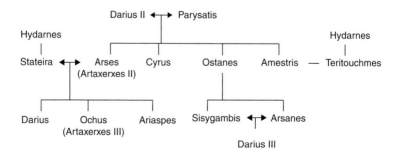

Appendix D – Further Readings

The specialized bibliography is wide-ranging. References to specific problems addressed in the text are included in the endnotes for each chapter. Selected examples of illustrative works cited here are primarily in English.

INTERNET RESOURCES

Achemenet: http://www.achemenet.com/
Encyclopaedia Iranica: http://www.iranicaonline.org/
Livius: http://www.livius.org/persia.html

ACHAEMENID HISTORY AND HISTORIOGRAPHY

Achaemenid History Series, multiple volumes with different editors, published by Nederlands Instituut voor het Nabije Oosten, Leiden
L. Allen, *Persian Empire*, 2005
J. Álvarez-Mon and M. Garrison (eds.), *Elam and Persia*, 2011
P. Briant, *From Cyrus to Alexander: A History of the Persian Empire*, translated by P. Daniels, 2002
P. Briant, W. Henkelman, and M. Stolper, *L'archive des Fortifications de Persépolis. État des questions et perspectives de recherches*, 2008
M. Brosius, *The Persians: An Introduction*, 2006
M. Brosius, *Women in Ancient Persia (559–331 B.C.)*, 1996
J. M. Cook, *The Persian Empire*, 1983

J. Curtis and St. John Simpson (eds.), *The World of Achaemenid Persia: History, Art, and Society in Iran and the Ancient Near East*, 2010

J. Curtis and N. Tallis (eds.), *Forgotten Empire: The World of Ancient Persia*, 2005

M. Dandamaev, *A Political History of the Achaemenid Persian Empire*, translated by W. J. Vogelsang, 1989

E. Dusinberre, *Empire, Authority, and Autonomy in Achaemenid Anatolia*, 2013

K. Farroukh, *Shadows in the Desert: Ancient Persia at War*, 2007

L. Fried, *The Priest and the Great King: Temple-Palace Relations in the Persian Empire*, 2004

R. Frye, *The History of Ancient Iran*, 1984

T. Harrison, *Writing Ancient Persia*, 2011

K. Hoglund, *Achaemenid Imperial Administration in Syria-Palestine and the Missions of Ezra and Nehemiah*, 1992

B. Jacobs and R. Rollinger (eds.), *Der Achämenidenhof/The Achaemenid Court*, 2010

A. Kuhrt, *The Persian Empire: A Corpus of Sources from the Achaemenid Period*, 2007

A. T. Olmstead, *History of the Persian Empire*, 1948

S. Ruzcka, *Trouble in the West: Egypt and the Persian Empire 525–332 BCE*, 2012

C. Tuplin, "The Administration of the Achaemenid Empire, in *Coinge and Administration in the Athenian and Persian Empires*, ed. I Carradice, 1987, 119–66

W. J. Vogelsang, *The Rise and Organisation of the Achaemenid Persian Empire: The Eastern Iranian Evidence*, 1992

J. Wiesehöfer, *Ancient Persia*, translated by A. Azodi, 1996

E. Yamauchi, *Persia and the Bible*, 1990

ART, ARCHAEOLOGY, CULTURE, AND RELIGION

J. Álvarez-Mon, *The Arjān Tomb: At the Crossroads of the Elamite and Persian Empires*, 2010

E. Bridges, E. Hall, and P. J. Rhodes (eds.), *Cultural Responses to the Persian Wars: Antiquity to the Third Millennium*, 2007

A. DeJong, *Traditions of the Magi: Zoroastrianism in Greek and Latin Literature*, 1997

M. Garrison, "The Heroic Encounter in the Visual Arts of Ancient Iraq and Iran c. 1000–500 B.C.," in *The Master of Animals in Old World Iconography*, ed. D. B. Counts and B. Arnold, 2010, 151–74

M. Garrison, "Visual Representation of the Divine and the Numinous in Early Achaemenid Iran: Old Problems, New Directions," *Iconography of Deities and Demons*, University of Zurich, electronic pre-publication available at http://www.religionswissenschaft.uzh.ch/idd/prepublications/e_idd_iran.pdf

M. Garrison and M. Root, *Seals on the Persepolis Fortification Tablets, Volume 1, Images of Heroic Encounter*, 2001

W. Henkelman, *The Other Gods Who Are: Studies on Elamite-Iranian Acculturation Based on the Persepolis Fortification Texts*, 2008

B. Lincoln, *"Happiness for Mankind": Achaemenian Religion and the Imperial Project*, 2012

W. Malandra, *An Introduction to Ancient Iranian Religion: Readings from the Avesta and Achaemenid Incriptions*, 1983

P. de Miroschedji, "Susa and the Highlands: Major Trends in the History of Elamite Civilization," in *Yeki bud, yeki nabud: Essays on the Archaeology of Iran in Honor of William M. Sumner*, ed. N. Miller and K. Abdi, 2003, 17–38

A. Mousavi, *Persepolis: Discovery and Afterlife of a World Wonder*, 2012

M. Root, *The King and Kingship in Achaemenid Art*, 1979

E. Schmidt, *Persepolis I: Structures, Reliefs, Inscriptions*, 1953

E. Schmidt, *Persepolis II: Contents of the Treasury and Other Discoveries*, 1957

E. Schmidt, *Persepolis III: The Royal Tombs and Other Monuments*, 1970

P. O. Skjærvø, "The Achamenids and the *Avesta*," in *Birth of the Persian Empire*, eds. V Curtis and S. Stewart, 2005, 52–84

D. Stronach, *Pasargadae*, 1978

C. Tuplin (ed.), *Persian Responses: Political and Cultural Interaction with(in) the Achaemenid Empire*, 2007

M. L. West, *The Hymns of Zoroaster: A New Translation of the Most Ancient Sacred Texts of Iran*, 2010

PERSIAN INVASIONS OF GREECE, PERSIAN-GREEK RELATIONS, ALEXANDER AND PERSIA

A. B. Bosworth, *Conquest and Empire: The Reign of Alexander the Great*, 1988

P. Briant, *Alexander the Great and His Empire: A Short Introduction*, translated by A. Kuhrt, 2010

A. R. Burn, *Persia and the Greeks*, 1984

G. Cawkwell, *The Greek Wars: The Failure of Persia*, 2005

T. Harrison (ed.), *Greeks and Barbarians*, 2002

W. Heckel, *The Conquests of Alexander the Great*, 2008

C. Hignett, *Xerxes' Invasion of Greece*, 1963

P. Krentz, *The Battle of Marathon*, 2010

D. Lewis, *Sparta and Persia*, 1977

M. Miller, *Athens and Persia in the Fifth Century B.C.: A Study in Cultural Receptivity*, 1997

H. Wallinga, *Xerxes' Great Adventure: The Naval Perspective*, 2005

Notes

CHAPTER 1. INTRODUCTION. TRACKING AN EMPIRE

1 Area as estimated in George Rawlinson's classic *The Five Great Monarchies*, Vol. III, 1870, 84–85.

2 Compare M. Waters, "Cyrus and the Achaemenids," *Iran* 42, 2004, 91–102; D. T. Potts, "Cyrus the Great and the Kingdom of Anshan," in *The Idea of Iran: Birth of the Persian Empire*, eds. V. S. Curtis and S. Stewart, 2005, 7–28; A. Kuhrt, "Cyrus the Great of Persia: Images and Realities," in *Representations of Political Power. Case Histories from Times of Change and Dissolving Order in the Ancient Near East*, eds. M. Heinz and M. H. Feldman, 2007, 169–191; and W. Henkelman, "Cyrus the Persian and Darius the Elamite: a Case of Mistaken Identity," in *Herodot und das Persische Weltreich*, eds. R. Rollinger, B. Truschnegg, and R. Bichler, 2011, 577–634.

3 For example, C. Waerzeggers, *The Ezida Temple of Borsippa*, 2010, analyzes administrative records of several generations of priests who worked in the temple of Nabu (god of writing) in Borsippa, near Babylon. These records provide enormous detail about the particulars of the priesthood's responsibilities, organization, and social networks.

4 M. W. Stolper and J. Tavenier, "From the Persepolis Fortification Archive Project, 1: An Old Persian Administrative Tablet from the Persepolis Fortification," ARTA 2007.001.

5 Note for example discussions in E. Hall, *Inventing the Barbarian: Greek Self-Definition through Tragedy*, 1989.

CHAPTER 2. FORERUNNERS OF THE ACHAEMENIDS.
THE FIRST HALF OF THE FIRST MILLENNIUM BCE

1 Herodotus 1.125 lists the main Persian tribes and names the Achaemenid clan as members of the Pasargadae tribe, the noblest of them. The passage generates a number of historical questions. See P. Briant, *From Cyrus to Alexander: A History of the Persian Empire*, translated by P. Daniels, 2002, 18–19 and 878 for discussion.

2 "Indo-Iranian" is primarily a linguistic term, synonymous with "Indo-Aryan." "Iranian" is the literal normalization of "Aryan," the term that the Iranians used to describe themselves. It has little connection to the usual meaning of the word in modern contexts applied, for example, to Nazi Germany. The literature on this phenomenon is extensive, for an overview see I. Good, "When East Met West: Interpretative Problems in Assessing Eurasian Contact and Exchange in Antiquity," in *Archäologische Mitteilungen aus Iran und Turan*, Band 42, 2010, 23–45.

3 For an overview of the Elamite language, see M. W. Stolper, "Elamite," in *The Cambridge Encyclopedia of the World's Ancient Languages*, ed. R. Woodard, 2004, 59–94.

4 For a discussion of the links between Assyrian and Achaemenid art, see M. C. Root, "Elam in the Imperial Imagination: From Nineveh to Persepolis," in *Elam and Persia*, eds. J. Álvarez-Mon and M. Garrison, 2011, 418–474.

5 M. Cogan and H. Tadmor, "Gyges and Ashurbanipal: A Study in Literary Transmission," *Orientalia* 46, 1977, 68.

6 E. Dusinberre, *Aspects of Empire in Achaemenid Sardis*, 2003.

7 Herodotus 1.73–74. Cannabalism is a recurrent motif in Greek literature and need not be taken at face value here; cf. the Greek myths of Tantalus and Pelops as well as Atreus and Thyestes' sons; the motif recurs in Herodotus in the story of Astyages and Harpagus' children, because Harpagus did not make certain that the infant Cyrus had been killed.

8 Note the various contributions to the volume *Continuity of Empire(?): Assyria, Media, Persia*, eds. G. Lanfranchi, M. Roaf, and R. Rollinger, 2003.

CHAPTER 3. PERSIA RISING. A NEW EMPIRE

1 Akkadian text is available in R. Borger, *Beiträge zum Inscriftenwerk Assurbanipals*, 2006, 191–192. Another text relays this same episode and Cyrus' obeisance

to Assyria, but it does not mention Arukku; see Borger, 280–281, lines 115–118.

2 See M. Waters, "Parsumash, Anshan, and Cyrus," 286–296 and M. Garrison, "The Seal of 'Kuraš the Anzanite, Son of Šešpeš' (Teispes), PFS 93*: Susa – Anšan – Persepolis," 375–405, both in *Elam and Persia*, eds. J. Álvarez-Mon and M. Garrison, 2011.

3 Akkadian text available in H. Schaudig, *Die Inschriften Nabonids von Babylon und Kyros' de Großen*, 2001, 417. Whether or not this threat was real or manufactured is a matter of debate: note R. Rollinger, "The Western Expansion of the Median 'Empire': A Re-examination," in *Continuity of Empire(?): Assyria, Media, Persia*, eds. G. Lanfranchi, M. Roaf, and R. Rollinger, 2003, 291–305.

4 Text from A. K. Grayson, *Assyrian and Babylonian Chronicles*, 107 and see 282. Note also on this issue R. Rollinger, "The Median 'Empire,' the end of Urartu, and Cyrus the Great's Campaign in 547 BC (Nabonidus Chronicle II 16)," *Ancient West&East* 7, 2008, 51–65.

5 A translation of Bacchylides poem may be found in A. Kuhrt, *The Persian Empire: A Corpus of Sources from the Achaemenid Period*, 2007, 65–66.

6 Among others, S. Zawadzki, "The End of the Neo-Babylonian Empire: New Data Concerning Nabonidus's Order to Send the Statues of Gods to Babylon," *Journal of Near Eastern Studies* 71, 2012, 47–51, with references.

7 For the Dynastic Prophecy, column ii, lines 20–21, A. K. Grayson, *Babylonian Historical-Literary Texts*, 1975, 32–33.

8 Translation slightly adapted from Kuhrt, *Persian Empire*, 84–85. The first version of the decree is in Hebrew, the second in Aramaic; the Aramaic version is held to be the more reliable. Doubts of the decree's authenticity persist, and the bibliography is enormous. Among others see P. Bedford, *Temple Restoration in Early Achaemenid Judah*, 2001.

9 See for a balanced treatment of this issue, A. Kuhrt, "The Problem of Achaemenid 'Religious Policy,'" in *Die Welt der Götterbilder*, eds. B. Groneburg and H. Spieckermann, 2007, 117–142.

10 J. Westenholz, *Legends of the Kings of Akkade*, 1997, 36–50 for the Sargon Legend. Herodotus indirectly taps further into this legend through his etymology of Cyrus' adoptive mother's name: Spako, a Median word that Herodotus explains (1.110) meant a female dog. By extension, Cyrus could be understood to have been raised in the wild by a wolf, just as later Roman tradition portrayed Romulus and Remus.

CHAPTER 4. FROM CYRUS TO DARIUS I. EMPIRE IN TRANSITION

1   Xenophon's *Cyropaedia* (8.7) offers a notable exception to most other Greek writers' claims that Cyrus died in battle at the ends of the earth. Therein the dying Cyrus is the philosopher-king dispensing speeches, gifts, and advice to his family and courtiers, an idealized picture that befits Xenophon's projected image of the man.

2   One may wonder what other diplomatic marriages Cyrus may have made earlier in his career, to incorporate various Iranian groups under to his rule. See M. Waters, "Cyrus and the Achaemenids," *Iran* 42, 2004, 91–102 and note M. Brosius, *Women of Ancient Persia*, 1996, 35–38 for Cyrus' wives.

3   The cuneiform evidence is collected and discussed in J. Peat, "Cyrus 'King of Lands,' Cambyses 'King of Babylon': The Disputed Co-Regency," *Journal of Cuneiform Studies* 41, 1989, 199–216.

4   W. Henkelman, "An Elamite Memorial: The *šumar* of Cambyses and Hystaspes," in *A Persian Perspective: Essays in Memory of Heleen Sancisi-Weerdenburg*, eds. W. Henkelman and A. Kuhrt, 2003, 101–172.

5   The archive of Aramaic documents recovered from the Jewish community stationed there is a key source for the Persian administration of Egypt, see B. Porten, *Archives from Elephantine: The Life of an Ancient Jewish Military Colony*, 1968 and Porten et al. (eds.), *The Elephantine Papyri in English: Three Millennia of Cross-Cultural Continuity and Change*, Second Revised Edition, 2011.

6   Translation from the French of G. Posener, *La Première domination perse en Égypte*, 1936, 36. The name "Sma-Towy" (spellings differ) is Cambyses' Egyptian name as king. For the difficulties surrounding the interpretation of the evidence, see L. Depuydt, "Murder in Memphis: The Story of Cambyses's Mortal Wounding of the Apis Bull (ca. 523 B. C. E.)," *Journal of Near Eastern Studies* 54, 1995, 119–126; P. Briant, *From Cyrus to Alexander: A History of the Persian Empire*, translated by P. Daniels, 2002, 55–57, 60–61, and 887–888; and A. Kuhrt, *The Persian Empire: A Corpus of Sources from the Achaemenid Period*, 2007, 122–124 with notes.

7   An excellent overview may be found in J. Wiesehöfer, *Ancient Persia*, translated by A. Azodi, 2001, 223–242.

8   The Old Persian terms are *arika* ("disloyal") and *drauga* ("Lie"), both terms replete with symbolic significance. Darius moralistic perspective became a linchpin of Achaemenid royal ideology. The term Mazdaean – from the god's

name, Ahuramazda – is preferred here over the more typical "Zoroastrian," but the two are closely linked (see pp. 152–154).

9 The figures are not only impossible to verify but in many instances difficult to read confidently. See Briant's discussion, *From Cyrus to Alexander*, 118–119.

10 The exception was Aspathines, who became prominent later. He was given a prominent place on Darius' tomb relief, so there is some explanation for Herodotus' confusion here. The summary version of Ctesias (Fragment 13 §15–18) also relates essentially the same story, though his list of the Seven has significant differences – it may reflect later offspring of the original Seven. See Briant, *From Cyrus to Alexander*, 107–112.

11 This Dadarshi was different than the homonymous individual, an Armenian, who was sent against rebels in Armenia (DB §26).

12 Note J. Wiesehöfer's discussion, with all appropriate caveats, "The Achaemenid Empire," in *The Dynamics of Ancient Empires*, eds. I. Morris and W. Scheidel, 2009, 76–78.

CHAPTER 5. DARIUS, THE GREAT KING

1 The literary motif of one year was widespread in the ancient Near East. For Darius' claims, note E. Bickerman and H. Tadmor, "Darius I, Pseudo-Smerdis and the Magi," *Athenaeum* 56, 1978, 239–261; W. Vogelsang, "Four Short Notes on the Bisitun Text and Monument," *Iranica Antiqua* 21, 1986, 121–140; and C. Nylander, "Xenophon, Darius, Naram-Sin: A Note on the King's 'Year,'" in *Opus Mixtum: Essays in Ancient Art and History*, 1994, 57–59.

2 For the Naram-Sin stele and its Elamite context, see *The Royal City of Susa: Ancient Near Eastern Treasures in the Louvre*, eds. P Harper, J. Aruz, and F. Tallon, 1992, 166–170. For Naram-Sin's inscriptions, see D. Frayne, *Sargonic and Gutian Periods (2334–2113 BC)*, 1993, especially pp. 116–117 for the Susa statue base inscription. Notably, Naram-Sin's nine battles occurred against only three kings. Darius defeated nine: to outdo your predecessor is always a good thing.

3 Among others M. Liverani, "'Untruthful Steles': Propaganda and Reliability in Ancient Mesopotamia," in *Opening the Tablet Box: Near Eastern Studies in Honor of Benjamin R. Foster*, eds. S. Melville and A. Slotsky, 2010, 229–244 and references.

4 See S. Parpola, "Excursus: The Substitute King Ritual," in his *Letters from Assyrian Scholars to the Kings Esarhaddon and Assurbanipal Part II*, 1982, xii–xxxii

and K. Radner, "The Trials of Esarhaddon: The Conspiracy of 670 BC," *ISIMU: Revista sobre Oriente Próximo y Egipto en la Antigüedad* 6, 2003, 171–172.

5 A. Kuhrt, *The Persian Empire: A Corpus of Sources from the Achaemenid Period*, 2007, 477–479 and 485–486 has full English translations of the Darius statue and stele inscriptions from Egypt, with references.

6 On the Skudrians, see W. Henkelman and M. Stolper, "Ethnic Identity and Ethnic Labelling at Persepolis: The Case of the Skudrians," in *Organisation des pouvoirs et contacts culturels dans les pays de l'empire achéménide*, eds. P. Briant and P. Chauveau, 2009, especially 288–289.

7 Getting one's adversaries drunk before disposing of them was a popular motif in Greek literature. In this case, as many scholars have noted, the story is probably a later revision that attempted to spin Macedon's pro-Persian stance. This would have applied especially during the fifth century and Herodotus' time, when Macedon's past as a Persian subject-state would place it in an often uncomfortable light.

8 This Datiya is identified with the Datis who led the campaign that ended at Marathon in 490. The record is from a Persepolis Fortification Tablet (PF-NN 1809), see Kuhrt, *Persian Empire*, 224 for translation and references.

CHAPTER 6. MECHANICS OF EMPIRE

1 A minutely detailed account of the foodstuffs for the King's feast is preserved by the Greek author Polyaenus 4.3.32, probably from a fourth-century BCE writer such as Ctesias. A translation of the text may be found in A. Kuhrt, *The Persian Empire: A Corpus of Sources from the Achaemenid Period*, 2007, 604–607 with references in footnote 1. Note also the thorough discussion in W. Henkelman, "Parnakka's Feast: *šip* in Parsa and Elam," in *Elam and Persia*, eds. J. Álvarez-Mon and M. Garrison, 2011, 89–166.

2 Babylonian documents also mention high-ranking Persian women. Kuhrt, *Persian Empire*, 595–604 contains a sampling of relevant translated texts. See in general the treatment of Brosius, *Women in Ancient Persia (559–331 B.C.)*, 1996.

3 The Athenaeus passage is from his only extant work, *Deipnosophistai* ("the Learned Banquet") 12.514b. For concubines in Esther, note in particular passages 2.2–3 and 2.12–14. The story of Esther, and how her influence with

the king saves the Jewish people from annihilation, is the foundation for the Jewish festival of Purim.

4 Another inscription from Susa (DSaa) and the Darius statue also contain *dahyu* lists, and there is disagreement about the translation of some of the terms. For discussion see W. J. Vogelsang, *Rise and Organisation of the Achaemenid Empire: The Eastern Iranian Evidence*, 1992, 96–119 and P. Briant, *From Cyrus to Alexander: A History of the Persian Empire*, translated by P. Daniels, 2002, 172–175.

5 See O. Armayor, "Herodotus' Catalogues of the Persian Empire in the Light of the Monuments and the Greek Literary Tradition," *Transactions of the American Philological Association* 108, 1978, 1–9 and see Briant, *From Cyrus to Alexander*, 390–393 and chapter 10. Kuhrt, *Persian Empire*, chapter 14 contains a variety of examples on collection of tribute and revenue – note in particular a lengthy Aramaic document from Elephantine in Egypt, which gives examples of harbor dues (pp. 681–703).

6 D. Kaptan, The *Daskyleion Bullae: Seal Images from the Western Achaemenid Empire*, 2002. For the Bactria documents, see S. Shaked, *Le satrap de Bactriane et son gouverneur: documents araméen du IV s. av. notre ère provenant de Bactriane*, 2004, also J. Naveh and S. Shaked, *Ancient Aramaic Documents from Bactria*, 2012.

7 PF 1404 in R. Hallock, *Persepolis Fortification Tablets*, 1969, 396.

8 Translated by Hallock, *Persepolis Fortification Tablets*, 205, 207, 209 and Kuhrt, *Persian Empire*, 782–783.

9 Note the discussion in Briant with tablet data and citations, *From Cyrus to Alexander*, 429–442.

10 See for example E. Dusinberre, *Aspects of Empire in Achaemenid Sardis*, 2003, especially chapter 8 for nonelites.

11 Xenophon also made reference to this extensive system, *Cyropaedia* 8.6.17–18. Engraved on the Post Office building at 8th Avenue and 33rd Street in New York is the saying: "Neither snow nor rain nor heat nor gloom of night stays these couriers from the swift completion of their appointed rounds" – it is widely but erroneously considered the United States Postal Service's official motto. That inscription is an adaptation of the Herodotus passage about the Persian messenger system along the Royal Road. For remains of one of these staging posts, see A. Mousavi, "The Discovery of an Achaemenid Station at Deh-Bozan in the Asadabad Valley," *Archäologishe Mitteilungen aus Iran* 22, 1989, 135–138.

CHAPTER 7. XERXES, THE EXPANDER OF THE REALM

1 Also called the Audience Relief, this sculpture is the subject of much debate beyond simply the identity of the figures portrayed. See A. Kuhrt, *The Persian Empire: A Corpus of Sources from the Achaemenid Period*, 2007, 536 for a succinct summary and references.

2 C. Waerzeggars, "The Babylonian Revolts against Xerxes and the 'End of Archives,'" *Archiv für Orientforschung* 50, 2003/2004, 150–173 has analyzed all the relevant tablets to confirm a 484 BCE date.

3 See W. Henkelman, "Der Grabhügel," in *Ktesias' Welt*, eds. J. Wiesehöfer, R. Rollinger, and G. Lanfranchi, 2011, 111–139.

4 The final part of the translation "as appropriate" glosses a number of convoluted translation issues best referred to the specialist literature, including how to interpret the Old Persian word *arta* here, often translated as "truth" (in opposition to *drauga*). See Kuhrt, *Persian Empire*, 304–306 with notes and references. The religious sensibilities expressed in XPh find forerunners in both Elamite and Mesopotamian traditions. For example, the Assyrian king Esarhaddon (reigned 680–669) refers to people telling lies and abandoning their gods and rites, see E. Leichty, *The Royal Inscriptions of Esarhaddon, King of Assyria (680–669 BC),* 2011, 203, lines 23f.

5 Artabanus' acting the part of Xerxes, to see if he too would be visited by the ominous dream (7.15–18), is another Greek variation of the Mesopotamian substitute-king ritual (p. 75).

6 D. Graf, "Medism: The Origin and Significance of the Term," *Journal of Hellenic Studies* 104, 1984, 15–30 and C. Tuplin, "Medism and Its Causes," *Transeuphratène* 13, 1997, 155–185.

7 H. Diels and W. Kranz, *Die Fragmente der Vorsokratiker*, Vol. 1, 1956, Fragment 22, 134.

8 See A. Kuhrt, "Earth and Water," in *Achaemenid History III: Method and Theory*, eds. A. Kuhrt and H. Sancisi-Weerdenburg, 1988, 87–99.

9 Note T. Harrison, *Writing Ancient Persia*, 2011, 61 for discussion of Xerxes' whipping of the Hellespont and the army's marching through Pythius' son's corpse.

10 On the return trip, Xerxes built a palace at the important city of Kelainai (Celaenae), in southwestern Phrygia of central Anatolia. An Achaemenid era tomb has revealed a spectacular monument and tomb with painted scenes including one of a Persian battle. See for discussion and references C. Tuplin,

"Historical Significance of the Tatarli Tomb Chamber" and L. Summerer, "Wall Paintings," both in *Tatarli: The Return of Colors*, eds. L. Summerer and A. Kienlin, 2010, 186–195 and 120–185, respectively.

CHAPTER 8. ANATOMY OF EMPIRE

1 Two prominent examples of such are the inscriptions of Darius I's grandfather Arsames and great-grandfather Ariaramnes, on gold tablets, purportedly from Hamadan. Most scholars consider them forgeries. See R. J. Kent, *Old Persian: Grammar, Texts, Lexicon*, 1953, 12 n. 2, 107, and 116 and also L. Allen, *The Persian Empire*, 2005, 64 and 188, n. 12.

2 The free translation "in need of attention" interprets the problematic Old Persian phrase rendered by various translators as "which was not complete" or "was put out of its place." After Kent, *Old Persian*, 142 and note A. Kuhrt, *The Persian Empire: A Corpus of Sources from the Achaemenid Period*, 2007, 491–492 with notes.

3 It is a matter of debate what specific event this relief sequence may have portrayed, the Iranian *Nō Rūz* (New Year) festival, various religious ceremonies, or even a celebration of the King's birthday.

4 Strabo (15.3.1) identifies the Pateischoreans as one of the Persian tribes.

5 These inscriptions are a linchpin of modern Achaemenid historiography, and the bibliography is enormous. For summaries and discussions of the problem, see inter alia D. Stronach, "Darius at Pasargadae: A Neglected Source for the History of Early Persia," *Topoi*, Supplement 1, 1997, 351–363. Another inscription labeled "CMb" in the scholarship consists of roughly thirty fragments that are not able to be confidently reassembled. It is not clear that the various fragments are even from a single inscription.

6 "Where it is necessary that a lie be told, let it be told." This occurs during the plot to overthrow the magus-imposter and as part of Darius' suggestion to gain access to the palace. That Herodotus has Darius so blithely advocate lying may be read as Herodotus' play against Achaemenid ideology and Darius' central place in creating it.

7 The term "religion" comes from the Latin term *religio*, a later context than the Achaemenid period. A number of scholars have noted that the term "religion" is anachronistically applied to any period of the ancient Near East. The term is used herein in its wider, standardized, application to beliefs and attitudes about the divine, cultic practices, and associated traditions.

8 The term "Mazdean" is sometimes employed to refer to a system that plainly emphasizes Ahuramazda, but that is not "Zoroastrian" per se; the latter term is reserved for the later form of the religion.

9 Note M. Garrison's seminal discussion, "Visual Representation of the Divine and the Numinous in Early Achaemenid Iran: Old Problems, New Directions," Iconography of Deities and Demons, University of Zurich, electronic pre-publication available at http://www.religionswissenschaft.uzh.ch/idd/prepublications/e_idd_iran.pdf

10 See the overview in A. de Jong, *Traditions of the Magi*, 1997, 387–394, with references.

CHAPTER 9. EMPIRE AT LARGE. FROM THE DEATH OF XERXES TO DARIUS II

1 Abu is the fifth month of the Babylonian calendar, so our July-August in 465. The sign for the number of the day is partially broken, so reading the "14th" is uncertain. See M. Stolper, "Late Achaemenid Babylonian Chronology," in *Nouvelles assyriologiques brève et utilitaires*, 1999, Note 6.

2 Megabyxos is a slight variation in the spelling of the same name. Ctesias credits Megabyzus with recapturing Babylon after its revolt during Xerxes' reign (Fragment 13 §26), perhaps the same sequence attributed by Herodotus to Megabyzus' father Zopyrus during Darius I's reign (3.153–160).

3 The bibliography is enormous. Note in particular the seminal commentaries to the Books of Nehemiah and Ezra by R. Bowman, *Interpreter's Bible* III, 1954. Among others note K. Hoglund, *Achaemenid Imperial Administration in Syria-Palestine and the Missions of Ezra and Nehemiah*, 1992; H. Williamson, "Judah and the Jews," in *Studies in Persian History: Essays in Memory of David Lewis*, eds. M. Brosius and A. Kuhrt, 1998, 145–163; and L. Fried, *The Priest and the Great King*, 2004, 156–233.

4 Note especially M. Miller, *Athens and Persia in the Fifth Century BC: A Study in Cultural Receptivity*, 1997. The diffusion of status objects and the values that accompanied them may be traced from satrapal courts, modeled on the King's court, which in turn served as models throughout the Empire.

5 M. Root, "The Parthenon Frieze and the Apadana Reliefs at Persepolis: Reassessing a Programmatic Relationship," *American Journal of Archaeology*

89, 1985, 103–120 and Miller, *Athens and Persia*, especially. 218–242 for the Odeion.

6 M. Stolper, *Entrepreneurs and Empire: The Muraša Archive, the Murašu Firm, and Persian Rule in Babylonia*, 1985, 70.

7 Stolper, *Entrepreneurs and Empire*, p. 96 for Arbareme and pp. 90–91 for Artoxares and Menostanes.

8 The correspondence between Strabo's "Agradates" and Ctesias' "Atradates" (according to Ctesias, Cyrus' father, Fragment 8d §3) is close enough to have been confused in the Greek tradition. Note W. Henkelman's discussion of Cyrus' name in "Persians, Medes and Elamites," in *Continuity of Empire(?): Assyria, Media, Persia*, eds. G. Lanfranchi, M. Roaf, and R. Rollinger, 2003, 196, n. 48. On Cyrus' name, compare also J. Tavernier, *Iranica in the Achaemenid Period: Lexicon of Old Iranian Proper Names and Loanwords, Attested in Non-Iranian Texts*, 2007, 528–530 and R. Schmitt, *Encyclopædia Iranica* online, "Cyrus. i. The Name," http://www.iranicaonline.org/articles/cyrus-i-name

9 Stolper, *Entrepreneurs and Empire*, 117–120.

10 Spartan ineptitude is manifest in the first treaty (8.18), the wording of which may be construed as ceding to the Persians all the territory the Empire held at its height – i.e., at the time of Xerxes' invasion of Greece – but it seems unlikely that anything further than Asia Minor was implied. See D. Lewis, *Sparta and Persia*, 1977, 90–107 for summary and insightful discussion.

11 Thucydides' account ends in 411, and the narrative is picked up by Xenophon in the *Hellenica*. For *karanos* (Xen. *Hell.* 1.4.3), see P. Briant, *From Cyrus to Alexander: A History of the Persian Empire,* translated by P. Daniels, 2002, 19, linking the term to the Old Persian word *kāra*, which can mean "army" or "people."

CHAPTER 10. MAINTAINING EMPIRE. ARTAXERXES II AND ARTAXERXES III

1 Hydarnes' family had been previously decimated, according to Ctesias (Fragment 15 §55–56) because of a love affair between Teritouchmes and his half sister Roxane, and Teritouchmes' subsequent rebellion. Teritouchmes was married to Amestris, the daughter of Darius II and Parysatis, and sister of Arses (Artaxerxes II). Whatever the truth behind this sordid tale of lust and

betrayal – some postulate an Achaemenid reaction to a potential rival's family – Stateira was spared at the behest of Arses before he became king. See P. Briant, *From Cyrus to Alexander: A History of the Persian Empire*, translated by P. Daniels, 2002, 589–590 for discussion of this curious episode.

2   This late testimony is likely colored by Mithraic ritual of the mystery cult popular during the Roman period, for which see the classic treatment by W. Burkert, *Ancient Mystery Cults*, 1987.

3   Diodorus' stereotypical description of battles and casualties has a check in this instance. Diodorus claims that more than 6,000 were killed in the exchange; a papyrus fragment from Egypt, part of the Oxyrnchus hoard (11.6), gives "about 600" killed for the same battle. P. McKechnie and S. Kern, *Hellenica Oxyrhynchia*, 1988, 63.

4   M. N. Tod, *Greek Historical Inscriptions*, Vol. II, 1948, no. 113.

5   See the treatment by R. Van der Spek, "The Chronology of the Wars of Artaxerxes II in the Babylonian Astronomical Diaries," in *Studies in Persian History: Essays in Memory of David M. Lewis*, eds. M. Brosius and A. Kuhrt, 1998, 240–241.

6   The core of this material is a group of roughly thirty documents in Aramaic. A seminar at Oxford University was dedicated to study of the archive http:// arshama.classics.ox.ac.uk/. For discussion and context of the letter A6.10, see C. Tuplin's paper "An Introduction to Arshama" available on that web site.

7   Assessment of the evidence from the Attic orators is included in Briant's important treatment of this period, *From Cyrus to Alexander*, 656–675.

8   Artaxerxes II also had several sons from his various concubines, 115 sons according to Justin 10.1.1. One may only speculate on the number of daughters of this inexhaustible king.

9   On Khababash, see S. Burstein, "Prelude to Alexander: The Reign of Khababash," *Ancient History Bulletin* 14, 2000, 149–154.

CHAPTER 11. TWILIGHT OF THE ACHAEMENIDS

1   Text treated by A. K. Grayson, *Babylonian Historical-Literary Texts*, 1975, 34–35; see also R. Van der Spek, "Darius III, Alexander the Great, and Babylonian Scholarship," in *A Persian Perspective: Essays in Memory of Heleen Sancisi-Weerdenburg*, eds. W. Henkelman and A. Kuhrt, 2003, 311–340.

2   Alexander used the same rationale during his invasion. A number of scholars
    have wondered whether these Greek cities truly wished to be "liberated" or
    not. See, for example, P. Briant, *Alexander the Great and His Empire: A Short
    Introduction*, 2010, 36 with references.
3   A. J. Sachs and H. Hunger, *Astronomical Diaries and Related Texts from Babylonia
    I: Diaries from 652 B.C. to 262 B.C.*, 1988, text no. 330.

CHAPTER 12. EPILOGUE

1   G. Rawlinson, *The Sixth Great Oriental Monarchy*, 1873, v.

Index